BETTER BIDDING

with

BERGEN

Volume I – Uncontested Auctions

by Marty Bergen

Published by
Devyn Press, Inc.
Louisville, Kentucky

FIRST PRINTING — DECEMBER, 1985
SECOND PRINTING — FEBRUARY, 1987
THIRD PRINTING — MARCH, 1988
FOURTH PRINTING — JUNE, 1989
FIFTH PRINTING — MARCH, 1992

Better Bidding with Bergen - Volume 1
ISBN No. 0-910791-36-8
Cover design — Pat Stoehr

TABLE OF CONTENTS

INTRODUCTION

Marty Bergen has certainly come a long way. Ten years ago he was thought of merely as a dangerous opponent. Although a young player with talent, he was considered too wild to be included on the good teams.

Five years later his excellent articles on conventions in *The ACBL Bulletin* had established him as a fine bridge writer. He had also made significant progress as a player with several high National finishes. However, he still lacked: a regular partner, the respect of the top echelon players, a National Championship, and his own book.

Today, all that he lacks is a World Championship, and that seems to be only a matter of time. His partnership with Larry Cohen has been phenomenally successful and shows no signs of cooling off, as evidenced by their recent victory in the Reisinger, the toughest of all team events. His "it's my turn, skip bid" philosophy is still far too radical for a solid citizen like myself, but the expert community has been duly impressed with the seven National Championships that Marty has amassed in the 1980's, four of which were in team competition.

In fact, the ACBL hierarchy was so impressed with Bergen-Cohen's sweep of the pair events at the Fall NAC in 1983 that they passed legislation intended to restrict the number of Bergen's very weak two bids. I understand that this has not fazed Marty in the least; he nows opens those hands with three bids!! At least it is comforting for me to know that I'll never lack swing hands when I need material for articles in *The Bridge World*.

I am forced to admit that I do take a look from time to time at Marty's articles, although I plan to have some other reading material handy when he writes about transfer preempts. Recently I even noticed some otherwise sensible people playing "Bergen raises." What is this world coming to?

Now we have Marty's first book, although he promises (threatens) that there are more to follow. I don't know how he could know so much about "uncontested auctions," as these never seem to occur when Marty's opponents have opened the bidding. Perhaps he rarely encounters opponents who practice the same competitive philosophy that he does.

As I look back over this introduction I can't fail to note that I have found myself saying some nice things about Marty's bridge, which isn't easy for me (after all, if his style is right, does that mean that mine...?). We will find out before long, for my coeditor has informed me that Marty and I will soon be adversaries in a *Bridge World* debate on preemptive tactics.

I highly recommend this book to players at all levels, although I do have one confession to make. I skipped the section on Bergen-Cohen agreements on weak two bids and three bids. If there is one thing that I don't need at this stage of my life it is more grey hair.

EDGAR KAPLAN
December, 1985

Foreword

Defining Treatments

Let's define what we mean by treatments. These are understandings that don't involve *conventions* but feature specific *partnership agreements*. For example, consider the 3♢ bid in the following auction:

PARTNER	RHO	YOU	LHO
1♡	1♠	2♡	2♠
3♢	Pass	?	

How does your partnership treat the 3♢ bid? Choose one from the following list which consists of various treatments in general use.

(1) Long-suit game try.
(2) Short-suit game try.
(3) Need-help game try.
(4) Long suit, not necessarily a game try.
(5) Lead director. Requests a diamond lead against an opponent's spade contract.

Which of these treatments should be Alerted? The ACBL says that any "unusual" treatment must be Alerted. Obviously, it is not always clear what is unusual and what isn't. But (2), (4), and (5) would deserve Alerts, and (1) would not. (3) is far from clear, in practice very few players Alert this.

We should be aware of the ACBL definition of the term. A treatment is "A call that indicates a desire to play in the denomination named (or promises or requests values in that denomination) but that also, by agreement, gives or requests information on which further action can be based." It seems that just about any call could be considered a treatment unless it is already a convention or a natural call.

Responding to 1♣ "Walsh"

We will take a look at this topic from the viewpoint of two distinct groups. The first group's view can be labeled as the "Standard" approach. They bid suits up the line and would always respond with a five-card diamond suit rather than a four-card major.

The second group includes those who agree with the Walsh and Kaplan-Sheinwold approaches. This group strains to respond in a major if possible, particularly on poor hands. For the moment we will refer to them as "Walsh." In comparing the two approaches, you will notice that the key for both is the *first response* and the theory behind the approved action. "Walsh" believes that responder should always show a four-card major immediately. The only exceptions are hands with very long diamond suits or very good hands that have slam potential.

Using the Walsh approach, let's try some hands in response to partner's opening bid of 1♣.

	PARTNER 1♣	RHO Pass	YOU ?	
1.	♠ KQ65	♡ Q874	◊ Q1042	♣ 8
2.	♠ 10743	♡ K53	◊ KQ974	♣ 8
3.	♠ 9	♡ A643	◊ Q87654	♣ 96
4.	♠ AK54	♡ A6	◊ K8743	♣ 93
5.	♠ 8	♡ Q953	◊ A1087432	♣ 8
6.	♠ 8	♡ 8654	◊ A654	♣ Q753
7.	♠ 654	♡ 863	◊ AQ5	♣ 8743
8.	♠ J954	♡ Q6	◊ 87	♣ A10654
9.	♠ 742	♡ 86	◊ AK874	♣ A65
10.	♠ Q104	♡ KJ5	◊ J6543	♣ Q9

(1) 1♡. "Walsh" players do go up the line as far as the majors are concerned. Diamonds are for children.

(2) 1♠. On a hand worth only one bid, make your bid in the most relevant suit. If you respond 1◊, you will have to bid 1♠ over 1♡ and then preference 2♡ over 2♣, which is much too much bidding on 8 HCP.

(3) 1♡. Even with six diamonds, the systemic response is to bid the major on a weak hand.

(4) 1 ◊. You are clearly strong enough to reverse, and you want partner to know that you have more diamonds than spades, in case the partnership is considering a choice of slams.

(5) 1 ◊. In this case 1 ♡ would really be going too far.

(6) 1 ♡. If we didn't bid diamonds on five or six, there is certainly no reason to bid them with only four.

(7) 1 ◊. This is not psych, but merely the lesser of evils. It would be wrong to bid 1 NT, since we don't wish to be declarer – and most partnerships require more than 6 HCP for a 1 NT response to 1♣. We obviously can't pass an opening suit bid with 6 points, and 2♣ does not seem right with no club honor and no ruffing value.

(8) 1♣. Very easy. A raise to 2♣ denies a four-card major.

(9) 1 ◊. Again, no problem.

(10) 1 NT. When you can show your hand in one bid, it is always a good idea to do so.

Is there a name for this style of responding, so that those who like to play this way can describe the style to potential partners? West Coast players refer to this as the "Walsh Diamond," named after Dick Walsh, West Coast expert of the 60's, who was one of the first successful practitioners of the style. Of course, Kaplan-Sheinwold adherents use this treatment in responding to 1♣, although in conjunction with weak notrumps.

When does a "Walsh" player respond 1 ◊ to 1♣? As our examples show, about the only hand types are (a) a hand with no major, usually with four or more diamonds, and (b) a full opening bid or better usually with five + diamonds as well as one or two four-card majors. The inferences that opener can draw from this can be very helpful.

Now we will concentrate on the rebidding by the opener from the point of view of both groups. Of course the rebidding style of each will be governed by their respective styles. After 1♣ – 1 ◊, Standard bidders must continue the up-the-line search for a major-suit fit. Responder could easily have a major as well as diamonds, so if opener doesn't show the major, a fit may be lost and responder may have a hand that is too weak for a second bid.

Walsh players are involved in a very different situation. A 1 ◊ responder has denied holding a four-card major unless preparing to reverse on a strong hand. Therefore, opener does not have to show a major if one is held. With a balanced hand, opener should take advantage of the methods used to show the minimum balanced hand by rebidding 1 NT. These players can't miss a major-suit fit since responder will now reverse into a major if one is held.

Let's zero in on this subject by bidding some hands. Bid each hand first from the Standard point of view (Answer "A") and then with the Walsh philosophy in mind (Answer "B").

SOUTH	NORTH
1♣	1 ◊
?	

1.	♠ AK109	♡ AQ9	◊ 87	♣ 10643
2.	♠ A874	♡ 10843	◊ A6	♣ AJ5
3.	♠ 9643	♡ K108	◊ A104	♣ AQ9
4.	♠ A64	♡ KQ95	◊ 8	♣ AQ743

(1) A – 1♠. Up the line we go.

B – 1 NT. Let partner know you have a weak notrump. North would have responded 1♠ if holding a weak hand containing four spades. If partner is about to bid spades now, holding a good hand, you will of course support spades. If none of this develops, you might get a favorable spade lead against your notrump contract.

(2) A – 1♡. Once again, up the line.

B – 1 NT. It is just as easy to suppress two major suits as one.

(3) A – 1♠. Partner could certainly have a hand like

$$\spadesuit K Q 7 2 \quad \heartsuit 9 \quad \diamondsuit Q J 6 5 4 \quad \clubsuit 8 7 4$$

where you belong in spades and this would be the only way to get there. Of course you may not like the idea of bidding two suits with 4 – 3 – 3 – 3 distribution or of suggesting a trump suit of 9 – 6 – 4 – 3, but it would be very dangerous to risk missing a 4 – 4 major-suit fit.

B – 1 NT. What's the problem?

(4) A – 1♡. This obvious rebid tells partner you have four hearts.

B – 1♡. This equally obvious call also shows four hearts, but guarantees an unblanced hand since we would always rebid 1 NT on a balanced hand.

We can now see that the sequence 1♣ – 1◊ – 1♡ or 1♣ – 1◊ – 1♠ means quite different things depending on whether the players are using Standard or Walsh. 1♣ – 1◊ – 1 NT is also an auction which might mean different things to different players. In Standard, 1♣ – 1◊ – 1 NT denies any four-card major. In Walsh, opener may have zero, one, or even two four-card majors.

Because of this I usually ask my opponents about such auctions when it might be relevant to the bidding, the defense, or the opening lead. Holding

$$\spadesuit 10 9 8 6 \quad \heartsuit K J 9 7 5 \quad \diamondsuit 8 2 \quad \clubsuit 9 5$$

in the balancing seat after

NORTH	EAST	SOUTH	WEST
1♣	Pass	1◊	Pass
1 NT	Pass	Pass	?

I would be less likely to balance with 2♡ against a Walsh pair whose opening bidder might have ♡A-Q-10-8!

Since the Walsh approach is so different from Standard, the Walsh bidders should Alert after 1♣ – 1◊ and also after 1♣ – 1◊ – 1 NT. As a Walsh player, I Alert a 1◊ response as denying a major (unless about to reverse) and a 1 NT rebid as possibly containing one or even two major suits. Also, a rebid of one of a major by opener after 1♣ – Pass – 1◊ should be Alerted as showing an unbalanced hand, since he would rebid 1 NT with a balanced hand.

The ACBL also encourages Walsh players to Alert after 1♣ – Pass – 1♡ and 1♣ – Pass – 1♠, informing the opponents that responder may have bypassed a diamond suit in order to show his major.

Let's move on to the matter of responder's rebids, where you will see that the early auction greatly affects the responder's thinking in planning the rebid.

In the following quiz, select your rebid using the Standard approach (A), then *Think Walsh* (B). In each case the auction begins.

1♣	1♢
1♠	?

1. ♠ A7   ♡ 864   ♢ A1074   ♣ 9743

2. ♠ KQ5   ♡ 653   ♢ 86542   ♣ K5

3. ♠ A   ♡ Q75   ♢ 976532   ♣ J106

(1) A – 1 NT or 2♣. 2♣ is probably the right bid in Standard American. You are not anxious to play notrump from your side – usually you should have the unbid suit stopped. Of course if partner has

♠ K Q J 9   ♡ K Q J   ♢ 8 6 5   ♣ J 5 2

or some similar hand, 2♣ should lead to a ridiculous contract with a cozy 1 NT available.

B – 2♣. Easy. Partner definitely has an unbalanced hand, and on this auction promises five or more clubs! Think about it. In order for partner to have an unbalanced hand, there must be a singleton, a void, or two doubletons. Therefore, partner's likely distributions are 4-2-2-5, 4-3-1-5, 4-1-3-5, 4-0-4-5, 4-?-?-6, 4-4-1-4, or 4-1-4-4. But with 4-4-1-4 he would rebid 1♡, and with 4-1-4-4 he would usually open 1♢. If he holds something like

♠ K Q 9 2   ♡ 9   ♢ 9 8 6 2   ♣ A K J 10

he will make sure we play in diamonds himself.

(2) A – 1 NT or 2♣ or Pass. 1 NT is not very attractive with no stopper in either red suit, but partner will expect four spades for the raise of a secondary suit. Many experts would go ahead and raise to two spades anyway, because of the location of the high cards, hoping that the 4 – 3 would be manageable. Pass will probably result in your playing in the correct strain, but even

♠ A J 6 4   ♡ 10 8 4   ♢ A   ♣ A Q J 6 4

in partner's hand is enough for a cold game.

B – 2♠. What's the problem? Partner will know we have only three-card support, since weak hands with diamonds and four spades would initially respond 1♠, not 1♢.

(3) A – 2♢. In Standard you really can't show preference for a minor with J-10-x when partner could have as few as three. Partner might retreat to 2♢ with 4 – 3 – 3 – 3 distribution, but certainly would not with 4 – 3 – 2 – 4

or 4-2-3-4. Therefore, 2 ◊ is the percentage action.

B — 2 ♣. As we observed earlier, partner must have five or more clubs. Prefer the known eight-card fit to rebidding your emaciated diamonds.

Since the auction

1 ♣	1 ◊
1 NT	

is also greatly effected by style, we must note a difference for responder's rebid between Standard and Walsh. Holding

♠ K 8 7 4   ♡ Q 6   ◊ A K 7 4 3   ♣ J 5

raise to 3 NT in Standard after 1 NT, since opener has denied a four-card major. But you must bid 2 ♣ using Walsh, since partner has said nothing about the presence or absence of majors in his hand.

What about

1 ♣	1 ◊
1 ♡	1 ♠?

In Standard, responder must rebid 1 ♠ with

♠ K Q 7 4   ♡ 8 4 2   ◊ K 9 6 5 3   ♣ 8

as opener could easily have four spades. Of course, those who use fourth suit forcing would also bid 1 ♠ with

♠ 6 5 3   ♡ A 6   ◊ A Q 8 6 4 2   ♣ A 7

being too strong for an invitational 3 ◊. Therefore

1 ♣	1 ◊
1 ♡	1 ♠

must be considered as ambiguous in Standard, possibly fourth suit forcing with a good hand, but quite possibly four spades and a weak hand.

With Walsh, responder would never use this auction with a weak hand. 1 ♠ would always have been bid at the first turn, so

1 ♣	1 ◊
1 ♡	1 ♠

guarantees a good hand in Walsh, eliminating opener's concern about the weak hand with four spades.

Although we haven't worried about them so far, what happens when the opponents get into the act? After opener bids 1 ♣ on

♠ 8 6 3   ♡ A K 7 4   ◊ 8   ♣ A Q 10 6 5

and responder bids 1 ◊ in Standard on

♠ 9 2   ♡ Q J 9 3   ◊ Q 10 6 5 4   ♣ J 8

how do we get to hearts after the opponents throw in a spade overcall and raise?

should opener reverse to 2♡ on 13 highs and a diamond misfit? Should responder commit the hand to the three level on a six count? It is not even obvious how to do so even if one wished to. (Some expert pairs would treat a double of 2♠ by responder as responsive, since the opponents have agreed on a suit, but they would not make the double on the garbage in question.) Meanwhile, we are probably cold for 3♡ or even 4♡, and are selling out to 2♠. Walsh players have no trouble getting to hearts – they respond in the major immediately.

What about trying to find a heart partscore after 1♣ – Pass – 1◇ – 2♠? Good luck. What about finding spades after 1♣ – Pass – 1◇ – 2♡, and being able to stop low if necessary?

So much for the Walsh vs. Standard argument. If the reader has received the impression that my experience with Walsh has convinced me of its superiority, I plead guilty. Of course, your choice is your own.

Walsh Questions

Question: **You say in your writings that there are two distinct groups when it comes to responding to 1♣, "Standard" and "Walsh." What is the preference these days of most good players?**

Answer: Years ago there would be no question in my mind that the Walsh players constituted a distinct minority. In the 1984 Bridge World Standard Poll, only 39% of experts, and 42% of subscribers responded 1◇ to 1♣ holding

♠ K J 6 2   ♡ 8 5 3   ◇ K J 6 2   ♣ 10 2.

Contrast that with over 50% of each group voting for 1◇ in 1967! And it is even clearer with hearts. Only 29% of experts voted for 1◇ with

♠ 5 3   ♡ K Q 10 2   ◇ Q 8 7 5 2   ♣ 6 4

with a mere 21% preferring 1◇ on

♠ 8 5 3   ♡ K J 6 2   ◇ K J 6 2   ♣ 10 2.

Question: **Holding**

♠ 8 6 4 3   ♡ A Q 5   ◇ –   ♣ K Q J 8 6 4

what would you rebid after 1♣ – 1◇?

Answer: Larry Cohen and I have discussed this situation, and we agreed to rebid 2♣. If partner passes 2♣, there is no danger of having missed a 4 – 4 spade fit, since partner can't have four spades. If partner has a good hand and bids again, there is time to get to spades later.

Question: **I agree with you that it is correct to suppress majors with a balanced hand after 1♣ – 1◇. But what about after 1♣ – 1♡? Should you bypass spades to rebid 1 NT?**

Answer: It is dangerous to rebid 1 NT over 1♡ holding four spades. If responder has four spades but is too weak to bid again, the partnership will languish in an inferior contract. Therefore I usually will rebid 1♠, as along as I have at least four clubs. With 4 – 3 – 3 – 3 I get into NT as fast as I can.

Question: **Holding**

♠ 9 4 2   ♡ K Q J 6   ◊ 8 5   ♣ A K J 10

would Walsh players still rebid 1 NT over 1 ◊? That looks like a case of overdoing it.

Answer: I agree. I would rebid 1♡ as if I had a two-suiter in clubs and hearts, which is what this hand looks like to me. When we Alert

1♣	1◊
1♡	

or

1♣	1◊
1♠,	

we announce "that opener is usually unbalanced, but could be balanced with extreme concentration." When I hold this hand, I want to play hearts rather than 1 NT opposite

♠ 8 7   ♡ A 8 7   ◊ 9 7 5 4 2   ♣ Q 9 5

or assorted other hands.

Question: **What inferences can opener draw about responder's length after an auction like**

1♣	1♠
1NT	2◊

playing Walsh.

Answer: Many players play 2◊ as "new minor forcing" where 2◊ is artificial and asks opener about spades and hearts. For many reasons I prefer 2♣ always as "checkback" also asking about majors. One reason is that the negative response is 2◊, as opposed to the 2 NT necessitated with this auction by "new minor" players. Secondly, my natural 2◊ rebid is nonforcing showing more diamonds than spades, uninterested in a correction back to spades. I would arrive at 2◊ with

♠ K 7 4   ♡ Q 6 4 3   ◊ K Q   ♣ K 7 5 4

opposite

♠ J 10 8 3   ♡ 9   ◊ J 10 9 7 6   ♣ A 3 2

on an auction of

1♣	1♠
1 NT	2◊
Pass	

I would bet that Standard bidders wallow in 1 NT or an even less elegant contract of 2♣.

Since 2 ◊ does not request a preference to spades, I have to rebid 2 ♠ with

♠ Q J 10 8 5   ♡ 6   ◊ A 6 5 4 2   ♣ 8 5

after

1 ♣	1 ♠
1 NT	

instead of 2 ◊. That doesn't bother me at all.

♧   ♤

Inverted Minors

Although many improvements in bidding have taken place in recent years, minor suit auctions are still a problem for many players. One reason is the lack of good methods. Many partnerships, even some involving top players, do not have a forcing raise available in the minors. Consider the following hand after partner has opened 1 ♣:

♠ A K 7
♡ A 8 4
◊ 9 4
♣ Q 10 8 7 5

If 3 ♣ shows a limit raise as many play, you are forced to respond 1 ◊ — better than bidding a 3-card major. Trying to recover after responding with two small cards in a suit may be an interesting, but unproductive, experience.

If you could bid 3-forcing-clubs you would have no trouble with the hand in question, but then what do you respond to 1 ♣ holding:

♠ Q 10 5
♡ K 6
◊ 8 3
♣ A 8 7 4 3 2

Forcing or limited? 3 ♣ must be defined as one or the other — one to a customer.

Not only is there an answer to this problem, but it's been around awhile. It comes to us from two of the best known personalities in bridge, Edgar Kaplan and Alfred Sheinwold — the originators of Kaplan-Sheinwold. Inverted minors were designed to work together with weak notrumps (a cornerstone of K-S), but they can also be used with strong notrumps. Since most players use a strong notrump, our discussion of inverted minors will be from the point of view of those players.

What do the various bids mean when you are using Inverted Minor Suit Raises?

1♣-2♣ and *1♢-2♢* show a *good raise,* while *1♣-3♣* and *1♢-3♢* are *weak preemptive raises.* Although this is the opposite of "standard," there are good logical reasons to play this way. With good hands you should try to keep the bidding low to allow more room for both opener and responder to describe their hands. When you have a fit in partner's minor and a bad hand, you don't mind taking bidding room away from your partner as it is unlikely that your side has a future in the auction. You also take valuable bidding room away from your opponents who have yet to enter the auction, but who could easily have the balance of power. The best analogy to help explain inverted minors is the major suit raise to the 4-level showing a weaker hand than the jump raise to the 3-level.

What, exactly, is a good raise? The minimum is roughly a limit raise, while there is no real maximum. The bid denies a 4-card major while showing at least good 4-card support for the minor. It is not forcing to game – only to 2 NT or three of the agreed minor. Of course, the partnership may eventually play game or slam.

The weak raise to 3♣ or 3♢ indicates very good support (almost always at least five cards), denies any 4+ card major, and shows fewer than 9 HCP. In fact, a near yarborough is possible if the vulnerability is right. Usually responder would have *a lot less* than 9 HCPs.

Before going further, let's try responding to 1♢ (neither side vulnerable and the next hand passes) to make sure we are still together.

Dealer	RHO	You
1♢	Pass	?

(1) ♠ 10 8 4 3
  ♡ K 8
  ♢ A Q 9 5 4
  ♣ 7 2

1♠. Never support an opening bid in a minor before showing a 4-card or longer major.

(2) ♠ A K 5
  ♡ 6 4
  ♢ K Q J 7 5
  ♣ Q 8 5

2♢. Your best move on this promising hand is to show your good support immediately.

(3) ♠ 8 6 3
  ♡ 9
  ♢ K Q J 5
  ♣ 10 8 7 4 3

3♢. This is the rare hand where you jump raise holding only four trumps.

(4) ♠ 9 5 4
♡ 8 7 6
◇ A K Q 6
♣ 9 6 5

1 NT. This may seem repulsive, but you are too weak for 2 ◇ and too strong and/or balanced for 3 ◇. You may not be playing notrump from the best side, but at least you are giving an accurate picture of your distribution and strength. All conventions occasionally give up something.

(5) ♠ 8 6
♡ 9 4
♠ Q 8 6 4 3 2
♣ 10 7 3

3 ◇. By all means! You are delighted to show your excellent support, lack of high cards, and desire to make life difficult for the opponents.

(6) ♠ A 7
♡ K 5 4
◇ Q J 10 9 4
♣ 8 7 5

2 ◇. With this limit raise type hand you don't intend to force to game, but are not embarrassed to show a *good* diamond raise.

This time assume both sides are vulnerable as partner opens 1♣ and the next hand passes.

(1) ♠ K 5
♡ K 7 4
◇ Q 10 3
♣ 9 8 6 5 4

1 NT. 3♣ is misleading with so much outside of clubs and a fair hand. You may get a chance to support clubs later.

(2) ♠ K J 5
♡ A Q 3
◇ K J 8
♣ 10 9 4 3

2 NT. With such bad clubs and such good stoppers, this must be more to the point than 2♣.

(3) ♠ 9 4
♡ 8 5
◇ A K Q 8 6
♣ A K 10 5

2 ◇. Your hand is so perfect for a jump shift followed by supporting clubs that 2♣ would be *per*verted, not *in*verted.

(4) ♠ A 6 5
♡ Q 7
◇ A J 8 5
♣ J 6 4 3

1 ◇. The clubs are too weak for 2 ♣, so wait for partner's natural rebid.

Opener's Rebids

After the Jump Raise. Opener usually passes the jump raise; after all responder is very weak. Occasionally however, game and even slam are possible. Opener can show a stopper trying for 3 NT – which could turn out to be the first move on a hand interested in slam. Even splinter bids may be employed; opener may have a big hand with a long minor and the determination of fit can be crucial.

Try rebidding these hands after your 1 ♣ opening bid has been preemptively raised to 3 ♣. Assume that neither side is vulnerable for all of these problems.

1) ♠ A Q
♡ K 10 6
◇ A Q
♣ A 9 7 4 3 2

2) ♠ A J 8 5
♡ Q 6
◇ A 5
♣ A Q 7 4 3

3) ♠ J 8
♡ A K 6 4
◇ A 8
♣ A K 9 5 3

4) ♠ A K 8 7
♡ A 8 6 3
◇ –
♣ A J 9 5 4

1) *3 NT.* This must have some play. You have a good chance to run clubs even if partner's five clubs lack the king.

2) *Pass.* A nice hand, but no game rates to be good. Partner could have as much as ♠ 94 ♡ 105 ◇ K1074 ♣ KJ1062 and no game has a play.

3) *3 ♡.* You can't bid 3 NT without a spade stopper, or even drive to a game, but you are too good to pass. Partner will bid 3 ♠ with a spade stopper, 3 NT with stoppers in spades and diamonds (unlikely), otherwise 4 ♣ or 5 ♣. All are okay with you.

4) *4 ◇ (Splinter).* Only 16 HCP, but chance for slam is excellent for the known big fit. This splinter bid will get partner to concentrate on major-suit honors and shortness as well as club strength. After all, you have a fair play for a grand slam opposite: ♠ Q6 ♡ 94 ◇ J874 ♣ K10862. Of course you would be content to get to a *small* slam on these cards.

After the Single Raise (1 ♣-2 ♣; 1 ◇-2 ◇). Most play that this auction is forcing to 2 NT or three of the minor, but not necessarily any further.

In Kaplan-Sheinwold or any system using weak notrumps, a 2 NT rebid shows a strong notrump and, logically, is forcing. However, after 1 ◇-2 ◇ strong notrumpers may rebid 2 NT on:

♣ K5 ♡ KJ6 ◇ A864 ♣ Q1053

and have responder pass holding

♠ QJ8   ♡ Q9   ◇ K973   ♣ K842

or bid a nonforcing 3◇ on

♠ 94   ♡ 93   ◇ KQJ75   ♣ A864

Let's take a look at other rebids and their meanings.

After 1◇-2◇, 2♡-2♠. Often a four-card suit, but could be the cheapest stopper. Guarantees at least four diamonds.

2 NT. Natural, nonforcing. Shows a balanced minimum, usually with lots of stoppers. Opener always rebids notrump with an original three-card minor.

3♣. Usually four plus club cards, suggests an unbalanced hand.

3◇. Nonforcing, an unbalanced minimum.

3♡, 3♠, 4♣. Splinter bid. Slam-try strength.

3 NT. Shows a balanced hand too good to open 1 NT. Slam is certainly possible.

Try these now after 1♣-2♣:

1)	♠ A 10 6 4	2)	♠ A Q 5
	♡ 9		♡ K J 6
	◇ 10 7 4		◇ K 8 5
	♣ A K Q 8 5		♣ A J 9 6
3)	♠ A Q 5	4)	♠ A J 7 4 3
	♡ A 10 6		♡ K 5
	◇ 8 3		◇ 8
	♣ K J 7 4 2		♣ A J 7 4 2

1) *2♠*. The next move is up to partner.
2) *3 NT*. Giving a very good picture of the hand.
3) *2♡*. The cheapest stopper.
4) *2♠*. We will rebid spades next to show the long suit.

Responder's Second Bid

Responder's rebids follow common sense lines rather than strict rules. Responder should try to avoid "closeout" bids when the hand still has slam potential. Of course responder must keep in mind which bids are forcing and which are not.

What should responder rebid after

    1◇-2◇
    2♡-?

1)	♠ A K 8	2)	♠ K J 7
	♡ K 5		♡ J 4
	◇ K 8 7 4 3		◇ Q 8 6 4 3
	♣ 10 8 3		♣ K J 5

3)	♠ A 5	4)	♠ J 7
	♡ 9 3		♡ K Q 8
	◇ Q J 8 7 4		◇ A K 8 6 4 3
	♣ A K 7 4		♣ 9 4

1) *2♠*. No problem for the time being; opener can now clarify his intentions.

2) *2 NT*. Not forcing, showing stoppers in both black suits without a great hand.

3) *3♣*. Too good a hand to say 3 NT. We have an excellent hand for slam. 3♣ is preferable to 2♠ in order to emphasize the clubs and possibly allow a subsequent spade bid beneath 3 NT.

4) *3♡*. Shows a good hand without black suit stoppers.

In Competition

Most players abandon inverted minors in competition and play fairly traditional methods. After 1♣-Dbl.-? 2♣ is weak and 3♣ shows at least five clubs with a weak hand. (This bid is virtually unchanged.) 2 NT can be used as Jordan, showing a limit raise in clubs or better with very good support. With lesser support, responder can redouble and then support.

After an overcall, such as 1◇-1♠-? 2◇ should be natural and competitive and there are two popular schools of thought regarding the jump to 3◇. Some play this as a limit raise, reserving the cuebid for the forcing raise. More aggressive players retain the jump to 3◇ as preemptive, with the cuebid signifying a limit raise or better. This can present ambiguities which may be difficult to resolve in the limited bidding space available.

Defense Against Inverted Minors

Be careful against a 1 minor–2 minor auction since both opponents may be very strong. Of course with a good long suit or lots of shape, it's usually right to bid.

Try to be aggressive with good distribution against the 1 minor–3 minor bid, although the level at which you have to bid is uncomfortably high. Of course, that's one of the reasons people use inverted minors.

Although inverted minors are not for everyone, it is important to understand them in order to be prepared for those opponents who employ the convention. A study of inverted minors can improve everyone's knowledge of minor-suit auctions, where there's a lot more involved than simply guessing whether to play 3 NT, 6♣ or 6◇.

Artificial Raises (Minor Suits)

Raising opener's suit after one-of-a-major presents a totally different problem than after one-of-a-minor. Since the major suit opening bid shows five card or greater length, we designate various auctions to distinguish the various raises of partner's suit. We are able to show and distinguish each of the following:

(1) A bad three-card raise
(2) A good three-card raise
(3) A preemptive four-card raise
(4) A good four-card raise
(5) A three card limit raise
(6) A four-card limit raise
(7) A balanced forcing raise
(8) A very big balanced raise
(9) A splinter raise
(10) A bad raise to 4
(11) A good raise to 4

After a minor-suit opening bid, we have less work to do. We can forget all the three-card raises, since we never want to make a direct raise of a minor suit opening bid on only three cards. Also, splinter bids will play a much less important role since —

1. We'll never make this bid holding a four-card major.
2. We need at least five trumps to splinter over a minor.
3. It's far from clear that 1 ♣ – 3 ♣ shouldn't show a preemptive spade hand.

Therefore, we have four main hand types to worry about in response to a one-of-a-minor opening bid. They are (assume here that partner opens 1 ◊):

1. The normal raise —

  ♠ 10 6   ♡ 9 3 2   ◊ A K 7 5   ♣ J 6 4 2

2. The preemptive raise —

  ♠ 10 6   ♡ 9 3   ◊ Q J 7 4 2   ♣ 10 6 4 2

3. The limit raise —

  ♠ A 10 2   ♡ 9 3   ◊ K Q J 4   ♣ 10 8 7 4

4. The forcing raise —

  ♠ A 6 2   ♡ 9 3   ◊ K Q J 4   ♣ A 8 7 4

How are minor suit raises handled by most duplicate players?

In Standard American, a single raise shows at least four-card support and modest values, about 6 – 10 points, while the jump raise shows a limit, invitational raise with 11 – 12 points. However, that leaves no way to show a forcing raise. Some players therefore choose to treat the jump raise as forcing, but they have a problem with a limit raise.

In *Aces Scientific,* Bobby Goldman suggested that 3-of-the-other-minor (i.e., 1 ◊ – 3 ♣ and 1 ♣ – 3 ◊) be employed as the forcing raise. This is definitely an improvement on standard methods, allowing the partnership to have both a limit raise and a forcing raise. Notice though that no standard methods allow for a preemptive raise short of the 4-level, although these can be devastating when it is the opponents' hand.

Kaplan-Sheinwold does feature a preemptive raise. They jump raise the minor-suit opening bid to the 3-level on bad hands. They start the limit raises and forcing raises with a constructive single raise and hope to sort them out later. This approach is popular among the expert community and may well represent an improvement on standard methods. However, hands worth a normal single raise like

♠ Q 8 4   ♡ 8   ◊ J 5 3 2   ♣ A 9 7 4 3

must respond 1 NT, which is a serious price to pay.

Isn't there a way to do better?

Since each of the above has some good features, let's borrow a little from each to achieve a more desirable framework.

Our single raises will be the standard variety, non-forcing, with 6 – 10 points including distribution. Our jump raises will be preemptive, as in K – S.

Holding a limit raise, we will jump to one step *below* 3 of opener's minor. Therefore 1 ♣ – 2 NT and 1 ◊ – 3 ♣ will be Alerted as artificial limit raises. Holding a natural 2 NT response to 1 ♣ we will temporize with 1 ◊.

Once you have accepted this idea, it's merely one small step to our forcing raise. With this hand, we jump to one step *above* 3 of opener's minor suit – 1 ♣ – 3 ◊ or 1 ◊ – 3 ♡.

Here's the structure.

Raises After an Opening Bid of 1 ♣ or 1 ◊.

	1 ♣	1 ◊
Normal single raise	2 ♣	2 ◊
Limit raise	2 NT	3 ♣
Preemptive raise	3 ♣	3 ◊
Forcing raise	3 ◊	3 ♡

Now try responding with the following hands. In each case partner has opened 1 ♣.

1.   ♠ A K   ♡ J 4   ◊ 8 7 4 3   ♣ K Q 10 5 4

Bid 3 ◊ showing a forcing club raise.

2.   ♠ A 10 6   ♡ K J 9   ◊ K 8 7 4   ♣ K 9 5

Bid 1 ◊. You would prefer to jump to 2 NT showing a good balanced hand but we're using that as a limit raise. Temporize with 1 ◊ and jump later.

3.   ♠ 10 6   ♡ 9 4 2   ◊ 7 6 4 2   ♣ A Q 7 4

Bid 2 ♣ and tell it all in one bid.

4.   ♠ 9   ♡ 6 5 4   ◇ J 7 4 2   ♣ K 10 9 7 4

Bid 3♣, preemptive. This is the indicated action at any vulnerability.

5.   ♠ K 7   ♡ K 7   ◇ Q 10 4   ♣ J 10 9 6 4 2

Bid 2 NT, our limit raise. Partner can sign off in 3♣ holding a minimum. So much for minor suit raises. With this structure we should be able to clue partner in as to our minor suit fit while making it difficult for the opponents to explore for their own fit.

♧ ─── ♧

1NT Forcing Response

For the last 15 years in this counntry, the trend has been to avoid opening in a major suit without at least five-card length. The popularity of five-card major systems, such as Precision, Kaplan-Sheinwold, and Roth-Stone offer proof that thoughts have changed since the heyday of Charles Goren when four-card majors were commonly opened.

The current popularity of five-card majors is not likely to be a passing fancy either. Since it is generally agreed that five-card majors are easier to play, bridge teachers all over the country are instructing students to open their better minor unless the major suit is five cards long. This is especially advisable for beginners who do not yet possess the judgment and understanding necessary to know when a four-card major suit should be opened.

Most players who play five-card majors have found it advantageous to use a response of 1 NT to an opening bid of 1♡ or 1♠ as forcing. The reasons for this are sound. If responder has three or more cards in opener's major, that suit probably should be trump. If responder has a singleton or void in the major, then play in another suit is usually preferable to notrump. It is only when responder has a minimum (6–10 high-card points) with exactly two cards in the major suit that 1 NT will be the correct contract. Since these hands occur rather infrequently, missing a possible 1 NT contract seems a small price to pay in exchange for a tool that works better on most hands.

For example, you hold

♠ 8 4   ♡ K J 9 4 3 2   ◇ 7   ♣ Q 7 6 3

and hear your partner open 1♠. Since you are not strong enough to bid at the two level, you respond 1 NT. If you play this as nonforcing, you will play there opposite hands like

♠ A K 7 5 2   ♡ Q 6   ◇ K 5 4   ♣ J 4 2

16

with no chance of making your contract. However, if 1 NT is forcing, you can plan on bidding 2 ♡ over two of a minor and either play it there or pass 2 ♠ if partner rebids to show a six-card suit.

Let's see what other kinds of hands responder may hold for his 1 NT response to a major-suit opening bid. All 1 NT responses fit into the following categories:

(1) Hands that would respond a nonforcing 1 NT, i.e. those hands with 6 – 10 high-card points, no suit to bid at the one level, not enough trumps to raise, and not worth venturing to the two level.

(2) Hands with 10 – 12 points that may even include trump support and are relatively balanced.

(3) Weak hands containing a long suit (six or more).

(4) Very weak hands that are worth a raise of partner's suit.

Here are some examples of 1 NT responses to 1 ♠ :

1.   ♠ K 6 3   ♡ A 5 4 2   ◇ 8 7   ♣ K 10 8 4

Bid 1 NT then jump raise spades. This auction shows a limit raise (10 – 12) with three-card support. However, if partner bids hearts, you will raise that suit.

2.   ♠ 8 5   ♡ 9 4   ◇ 8 7 2   ♣ K Q J 10 8 4

Bid 1 NT. Your next bid will be 3 ♣ showing a weak hand with a good suit. If one of your small cards was an ace, you would bid 2 ♣ then 3 ♣, invitational.

3.   ♠ 6 4   ♡ Q J 7   ◇ K J 5 2   ♣ A 10 6 4

Bid 1 NT, then 2 NT over partner's two-level bid. This shows a balanced 10 – 12 with fewer than three spades.

Because large numbers of hands call for a rebid over 1 NT regardless of whether it is forcing, 1 NT forcing is not that much of a change. Nevertheless, there are certain considerations with which all practitioners of the convention should be familiar.

Since opener has already promised five-card length with his major suit opening bid, rebidding his suit after the forcing notrump shows extra length – at least six. Therefore, with a hand of 5 – 3 – 3 – 2 distribution, opener must bid his cheaper three-card minor suit. After 1 ♠ – 1 NT, bid 2 ◇ on

               ♠ A K 8 4 2   ♡ 10 6 3   ◇ A 8 4   ♣ Q 9

and 2 ♣ on

               ♠ A Q 7 4 3   ♡ K 8   ◇ A 5 4   ♣ J 3 2.

The other type of problem hand is one containing four spades and five hearts which isn't good enough to reverse. For those who don't play Flannery 2 ◇, the general idea is to bid your longer minor if your minor suit cards are divided 3 – 1 or 4 – 0, and to lament if they are distributed 2 – 2. With a hand such as

               ♠ A 8 6 3   ♡ K J 8 5 4   ◇ K 4   ♣ Q 8

bid 2♣, but if your hearts are very good, a lie of 2♡ is probably better.

Since auctions such as 1♠ – 1 NT – 2♡ and 1♠ – 1 NT – 2♠ are not affected by the forcing notrump, responder's rebids over these are unchanged. However, since his maximum is greater with the forcing notrump, he makes bids like 2 NT more often than opposite the nonforcing notrump.

However, after an auction such as 1♠ – 1 NT – 2♣, the situation is quite different because of the possibility of a three-card suit. Responder never passes with less than four-card support, and even with four is reluctant to pass since the partnership may have only seven trumps. With five to nine high card points, responder will either pass 2♣, prefer 2♠ on a doubleton, or bid a suit of his own. Also, with a very weak raise of partner's major, responder now gives a preference for that suit at the two level. This is an effective way to bid

♠ J 8 4   ♡ A 7 2   ◇ 9 8 4 3 2   ♣ 4 3

after a 1♠ opening bid. This way you keep the bidding open in case partner has a monster, make it tough for the opponents to come in, and insure playing in spades, yet your action does not encourage partner the way a direct raise would.

When responder holds 10–12 points after 1♠ – 1 NT – 2♣, he has the following bids available:

(1) Jump raise to 3♠ showing the delayed limit raise with three trumps.
(2) Bid 2 NT with red-suit stoppers.
(3) Raise to 3♣ with support, usually five-card length.

Now that we have seen some of the ramifications of 1 NT forcing, let us try some examples of rebidding by the 1 NT bidder.

In each case the auction has gone

1♠   1 NT;
2◇   ?

1.   ♠ 4   ♡ K Q J 6 5   ◇ 8 7 4 3   ♣ 9 6 5

Bid 2♡. Remember that partner may have only 3 diamonds.

2.   ♠ J 8   ♡ K 8 4 3   ◇ K 6 4   ♣ J 6 4 2

Bid 2♠. It is safe to give a spade preference when partner is known to have at least five.

3.   ♠ A 8 4   ♡ 6 3   ◇ Q J 9 4   ♣ A 9 7 5

Bid 4♠. You were intending to jump to 3♠, but now that you know partner has diamonds, you should insist on game because of the fit.

Now let us examine the effect of this convention on our two-level responses.

Since the 1 NT response can be made on a stronger hand and is forcing, the minimum requirement for a two-level response is a much better hand than in standard methods. In fact, after a two-level response to a major suit, the auction is considered to be forcing to game except when responder later rebids his suit at the three-level. Therefore, auctions like

$$1\spadesuit-2\clubsuit \qquad\qquad 1\spadesuit-2\clubsuit \qquad\qquad 1\spadesuit-2\clubsuit$$
$$2\heartsuit-2\spadesuit \qquad\qquad 2\heartsuit-3\heartsuit \qquad\qquad 2\heartsuit-2\,NT$$

are all game forcing with only

$$1\spadesuit-2\clubsuit$$
$$2\heartsuit-3\clubsuit$$

being invitational. Because of this, it is necessary to respond 1 NT after 1 ♠ instead of bidding at the two-level with such hands as:

    ♠ A 6 4   ♡ K Q J 10 6   ◊ 8 3   ♣ 9 4 2

    ♠ 8 4   ♡ 7 3   ◊ A 8 6 5   ♣ A Q J 8 6

    ♠ J 10 7   ♡ 4 2   ◊ 9 8   ♣ A K J 6 4 3

    ♠ J   ♡ 8 2   ◊ K Q 7 5 2   ♣ K Q 9 4 3

    When responder is a passed hand, the situation becomes quite different. Since responder should bid a good suit if he has one, the 1 NT response becomes similar to the nonforcing 1 NT response when made by a passed hand. 1 NT can now be passed by opener with a minimum 5-3-3-2 hand such as

    ♠ A Q 6 4 2   ♡ K 7 3   ◊ J 4 2   ♣ Q 6.

Therefore responder should no longer bid 1 NT with a three-card limit raise, but should prefer to play Drury.

    With a passed hand like

    ♠ 6 3   ♡ K J 7   ◊ A J 10 4   ♣ Q 10 7 6

after a third-hand 1 ♠ bid, you can jump to 2 NT as you would in standard methods. However, if your partnership allows bids on light hands in third seat, you just bid 1 NT followed by 2 NT, and if partner passes 1 NT on a balanced minimum, you should be in your best spot.

    Let's try a few examples of responding as a passed hand. Also consider what you would do as an unpassed hand. In each case the auction has been

$$\text{Pass}-1\spadesuit$$
$$?$$

1.   ♠ 6   ♡ K 7 3   ◊ A J 9 8 6 4   ♣ 8 4 2

    Bid 2 ◊. You would have bid a forcing notrump as an unpassed hand since your hand and suit are not worth bidding 2 ◊ then 3 ◊. However, as a passed hand you don't have to worry about rebids.

2.   ♠ J   ♡ 8 3   ◊ K Q 7 6 3   ♣ K Q 5 4 2

    Bid 2 ◊. You would like to bid 2 ◊ then 3 ♣ nonforcing, and that's exactly what you should do. If you hadn't passed though, that auction would be forcing, so you would have had to respond 1 NT first.

3.　　　　　♠ K 6 4　　♡ 8 5 3 2　　♢ K 7 2　　♣ 9 4 2

Bid 1 NT. You still respond 1 NT and not 2♠ with this, since the raise to 2♠ is too forward going for this hand.

Defense Against 1 NT Forcing

Is a special defense needed if your opponents use 1 NT Forcing? No, but it is important to be aware of the meaning and inferences of the opponents' auction. Since

$$1♠ - 1 \text{ NT}$$
$$2♣ - 2♠$$

usually shows doubleton support, you would not tend to balance very often, but you wouldn't tend to balance on this auction after a nonforcing notrump either. Double of the forcing notrump should remain for takeout, and the requirements for an overcall are also unchanged. It is also important to remember that

$$1♠ - 1 \text{ NT}$$
$$2♣$$

may be a three-card suit, but

1♠	Pass	1 NT	Pass
2♣	Dbl		

is still best employed as a takeout double for the red suits.

You must also be aware of auctions that don't include a forcing 1 NT response. If your opponents are playing 1 NT Forcing, beware of making an "automatic" balance after 1♠ – 2♠ since 2♠ always shows a pretty good raise. In addition, the minimum requirement for 1♠ – 2♢ is raised considerably with 1 NT Forcing. Therefore, you would probably pass on a hand such as

♠ 6 3　　♡ K Q 5 2　　♢ K 7　　♣ A 10 8 4 2

or

♠ 8 5 4 3　　♡ K Q 9 7 2　　♢ K 6 3　　♣ A

after 1♠ – 2♢, since it is much less likely to be your hand.

Let's sum up by taking a look at the advantages and disadvantages of the convention. Playing 1 NT Forcing has the following disadvantages:

(1) It is no longer possible to play in 1 NT, which may be the right contract. Not playing 1 NT can be a problem in that it may be your last chance for a plus score (unlikely) or can cause you to miss your best partscore at matchpoints.

(2) Responder occasionally won't be able to show his suit. With:

♠ A J 4　　♡ 9 2　　♢ J 7 3　　♣ K Q 9 6 4,

you will be unable to bid clubs on any of these auctions:

1♠ - 1 NT	1♡ - 1 NT	1♡ - 1 NT
2♢	2♡	3♢

1♡ - 1 NT	1♡ - P - 1 NT - 2♠
3♡	P - P

(3) The fact that opener sometimes must rebid in a three-card suit can create ambiguities and insoluble problems. After

$$1♠ - 1 \text{ NT}$$
$$2♣$$

if you hold

♠ A   ♡ 8 6 4 3   ♢ 9 7 5 2   ♣ K Q 10 6

you have a nice supporting hand if partner has four or more clubs, and game is still possible. If he has only three though, you may regret bidding after 2♣. Even worse, what do you do after

$$1♠ - 1 \text{ NT}$$
$$2♣$$

with

♠ 9   ♡ K J 7 2   ♢ 10 6 4 3 2   ♣ Q 7 4 ?

There is really nothing to do except pass (and pray for someone to balance), but if your partner makes a face when you put down the dummy and takes 10 minutes to play the hand, you are probably witnessing the play of a 3-3 fit.

Now that you're convinced you shouldn't play 1 NT Forcing, let's look at the convention's advantages, which suggest you should try it.

(1) You no longer have an impossible problem in responding with a weak distributional hand. After partner opens 1♠, there is no good response on

♠ 6 3   ♡ K J 9 7 4 2   ♢ Q 6 5 2   ♣ 10

in standard methods. Pass risks missing a game, 1 NT is almost always a silly contract whenever partner passes, and 2♡ will mislead partner as to your strength. With 1 NT Forcing, you don't have to worry about playing 1 NT. On the next round you can bid your hearts or pass 2♣ since partner will have six and a minimum hand for that bid.

(2) Opener need not worry about partner passing in the middle of the auction, which we've all seen happen with

♠ A 10 9 8 6 3   ♡ 9   ♢ A J 8 5   ♣ A 7

opposite

♠ J 5   ♡ A J 8 6 4 3   ♢ K 6   ♣ 8 6 3

after the auction

$$1♠ - 2♡$$
$$2♣ - \text{Pass.}$$

Remember that responder guarantees another bid after a two-over-one, so it is not necessary for opener to jump on all good hands. With

♠ A K 8 5 3 2   ♡ Q 2   ◇ A 7   ♣ A 6 3

after 1♠ – 2♣, opener can bid 2♦ or 3♣ secure in the knowledge that partner will not pass and that the search for the best game or slam can be explored at leisure.

(3) Another auction that is clarified with 1 NT Forcing is one like

1♠ – 2◇
2♡ – 3◇

In standard this can be anything from

♠ 6 3   ♡ J 7 2   ◇ Q J 10 7 4 3 2   ♣ A

to

♠ 8 5   ♡ 10 6 3   ◇ A K Q J 9 4   ♣ 7 2.

Playing 1 NT Forcing, this auction always shows a hand of invitational strength, so declarer will never be faced with a hopeless dummy in 3 NT.

(4) You are not forced to bid a terrible suit at the two-level. In standard you must respond 2♣ to an opening bid of 1♠ with

♠ A Q   ♡ A 6 3 2   ◇ J 4 2   ♣ J 7 4 3,

hardly an appetizing choice. With 1 NT Forcing you start off with 1 NT, which avoids sending a misleading message.

(5) The other two clarified sequences involve raises of opener's suit. When playing 1 NT Forcing, the simple raise is normally played as semi-constructive, meaning about 8 – 10 points counting distribution. Thus after 1♡ bid 2♡ on

♠ A 6 4   ♡ K 7 2   ◇ 6 4   ♣ J 8 5 3 2

or

♠ 10 8 2   ♡ K 10 4   ◇ A 8 6 5   ♣ Q 6 5,

but bid 1 NT on

♠ 7 4 2   ♡ K J 6 5   ◇ J 4 3   ♣ 10 6 5

or

♠ Q 6 3   ♡ K 5 2   ◇ J 9 4 3 2   ♣ 7 4.

This helps opener judge when to try for game.

(6) Limit raise auctions are also clarified. When playing that 1♡ – 3♡ shows four trumps, opener should bid game on all unbalanced hands, since responder will have the needed trumps to ruff out declarer's losers. After

1♡ – 1 NT
2♣ – 3♡

though, opener knows he will be facing only three-card support and needs more high cards in order to bid game. Holding

♠ 7   ♡ K 10 9 4 3   ◇ A 10 7 6   ♣ A 4 3

many players would pass after 1 ♡ - 3 ♡, but this is a clear-cut raise to game opposite four trumps because of the controls. However, after

1 ♡ - 1 NT
2 ◇ - 3 ♡

you should pass.

Questions on 1 NT Forcing

Question: **Playing 1 NT Forcing, is it still forcing if bid by a passed hand? If not, should this be alerted?**

Answer: If a passed partner uses 1 NT Forcing, opener can pass since partner can no longer be planning a big surprise on the next round of bidding. If he had a strong suit he could show it directly without sounding strong in high cards; and he could use Drury to show a limit raise in a major. Therefore, the 1 NT response can be passed if opener has a balanced minimum like

♠ A J 7 5 4   ♡ K 8   ◇ Q 10 5   ♣ K 10 4.

There is no reason for him to disturb 1 NT since game is so unlikely. Of course, with a distributional hand, he would make his normal rebid. However, the 1 NT bid should still be alerted. Responder could have a balanced hand with 10 - 12 high card points, which is not true in standard. Also opener may rebid 2 ♣ on

♠ A Q 10 5 4   ♡ A 6   ◇ K 7 2   ♣ K 6 4,

and the opponents would not expect a possible three-card suit without the alert. When I alert 1 NT Forcing by a passed hand I say that it is "forcing – except on a balanced minimum," which gets the message across.

Question: **What does opener rebid over 1 NT Forcing with a strong hand?**

Answer: Opener rebids over 1 NT Forcing similar to the way he would rebid over a nonforcing 1 NT bid. The only differences are:
a. a rebid of two of a minor may be a three-card suit;
b. the point range for a raise to 2 NT is slightly higher.
Remaining strong rebids are identical. The major differences caused by 1 NT Forcing are mainly reflected in responder's actions.

Question: **Is it possible to play 1 NT Forcing with four-card majors?**

Answer: 1 NT Forcing is playable only because responder can give a preference to opener's major on a doubleton in a pinch, knowing that partner has at least five. Therefore, play 1 NT Forcing only in conjunction with five-card majors.

Question: **What should you rebid on 6-4 hands after partner's 1 NT response?**

Answer: The general advice to follow is to bid the four-card suit on the better hands when you're hoping partner won't pass, and to simply rebid the six-card major on the weaker hands. Therefore, after 1♠-1 NT, bid 2◊ on

♠ A Q 10 6 4 3   ♡ K 7   ◊ A J 10 6   ♣ 9,

but with

♠ K Q J 7 4 3   ♡ 8 5   ◊ A J 6 2   ♣ 4

just bid 2♠.

Question: **What should 4♣ be on each of the following auctions?**

1. 1♠–1 NT	2. 1♠–1 NT	3. 1♠–1 NT
3♡–4♣	3♠–4♣	2♡–4♣

Answer: We're playing 1 NT Forcing, so that responder's maximum is a pretty fair hand. Although responder could have a lot of clubs for his 1 NT response, the four-level is kind of late to be introducing a new suit. Therefore, what all of these auctions have in common is that responder's 4♣ bid is a fit-showing cuebid. On auction (1) responder could have

♠ Q 6   ♡ K 10 7 4   ◊ 9 2   ♣ A J 7 4 3,

For auction (2)

♠ K 9 3   ♡ 9 2   ◊ 7 4 3   ♣ A K 10 6 5

is possible, since here we are supporting spades. Since auction (3) is least likely to lead to slam (opener didn't jump), responder might be as good as

♠ K 5   ♡ K 10 6 4 3   ◊ 8   ♣ A 10 7 4 2.

Question: **I've played against you when you've explained an Alert of a 1 NT response to a major as "almost forcing." What do you mean by that?**

Answer: We play two-over-one game forcing, so need 1 NT Forcing to show three-card limit raises, as well as other invitational hands. However, we also open light, so being always forced to bid over a 1 NT response may be inconvenient. The solution is to allow opener to pass 1 NT with a minimum balanced hand. Therefore, our maximum for a 1 NT response is 11 or a bad 12 HCP. Opener is therefore relatively safe in passing 1 NT with 11-13 balanced. Also, by opening 1 NT with 14–16 and not hesitating to open 1 NT with a five-card major, we almost never need to rebid in a three-card minor, which is useful information for responder in evaluating his fit for opener's second suit.

These hands would open 1♡ and pass a 1 NT response.

1.   ♠ K J 7   ♡ K J 7 4 2   ◊ A 6   ♣ 9 5 4

2.   ♠ K 5 3   ♡ 8 6 4 3 2   ◊ A 7   ♣ A J 5

3.   ♠ K J 7 4   ♡ Q 8 6 4 2   ◊ A J   ♣ Q 5

Note that this solves the impossible rebid problem on hand (3) for those of us who play 1 NT Forcing but don't play Flannery 2◊.

Question: **How can you afford to pass 1 NT when responder might have a three-card limit raise? How can you risk missing a game?**

Answer: I've never found this to be a problem. If I have a balanced minimum, I'm going to be rejecting responder's game invitation by passing three-of-a-major, and it has never bothered me to play in a safe, cozy 1 NT trying for overtricks, as opposed to a touch-and-go three-level partscore with two balanced hands facing one another. Usually an unsuccessful finesse or a bad suit split will result in a minus score.

By the way, our results in this area have been quite good. We aren't always in the best contract, but we do seem to go plus because we are stopping so low. Besides the opponents do not always defend 1 NT perfectly.

♠   ♠

Bids Showing Fit

Following a Forcing Notrump Response

Suppose you hold

♠ A 10 5   ♡ 4 3   ◊ A 9 8 6   ♣ Q 7 4 2

and hear your partner open 1♡. Your partnership uses a response of 1 NT here as forcing, so that is your choice. Partner rebids 2♣, which could be a three-card suit. You are certainly worth another bid since even a slam is still possible opposite

♠ 4 2   ♡ A K 10 9 5   ◊ 7   ♣ A K 9 5 3.

However, it is not at all clear whether you should raise clubs or bid notrump. 2 NT will be a terrible contract opposite

♠ 8   ♡ Q J 7 5 2   ◊ K Q 4   ♣ K J 9 3,

while a raise to 3♣ will look ridiculous if partner holds

♠ Q 7 4   ♡ A K Q 5 2   ◊ Q 5   ♣ 8 5 3.

Is there any way to avoid a blind guess?

We need an alternate bid to show our hand when we can't decide whether to raise clubs or suggest notrump. Fortunately there's an idle bid – 2♠ – we can put to good use. 2♠ cannot show a real suit – if we had spades we would have responded 1♠, not 1 NT. Partner will Alert the 2♠ bid and explain, when questioned, that 2♠ shows clubs with values for 2 NT while saying nothing about spades.

With this in mind let us view life from opener's point of view. What would you bid with each of the following hands after an auction of

$$
\begin{array}{ll}
1\heartsuit & 1\ \text{NT} \\
2\clubsuit & 2\spadesuit \\
?
\end{array}
$$

1.   ♠ K 4 3   ♡ K 8 7 5 3   ◇ 9   ♣ A Q 8 6

Bid 3♣. Even at matchpoints, you would like to avoid notrump, especially now that you know you have a club fit.

2.   ♠ A Q 4   ♡ K Q 8 6 4   ◇ 9 4   ♣ A 7 4

Bid 3 NT. Clearly you wish to play in notrump, and since partner's auction is invitational to game, your extra values entitle you to accept.

3.   ♠ A 8 5   ♡ A Q 7 4 2   ◇ 9   ♣ K Q 7 5

Bid 3♠. Again you have extra values, but this time you are not at all sure where the hand belongs. Showing your spade "fragment" communicates your distribution and preserves all options.

Notice you can't show this kind of hand after a 1♣ opening bid. After 1♣ – 1 NT - 2♣ there is no convenient low level bid for us to borrow to indicate this type of problem hand. Therefore, when playing 1 NT forcing, responder may have four clubs for a 2 NT rebid after 1♣ - 1 NT - 2♣, but most likely will not after 1♡ - 1 NT - 2♣. This is also true when opener has rebid 2◇, keeping in mind that diamonds are less likely to be three long than clubs.

Are there other opportunities for responder to use a fit-showing spade bid after a 1♡ - 1 NT beginning? Certainly. Quite a few of them. Consider the following:

$$
\begin{array}{llll}
1\heartsuit & 1\ \text{NT} & 1\heartsuit & 1\ \text{NT} \\
2\heartsuit & 2\spadesuit & 2\ \text{NT} & 3\spadesuit \\
\\
1\heartsuit & 1\ \text{NT} & 1\heartsuit & 1\ \text{NT} \\
3\clubsuit & 3\spadesuit & 3\heartsuit & 3\spadesuit
\end{array}
$$

In each case, responder has produced the "impossible" spade bid at the second turn. My suggestion, assuming 1 NT forcing, is to define responder's spade bid as showing a hand with some support for partner's last-bid suit and notrump values, leaving it up to opener to decide which way to go. This is exactly the same interpretation we used in dealing with

$$
\begin{array}{ll}
1\heartsuit & 1\ \text{NT} \\
2\clubsuit & 2\spadesuit
\end{array}
$$

Here are some examples:

1♡	1NT	
2♡	2♠	responder might have

♠ K Q 6   ♡ K 3   ◊ J 9 5 4 3   ♣ Q 8 4.

It's not clear whether we belong in notrump or hearts. Partner should be in a good position to decide where and at what level the hand should be played.

The hand type that comes to mind for

1♡	1 NT
2 NT	3♠

is the three-card limit raise. 3♠ provides flexibility when holding a hand like

♠ A 8 4   ♡ 10 8 5   ◊ A J 4 3   ♣ Q 7 5.

That way you can get to 3 NT when opener holds

♠ K Q 5   ♡ J 6 4 3 2   ◊ K Q   ♣ A K 8

and to 4♡ opposite

♠ J 7   ♡ A K Q J 4   ◊ Q 7 5 2   ♣ A J.

For

1♡	1 NT
3♣	3♠	you might have

♠ K J 5   ♡ J   ◊ Q 7 5 4 3   ♣ Q 6 4 2

and have no idea what to do. Since game bidding is so vital in bridge, having an extra bid to describe our hand can make all the difference. Avoiding "unlucky guesses" is what bridge is all about.

Let's return to

1♡	1 NT
2♣	2♠

and see what other options responder has besides 2♠. Our methods are two-over-one game forcing and 1 NT forcing. The 2♣ bidder promises 3 + clubs without enough values to jump shift.

The first call to consider is pass, which is rare but certainly does not come as a shock. Other bids at the two-level besides 2♠ are natural and fairly obvious. 2◊ shows a good diamond suit while 2♡ is a preference, usually based on a doubleton. Neither of these bids shows much strength, although a fair hand is possible. 2 NT shows about 11 HCP, usually in a balanced hand with two hearts, often with 3 - 2 - 5 - 3 distribution..

As for three-level rebids, some show fits and some don't. 3♣ is almost always five-card support with fair values, maybe

♠ A 4   ♡ 9 3   ◊ 8 6 4 2   ♣ K J 8 7 5.

3◊ is also a natural bid, showing a maximum 1 NT response with good diamonds.

♠ J 4 2   ♡ 8   ◊ K J 10 9 7 4   ♣ A J 9

is a possibility, keeping in mind that an immediate 2◊ response would be game-forcing in our system.

3♡ is the three-card limit raise, an accepted bid in the 1 NT forcing framework. That leaves 3♠, 3 NT, 4♣, and 4♡ – anything more would be too remote to worry about. In fact, some of these bids are quite remote.

3♠ would probably be treated as a splinter bid, maybe based on

♠ 9   ♡ 6 4   ◇ A 8 7 5 4   ♣ A J 10 6 3.

Assuming a 1 NT response usually denies a full opening, you would need a good 12 to justify the jump to 3 NT – a hand that was improved by the 2♣ rebid. Perhaps a good example might be

♠ K Q 9   ♡ J 10   ◇ K 9 4 2   ♣ Q J 9 5.

4♣ could be justified only by a huge club fit, with some shape as well. Responder should have six-card support or better as well as a void or a singleton in hearts, opener's first suit. This bid is not forcing, but with responder's hand looking like

♠ A 7 4   ♡ 8   ◇ 9 4 3   ♣ K Q 8 7 4 2,

opener would pass only with a real dog.

4♡ shows a three-card raise which just got improved by the 2♣ response. I would insist on game with

♠ A 7 4   ♡ Q 10 9   ◇ 8 4   ♣ K Q 7 4 3

when partner rebid 2♣ after my forcing NT response.

♠ ——————————————————————————————— ♠

2/1 Game Forcing

Nowadays, more and more practitioners of 1NT Forcing are also treating any response in a new suit at the two level as game forcing. We argue that it is much more practical to play a system that is always on, rather than one with a major exception. Opener should be able to plan his auction based on the certainty that partner has a game-forcing hand, rather than worrying about the one-hand type where he does not.

Playing these methods,

1♠	2◇
2♡	3◇

is game forcing, so with

♠ A 5   ♡ 6 4   ◇ K Q J 9 7 3   ♣ 8 5 2

you respond 1NT, then bid 3◇. It is true that you would bid the same holding

♠ 5   ♡ 6 4   ◇ K Q J 9 7 3   ♣ 8 5 4 2

except if partner was intelligent enough to rebid 2♣, then you could jump to 3◊ with the first hand, and bid a weak 2◊ with the second.

So, although it is possible that you can miss a game after

$$
\begin{array}{ll}
1♠ & 1\ NT \\
2♡ & 3◊
\end{array}
$$

when opener passes, we believe that this is a small price to pay for the resulting ease and accuracy in our two over one auctions.

One subject that I believe to be crucial, yet is usually overlooked, is that of rebids after the game-forcing two over one response. It is easy for a partnership to be lazy when playing two over one game forcing, since so many auctions are clarified. However, defining auctions and style is still essential, we just have less work to do than standard players.

Experience has shown there to be a wide range of opinions here (reemphasizing the need for discussion), even among experts. What I will endeavor to do is to present the rules in my partnership with Larry Cohen. As with Roman Key Card, my aim in doing so is not to impose our views on you, but to illustrate what needs to be discussed, as well as some "intelligent" suggestions in a framework that we know to be compatible and successful.

Bergen-Cohen Rules After Game-Forcing 2/1 Response to One of a Major

A. OPENERS' REBIDS

1. Catchall bid when stuck (2NT)
I'm sure you've all had occasion to open one spade with a hand like

♣ 10 7 6 4 3　　♡ K　　◊ A K J　　♣ Q 6 4 3.

Were you brave enough to also plan your rebid if partner responded 2♡? Or would you, like most players, just hope that it wouldn't happen? By the way, what would you rebid?

Some pairs rebid their major when stuck, calling it a meaningless waiting bid. Others would rebid 3♣, saying that it didn't promise any extra values. Every pair must define which rebid is their "catchall" bid.

We prefer to rebid 2NT with these awkward hands, allowing all other bids to be meaningful. Not only do we rebid 2NT with a singleton in partner's suit, but we would also rebid 2NT with a worthless doubleton

♠ K 9 7 4 3　　♡ A K J　　◊ J 5 4　　♣ 10 7

or with 5-2-2-4

♠ A 8 6 5 2　　♡ A 7　　◊ Q 5　　♣ K 8 6 4.

after
$$
\begin{array}{ll}
1♠ & 2◊
\end{array}
$$

2. Original Major
We believe that this bid is meaningful, promising either six or a strong five-card suit. After 1♠–2♣, we would always have a six-card suit for a two spade rebid because of the room available to show any side four-card

29

suit. After any other two over ones, we are willing to rebid suits like AJ1095, KQJ74, AK1086, etc. On the other hand, suits like K8642, Q9543, A7432 are definitely excluded.

3. Two of a new suit (not a reverse)
Nothing special here, simply 4+. With 6-4's we usually show the second suit, but will tend to rebid the first suit with a minimum hand.

4. Two spades after opening one heart (only reverse at two level)
No extra values, just showing one's shape (we don't play Flannery 2♢). We tend to rebid two spades with 4-6 as well as 4-5.

5. Three of a new minor (nonjump)
Shows either a five-card suit, or a very, very strong suit such as AKQx, KQJ10. We do open one spade with all black 5-5's, and like to let partner know. For those who require extra values to go to the three level in a new suit and rebid two spades with

♠ A 7 4 3 2 ♡ 10   ♢ A Q J 10 6   ♣ 6 5,

to each their own.

6. Raise to the three level.
We don't go out of our way to make this bid, certainly never with xxx. We require either four trumps or three good ones, even for

1♠   2♡

3♡

with

♠ A Q 7 4 3   ♡ 8 6 4   ♢ K 5   ♣ K 9 4

We would rebid 2NT and later correct to 4♡, wary of over-encouraging responder with such bad trumps. We will raise with three fair trumps and a good hand

♠ A K 9 4 3   ♡ 8   ♢ Q 8 6   ♣ A J 5 4

after

2♡   2♠   /ꜱ - 2ᴰ - 3 ᴰ

where slam chances are lively. When we have four trumps, we tend to be 5-2-4-2, since we like to splinter when possible.

7. Jump to three of a new suit
This is a splinter bid, promising at least four cards in partner's suit, although no extra values. After 1♠ -2♢, we would bid 3♡ with

♠ K Q 9 7 4   ♡ 8   ♢ A J 6 3   ♣ K 5 4

or even

♠ A K 10 9 6   ♡ 6   ♢ K 10 8 4   ♣ 7 5 3.

There is no need to jump shift in a new suit, it only serves to crowd the auction. We never need to jump in a game-forcing two over one auction. We only do so to describe a specific type of hand where the trump suit is known.

8. Three of opener's original major
We restrict this to a solid suit, setting the trump suit. Suit quality must not be worse than AKQJxx or AKQxxxx or KQJ10xx or KQJxxxx, it is o.k. to be missing the ace. we don't guarantee a lot of extra values, but can't have an absolute minimum. We would rebid 3♠ with

| ♠ A K Q J 6 4 | ♡ K 7 | ◇ 8 5 3 | ♣ 6 4 or |
| ♠ A K Q J 7 5 3 | ♡ Q 10 3 | ◇ 6 4 | ♣ 8, |

but only two spades with

| ♣ K Q J 10 6 5 | ♡ K 8 3 | ◇ K 5 | ♣ 8 4 or |
| ♠ A K Q J 9 5 | ♡ 6 4 3 | ◇ Q 6 | ♣ J 5. |

Opener's jump guarantees that the hand will be played in spades (or possibly NT), so all of responder's bids are cuebids, and Blackwood will be keycard in spades.

9. 3NT.

This jump promises a balanced hand too good for a 1NT opening. Since we open 1NT with 14–16 (and don't mind doing so with a five-card major), 3NT here is about 16+ –18.

$$♠ A Q 10 9 6 \quad ♡ A K 6 \quad ◇ 9 2 \quad ♣ K 10 5$$

would be a good example of the sixteen pointer feeling too good to open 1NT, but right for 3NT over 2◇.

10. Single jump to four of new minor.

A splinter bid; just like the jump to a new suit at the three level.

11. Jump raise to the four level.

We are most unlikely to make this bid after responder bids a minor. Why take up all this bidding room? If we did, we would have a very good 5-2-4-2 hand. If we jump raised two hearts to four, we would have a minimum hand with four trumps, presumably with no singleton. If all opener needs for slam is

$$♠ A K 9 6 3 \quad ♡ K J 8 5 \quad ◇ 6 4 \quad ♣ 8 5,$$

so be it.

12. Double jump to four hearts (over two of a minor).

Another very rare bid, showing 6–6 or 5–6 in the majors with a minimum or even subminimum hand in a high cards. Notice that we guarantee six hearts, so responder should not go out of his way to correct to spades.

$$♠ A Q 8 6 4 2 \quad ♡ K 10 8 7 4 3 \quad ◇ 6 \quad ♣ -$$

looks about right.

13. Four of original major.

We don't go out of our way for this one either. We promise a minimum hand and a seven or eight-card suit, with at least one hole.

| ♠ A Q J 9 7 4 3 | ♡ A 6 | ◇ 8 5 | ♣ 6 4 and |
| ♠ Q J 10 7 6 4 3 | ♡ K 4 3 | ◇ A | ♣ 9 5 |

are reasonable examples.

B. RESPONDERS' REBIDS

1. 2NT.

He will also bid 2NT (when available) if he lacks an obvious action. This does show stoppers in unbid suits with a balanced or slightly unbalanced hand, waiting for opener's next move.

2. Jump to 3NT.

While we're on the subject of NT, a jump to 3 NT is used to promise extra values. This is the best way to show a hand with enough high card points to open 1NT, lacking an established fit, since experience has shown that the 16 – opposite – 16 hands can be tough to bid to slam until someone promises extras.

3. Two-level spade preference, such as

1♠	2♣
2◇	2♠

This is a bid we like to make, since it is so economical and establishes a fit. It usually shows three trumps (in fact, we have an agreement that failure to make a conventional raise at responder's first turn denies four), but a doubleton is acceptable when it contains two honors (J10 or better).

Opener will usually continue to bid out his pattern, and we have a lot of room to search out the best game (usually 4♠, possibly 3NT) and/or slam.

4. Raise to 3 diamonds.

1♠	2♣	or	1♡	2♣
2◇	3◇		2◇	3◇

Nothing special here, responder is promising 4+ diamonds without good support for opener's major. Subsequent bidding will attempt to ferret out the best game (first priority) not worrying until later about slam.

5. Jump preference to three spades.

This is a big bid, promising three good trumps and a strong hand, about 15+ including distribution. Opener is urged to cuebid toward slam, therefore, if he does bid 4♠, he won't have much.

6. Raise to three in openers major, for example

1♠	2♣	or	1♠	2◇
2♡	3♡		2♠	3♠

This is usually responder's choice with support. Responder does not promise any extra values (remember, opener is not limited by his failure to jump), just the opening bid he promised with his initial response. Cuebidding is also encouraged here.

7. Jump in a new suit to 3 or 4 level.

1♡	2♣	1♠	2♣	1♡	2♣
2♡	3♠	2♡	4◇	2◇	3♠

etc. Splinter raises of opener's last bid suit.

8. Jumps to four of opener's major.

1♠	2♣	1♠	2◇	1♠	2♡	1♠	2♣
2♡	4♡	2♠	4♠	3♣	4♣	2♡	4♠

etc.

32

These are rare, unusual bids (although I have a difficult time in convincing some of my students of that), since they unnecessarily take up so much bidding room. The only reason for responder to make this bid is with a "picture book" hand, a minimum game force with good trumps and a good side suit, and no control (ace, king, singleton, or void) in the other two suits. After

$$1\spadesuit \qquad 2\clubsuit$$
$$2\spadesuit ,$$

only bid 4♠ with something like

♠ K Q 5   ♡ 6 4 2   ◇ Q 3   ♣ A Q 7 4 3 or

♠ A J 4   ♡ 6 4 3   ◇ J 7 5   ♣ A K J 8.

Since these very specific hands will rarely occur, prefer the two level rebid in opener's major or raise partner's rebid of his suit to three with hands that do not conform to this high card placement.

9. New suit bids when no fit has been established.

These are natural, promising length (including bids in fourth suit, since we don't need the "fourth suit forcing" convention when already forced to game). No extra values are suggested.

10. New suit bids after a fit.

If the fit was in a minor suit, these are assumed to be probing for 3NT (although they could be revealed later as slam tries). If the fit was in a major, specifically

$$1\spadesuit \qquad 2\heartsuit$$
$$3\heartsuit ,$$

they are cuebids looking for slam.

11. Rebid of suit at three level promises 6 + .

12. Jump rebid of first suit (to four level).

If responder's suit is a minor, it promises a solid suit (possibly missing the ace) with strong slam interest and demands cuebidding (aces only) by opener.

If responder's suit is hearts, he is showing an independent (but not necessarily solid) suit, with slam interest. Since we don't use strong jump shifts at the three level (preferring artificial raises), some hands require subsequent effort to "catch up."

Jacoby 2 NT

Many ingredients are necessary for good slam bidding, and point count plays a relatively minor role. So it's no surprise that slams give the average player an especially tough time.

One of the most important requirements of good slam bidding is to set the trump suit early. The most desirable bid in bridge is raising partner's suit to signify the presence of a good trump fit. Once that is done, cuebids and probes toward slam can follow.

Another extremely important part of slam bidding is distributional information. It is almost always necessary for at least one player to have distributional information about his partner's hand. He must at least know where partner's short suit lies and evaluate the fit there, hoping that most of his honors are located opposite partner's length instead of being wasted oposite shortness.

These two requirements are achieved nicely by the use of splinter bids. Using splinter bids, a player can show support for his partner and show a singleton (or void) as well.

A convention with very similar objectives is Jacoby 2 NT. This is an artificial response to a major suit opening bid, showing at least a forcing raise of opener's trump suit with four or more trumps. This bid's economy factor is inescapable. Although each player has made only one bid, the partnership already knows at least a game will be bid in the agreed trump suit, and there's still plenty of room for exploration.

What must be given up to play Jacoby 2 NT? This is a most important test for any convention. Usually 1 ♠ - 2 NT shows 13–15 HCP in a balanced hand with stoppers in the unbid suits. It's a nice bid, but you can survive without it by bidding your best suit over 1 ♠ and then jumping to 3 NT (or by bidding 2 NT next if it is game forcing with 1 NT forcing).

OK, back to Jacoby 2 NT. Responder can make this bid any time he has a strong raise in partner's suit. After partner's opening 1 ♡ bid, responder would bid 2 NT with all of these hands:

♠ A 8	♠ A	♠ A 7 6 5	♠ A 8 5
♡ K Q 7 4	♡ A Q 8 4	♡ A J 6 4	♡ J 10 6 3
◇ A 9 5 3	◇ Q 10 6	◇ K 4 3	◇ A 9 4
♣ A 7 4	♣ J 8 7 5 4	♣ Q 8	♣ A 10 7

Notice that 2 NT is usually bid on a balanced hand. If responder has a singleton, he will usually choose to show it by splintering directly. The exception was made on our second example since our singleton was an ace, not the perfect holding with which to splinter.

The first example shows that responder's strength is not severely limited. Since opener is about to describe his own hand further, responder can make the 2 NT bid and then sit back and await developments, without worrying about his own point count.

For his rebid, opener's first responsibility is to show a singleton or void. The singleton is shown at the three level, the void at the four level. Opener identifies the singleton or void by bidding the suit with the shortness.

Therefore, after 1 ♠ - 2 NT:

3♣ = club singleton
3◊ = diamond singleton
3♡ = heart singleton
4♣ = club void
4◊ = diamond void
4♡ = heart void

What does opener do without a singleton or void? He uses one of the three remaining bids to identify the relative strength of his hand. The remaining actions are 3♠, 3 NT and 4♠. 3♠ is the most encouraging, 4♠ is completely discouraging, while 3 NT is for hands that fall in between these two extremes.

Here are some examples of each type of rebid by opener after 1♠-2 NT: These hands would rebid 4♠.

1) ♠ K J 6 5 3   2) ♠ J 7 6 5 4   3) ♠ 10 8 7 4 3
   ♡ A 10   ♡ A K 7   ♡ A K 6 3
   ◊ K 5   ◊ Q 10 6   ◊ A 5
   ♣ J 7 4   ♣ K 5   ♣ 6 4

The following would rebid 3 NT.

1) ♠ K J 8 7 6 3   2) ♠ A Q 8 7 4   3) ♠ A 10 8 6 3
   ♡ K 7   ♡ A 6   ♡ A Q J
   ◊ A 5   ◊ K J 4 2   ◊ K J 4
   ♣ J 6 3   ♣ 9 4   ♣ 8 5

These hands are all good enough for the most encouraging bid of 3♠. They all have serious slam interest.

1) ♠ A K J 7 4   2) ♠ A Q J 8 4 3   3) ♠ K Q 8 7 4
   ♡ A 10 6 5   ♡ A 10 6   ♡ K Q 6
   ◊ K 4   ◊ 9 4   ◊ A 8 4
   ♣ 9 2   ♣ K 5   ♣ K 5

The approximate point ranges for the three bids, including distribution, are: 4♠, 13-15; 3 NT, 15-17; 3♠, 18+.

Notice that opener follows the sound strategy of keeping the bidding low with the good hands, while employing fast arrival (signing off in game) on the weak ones. Fast arrival is also used by responder. Holding

♠Q 8 4 3   ♡K Q J 7   ◊A 8   ♣10 6 4, after

Opener	Responder
1♠	2 NT
3♡	?

responder should jump to 4♠ to show he has the worst possible hand for slam, which would be accurate if opener showed a singleton heart.

Jacoby 2 NT lends itself very well to cuebidding since there is so much room. Cuebids always show slam interest and a control (ace or king in the suit bid) with the emphasis on the first-round control. You usually make the cheapest available cuebid to save room. Don't be in a big hurry to use

Blackwood or jump to slam. Take advantage of your bidding space.

Let's practice some Jacoby 2 NT auctions. Your hand will always be

♠ 9 2   ♡ K 10 8 5   ◇ A 8 7 4   ♣ A K 7

and you have replied 2 NT to your partner's opening bid of 1 ♡. For each problem, opener's rebid will be shown. Choose your bid, making sure to plan ahead.

1) Opener	You
4 ♡	Pass

Partner is announcing that he has a minimum, so even with your nice hand, there's nothing you can do.

2) Opener	You
3 ◇	3 ♡

Perfect, just what we were hoping to hear. Opposite a diamond singleton, we can drive the hand to slam, as long as partner has a spade control, which is very likely. 3 ♡ is bid to mark time since it is more economical than 4 ♣ and allows a 3 ♠ cue by partner. 3 ♡ is encouraging, as is any action other than 4 ♡.

3) Opener	You
4 ♣	4 ◇

Partner's being void in clubs is not perfect for your hand, but your ♣ A–K are still tricks, useful for discards.

4) Opener	You
3 ♠	4 ♣

Partner's singleton spade is good since it doesn't duplicate any strength, but it would be nicer if we had more spades and therefore fewer minor suit cards. If partner also has diamond length, we may have an inescapable loser there.

5) 3 NT	4 ♣

Slam is quite doubtful now, but we are worth one try. If partner bids 4 ♡, we will pass.

Some players prefer to use opener's jump to the four level as a five-card side suit rather than a void. This obviously has merit, and is preferred today by most experts.

Jacoby 2 NT is considered to be one of the most valuable slam aids. A good percentage of experienced players use it, and it is easy enough so that it can be used by less sophisticated pairs also.

Question: **If we are playing Jacoby 2 NT, can we use it after an opponent's overcall?**

Answer: After

Partner	Opponent	You
1 ♡	1 ♠	?

I guess you could play 2 NT as Jacoby, using a negative double or two of a minor or even 3 NT on a hand that wanted to bid notrump naturally. However, after

Partner	Opponent
1 ♠	2 ◊ (or the
	equivalent),

2 NT has to be reserved for a balanced 11 count. The moral is to use this convention only in the absence of competition. This is also recommended for Jacoby Transfers when partner's opening notrump bid is overcalled or doubled.

Question: **Can I bid Jacoby 2 NT with three trumps?**
Answer: NO! For slam purposes, the extra trump is frequently crucial.

♠ ♠

Artificial (and other) Raises after One of A Major

How do you treat a jump shift at the three-level in response to a major suit opening bid? Most play that it shows a very good hand with slam interest. When was the last time you heard this kind of auction? Even with a very strong hand a player is often reluctant to make a three-level jump shift since it takes up so much bidding room. It is usually correct to make a non-jump response to keep the bidding low and allow for a more thorough exchange of information.

A smaller percentage of players uses jump shifts as preemptive bids, showing a very weak hand with a long suit. The hand may or may not have enough strength to warrant a simple response playing *Standard,* but the suit must be respectable enough to play adequately even if opener has no support.

How often does this come up? It is certainly true that responder is dealt more mediocre hands than powerhouses. However, it is not recommended that responder jump around without a good suit, particularly when the jump takes the partnership to the three-level. In fact, noncompetitive preemptive jump shifts at the three-level seem to occur only about once a year. It is impractical to reserve five bids (1♡ – 3♣, 1♡ – 3◊, 1♠ – 3♣, 1♠ – 3◊, 1♠ – 3♡) for auctions which rarely occur.

If you are willing to accept that it is not feasible to play three-level jump shifts as either strong or weak, I offer another application for the bid. As Ed Manfield wrote in *The Bridge World* some years ago, "We need more ways to raise partner." Well, Ed, I'm ready to present enough raises to satisfy almost any partner.

The first of the raises is the weakest one. Most experts use the following auctions to show a preemptive jump raise: 1♡ -2♣ -3♡, 1♡ -Dbl-3♡, 1♠ -1♡ -1♠ -3♡.

Such a hand as

♠ 9 4   ♡ Q J 10 6   ◊ 9 7 4 3 2   ♣ 8 5

would be just find for all three calls. This preemptive bid works fine, but its effectiveness is limited by the fact that the opponents are already in the auction. We all know it is more difficult to preempt opponents once they have bid.

If it is so desirable to have a preemptive three-level bid available after the opponents have entered the bidding, then it must be even more desirable to have a preemptive bid available to take advantage of the fact that the opponents know virtually nothing about each other's hands. Therefore we designate a jump response to three as preemptive after a major suit opening, showing at least four trumps (rarely five) with 0-6 points including distribution.

Holding a limit raise with 4+ trumps we now jump to 3◊.

Those who use 1 NT Forcing can distinguish between three and four-card support, which can make all the difference in the world.

Speaking of distinguishing between three and four-card support, it is time to discuss our raise to 3♣. First, though, we'll need to prepare you, since you may not be in a frame of mind to accept this one so readily. What do you bid with

♠ J 8 5 4 3   ♡ A 6   ◊ A K 8 4 3   ♣ 8

after your partner raises your opening 1♠ bid to 2♠? Isn't this a familiar problem? If you bid 3◊, how will you feel playing 3♠ opposite something like

♠ 9 6 2   ♡ Q 8 7 5   ◊ J 2   ♣ K Q 10 5?

If you choose to pass 2♠, won't you expect to make four, or even five, opposite

♠ K 10 9 6   ♡ K 5 3   ◊ 9 2   ♣ 10 7 4 2 ?

Of course, even if you bid 3◊ when partner holds the latter hand, would your partner know to go to 4♠ holding a weaker hand in high cards than the potential dummy which didn't even offer much play for 3♠)

It is frequently crucial for opener to know exactly how many trumps are opposite. The ninth trump is the most underrated concept in the game. So . . .

Let's play that the single major raise (1♠ -2♠ and 1♡ -2♡) promises exactly *three* trumps. With *four* trumps and a reasonable single raise (7+ to 10- including distribution) *bid 3♣*.

Now some of you are thinking: Marty has finally gone off the deep end. He's proposing that we get to the three-level with two-level values. My answers:

1) In all the years I have used the 3♣ bid, only once have I gotten to three, down one. On that occasion my opponents were cold for game.

2) The biggest advantage of the 3♣ raise is the negative inference each time it doesn't occur! When responder can only raise to the two-level, opener knows much more than other players in his seat – there is no fourth trump in dummy.

3) 3♣ raises don't occur nearly as often as the three-card single raise.

4) When we do play in three of a major after the 3♣ raise, we have enough offense to make it. If you should play in three down one, it is likely the opponents should have balanced. Since they almost certainly can make something, you may get a good score even for your small minus.

5) Every time responder bids 3♣, opener can judge the hand better, especially with an unbalanced hand or weak trumps.

A few notes on the above. When playing these raises, all are Alertable. In addition to the obvious Alerts for 3♣ and 3◊, you must Alert the single raise as "promising exactly three trumps." The 3♣ and 3◊ raises are off in competition, just like most conventional bids. Those who like to open four-card majors in third and fourth seat probably will not want to use these bids by passed hands, since they are based on a five-card major style. However, this is a choice each pair should make for themselves.

Try these hands in responding to partner's 1♡ bid with no interference. You are not a passed hand:

1.   ♠ A 7   ♡ K Q J 6   ◊ 9 5 4 3   ♣ 8 7 2

Bid 3◊. This is a limit raise. Remember that the 3♣ bid shows the strength of a single raise, always less than a limit raise.

2.   ♠ K 6 5   ♡ Q 10 6 5   ◊ 9 4 3   ♣ 8 7 2

Bid 3♡. No one said you promised any shape when you bid 3♡. You make this bid even when you are vulnerable. It is not intended for the faint of heart.

3.   ♠ A 4 3   ♡ J 9 5   ◊ K 8 7 4   ♣ 10 5 4

Bid 2♡, obviously. Your partner can start counting trumps immediately.

4.   ♠ Q 7 4   ♡ J 9 6 4 3   ◊ 8 5   ♣ J 7 4

Bid 3♡. It is even better to bid 3♡ with five trumps.

How does opener make a game try? Except for 1♡–3◊, there is always at least one game try available. You may be able to make the game try in a second suit, but usually you already know enough to be able to place the contract accurately. It should be easy to remember that 3♣ shows a better hand than the weak jump raise, since we prefer to keep the bidding "lower" with "better" hands.

If you are still skeptical, what have you got to lose by giving it a try? You'll like it, but your opponent sure won't.

Now we will continue to develop the system by defining the remainder of the three-level as well as the four-level bids. First, we must denote our forcing raise, usually a balanced hand. This is Jacoby 2 NT, which shows an opening bid in support and asks opener to describe his hand, beginning by showing a singleton (if he has one).

The next topic is Splinter Bids. Although these bids occur infrequently, they can be very effective for slam bidding. However, it seems impractical to reserve three bids for one infrequent hand type.

Instead, why not use one bid to show all three splinters? Therefore, after partner opens one of major, a response of three in the other major shows a game-forcing raise with shortness in one of the other suits. After partner opens 1♡, we respond 3♠, not only when we hold

♠ 8   ♡ K 8 7 2   ◇ A 10 6 4   ♣ A J 7 3,

but also when the singleton is in either diamonds or clubs.

Having defined 1♠ – 3♡ and 1♡ – 3♠ as ambiguous splinter auctions, we now need a way to allow opener to identify the singleton (or void). We use what we refer to as "Splinter Relays."

These involve opener relaying with the cheapest bid (when he is interested in discovering the location of the splinter) and responder replying in steps. Here is how it works:

After 1♡ – 3♠		After 1♠ – 3♡
3 NT		3♠
4♣ = Clubs	Step 1	3 NT = Clubs
4◇ = Diamonds	Step 2	4♣ = Diamonds
4♡ = Spades	Step 3	4◇ = Hearts

Let's try a couple of these as opener. In each case you've opened 1♠ and received a 3♡ response, showing a game-forcing raise with shortness somewhere.

1♠ – 3♡
?

1.   ♠ K Q 10 6 4   ♡ A K 4   ◇ 8 7 3 2   ♣ 8

3♠. If partner shows a diamond splinter (via 4♣) you can head for slam, presumably by bidding Blackwood. If partner is short in hearts or clubs, you will be satisfied with game.

2.   ♠ Q 8 7 4 3   ♡ K J 8   ◇ K 10 4   ♣ A 6

4♠. No matter what splinter partner was dealt, you are not interested.

3.   ♠ Q 8 7 4 3 2   ♡ K Q 6 5   ◇ A K 7   ♣ –

4◇. You are more interested in discovering the location of partner's high cards than in his shortness.

The last three-level response is 3 NT. We play this as a balanced non-forcing three-card raise, offering a choice of contracts. Partner can pass, sign off in four of the trump suit, or even cuebid toward slam. We try to be 4 – 3 – 3 – 3 with stopper in all unbid suits. In response to 1♡ bid 3 NT on

♠ K Q 5	♡ Q 7 4	◇ A 19 6 4	♣ K 4 3 or
♠ A 6 4	♡ 7 4 3	◇ Q 9 7 2	♣ A K 9

or even

♠ A Q   ♡ 9 8 5   ◇ K 9 4 3   ♣ A 10 7 2.

We're now ready to move on to the four-level. We are free to play 4♣ and 4◇ any way we wish, since we don't need them as splinters. 4♣ is used as a big balanced Swiss raise with at least good three-card support. It is definitely a hand too good for 3 NT. Respond 4♣ after partner opens 1♠ holding

♠ K J 7 2	♡ K Q	◇ K 7 4	♣ K J 7 3 or
♠ A K 9	♡ Q J 7	◇ A Q 5	♣ Q 10 7 4.

4◇ shows a considerably weaker hand than 4♣. It is what I call a good 1–4, a good raise to four of opener's major. That gives us two ways to raise one of a major to four, "constructively" via 4◇, or very weakly with a direct 4-of-the-major. Therefore in response to 1♡, bid 4◇ holding

♠ 9	♡ K Q 7 4 3	◇ K 10 5 4	♣ 8 4 3,

but bid 4♡ with

♠ 9	♡ K 10 7 4 3	◇ 10 7 4 3	♣ 8 5 4.

Opener is now in a better position to judge whether to try for slam, or whether to bid on or double if the opponents compete.

A word about playing against these artificial raises, in case you are unfortunate enough to confront opponents enlightened enough to use these or similar bids. It is not clear to me whether it is correct to define a double of the artificial raise as lead-directing or takeout, in those cases where it denotes a weak hand. It is clear that it should be lead-directing when a strong hand is promised. Fortunately I have not yet been confronted with this problem, but if some of you choose to take up these artificial raises, I may rue the day I shared all this "good stuff."

As we stated earlier, since 4◇ shows a good 1–4, the actual raise to four shows real garbage. The only remaining bid is the response of four of the other major. Those of you who think I have gone too far already will be relieved to hear that this is a purely natural bid. 1♠–4♡ and 1♡–4♠ are played as natural and preemptive. If partner opens 1♠, respond 4♡ holding

♠ 9	♡ K Q 9 7 6 5 4 2	◇ 8 7	♣ 9 2 or
♠ 6 4 3	♡ K Q J 10 9 4 3	◇ 9 7	♣ 8.

That concludes our discussion of artificial raises by an unpassed hand. Those readers who feel inclined to try out these bids are urged to experiment by devising their own types of raises, as well as mixing up the sequence, and I would be interested in hearing from those who have bids they consider worthwhile. Indeed, I have already modified the structure several times, searching for the most effective combination.

Here is a summary of the existing structure.

	1 ♡		1 ♠
2 ♡	3-card raise		Natural
2 ♠	Natural		3-card raise
2 NT	Jacoby 2 NT		Jacoby 2 NT
3 ♣	4-card constructive raise (7+ to 10 −)		4-card constructive raise (7+ to 10−)
3 ◊	Limit Raise		Limit Raise
3 ♡	4-card preemptive raise (0-6)		Splinter raise with relays
3 ♠	Splinter raise with relays		4-card preemptive raise (0-6)
3 NT	3-card balanced non-forcing raise		3-card balanced non-forcing raise
4 ♣	Big balanced raise		Big balanced raise
4 ◊	Good raise to 4 ♡		Good raise to 4 ♠
4 ♡	Weak preemptive raise		Natural, preemptive
4 ♠	Natural, preemptive		Weak preemptive raise

All of the above include distribution. How do you play this auction:

Pass	Pass	1 ♠	Pass
2 NT ?			

Should you ever jump to 2 NT opposite a third-seat opener with 11 or 12 HCP if using 1 NT Forcing? It is unnecessary, since you can bid 1 NT which partner will pass only with balanced garbage. After all, why hang partner? Surely we can find a better meaning for 2 NT. After

Pass	Pass	1 ♠	Pass
?			

♠ A 9 5 4   ♡ K 10 7 3   ◊ J 10 4 3   ♣ 9

We would like to show a limit spade raise with 4 + trumps and shortness in clubs, but there is no standard way to do so. We can hardly splinter to 4 ♣ opposite a potential light opener with only 8 HCP. I define a passed-hand 2 NT as a limit raise with a singleton (or void) in an unspecified suit. Opener can bid 3 ♣ to ask where the shortness is. The responses after

Pass	1 ♠
2 NT	3 ♣
?	

are once again based on splinter relays.

Step 1 – Club shortness. Bid 3 ◊
Step 2 – Diamond shortness. Bid 3 ♡
Step 3 – Heart shortness. Bid 3 ♠.

Once again, the actual bids do not conform to the suits shown.

Does opener always ask for the shortness? Of course not. You would jump to 4 ♠ with

♠ A Q 8 7 4   ♡ K 7 3 2   ◊ K J 8   ♣ 9

since you want to be in game regardless and can't have enough for slam. With

♠ Q 7 4 3 2   ♡ K J 6   ◊ K 8   ♣ K 5 4

you would sign off in 3 ♠, since you wouldn't want to be in game no matter where partner's splinter was. But wouldn't it be nice to hold

♠ A Q 8 7 4   ♡ K J 8   ◊ 8 7 4 3   ♣ 9

and discover that partner had diamond shortness? You could then bid a confident 4 ♠ and make it opposite

♠ J 10 6 3   ♡ Q 10 7 4   ◊ 9   ♣ A 7 5 3.

What's the splinter bid if partner opens 1 ♡? If we bid 2 NT, there isn't room to get them all in ending with 3 ♡. If responder has a spade splinter, the auction would go

Pass	1 ♡
2 NT	3 ♣
3 ♠	

and we'd be forced to play 4 ♡ even if opener was turned off by the location of the splinter. Therefore over 1 ♡ we play 2 ♠ as a passed hand to show a SPLimit (*SP*linter *Limit* Raise). The relays work on the same principle. 2 NT asks for shortness.

Pass	1 ♡
2 ♠	2 NT

Step 1 – Club shortness. Bid 3 ♣ *
Step 2 – Diamond shortness. Bid 3 ◊ *
Step 3 – Spade shortness. Bid 3 ♡
*Note that here the bids are the same as the splinter.

Question: **My favorite article of those you've written in the** *Bulletin* **was your April, 1982 article on artificial three-level raises after an opening bid in a major. Someone told me that you were no longer playing them. What went wrong?**

Answer: I did suggest that 3 ♣ and 3 ◊ be used as artificial responses to a major suit opening bid. This has worked out well, getting to the three-level with 9 + trumps "never" seems to be a problem.

We have also enjoyed some real triumphs after the direct raise to the two-level. In several cases we were able to pass with distributional hands, while the other players made game tries. We knew that partner had only three trumps, but they did not.

However, several of my partners suggested that as long as I was going to use a three-level raise as preemptive, why not take up the maximum available space. This made sense to me, so I inverted the preemptive raise with the limit raise. But we (as well as others) are still playing "Bergen Raises" and will continue to do so.

Drury

You're playing at the local duplicate game where you and your partner are the acknowledged experts, having won for four consecutive weeks. On the first board you, as South, gaze at

♠ A 8 7 5   ♡ K 9 4 2   ◇ 8 6   ♣ K 7 3.

You pass of course, then hear your partner open 1♠ in third seat. You bid 3♠, since you have a maximum for a passed hand in support of spades. Your bid is not forcing, and partner duly passes. You notice with surprise that partner's usual "thank you" is not forthcoming when you put down the dummy, and the eventual result is down one. You ask to see partner's hand which is a perfectly sound third-seat opening:

♠ K Q J 10   ♡ J 8 5   ◇ A J 7 2   ♣ 9 4.

You decide that next time you'll simply bid 2♠ with your 11 points.

Things proceed smoothly for the next few rounds, and you and partner are having your usual solid game. Then you pick up:

♠ K 6 5 4   ♡ A 8 7 3   ◇ 9 2   ♣ K 6 3.

You pass and again partner opens 1♠ in third seat. Having learned your lesson, you bid only 2♠. You confidently put down your dummy, but for some reason partner again does not seem pleased. He takes 11 tricks in rapid fashion, and you question why he didn't invite with 3♠, since you would have accepted his game try.

"Do you really think I should with

♠ A J 9 7 3   ♡ 4   ◇ A 7 5 4   ♣ Q J 8?"

partner asks. You're forced to admit that his pass can't be criticized. However, you decide that in this situation it pays to be aggressive in trying for game.

Once again your results pick up and you are glad that your luck has changed—until you find yourself looking at

♠ K Q 7 5 2   ♡ 4   ◇ A 8 7 3   ♣ Q J 6.

After two passes you naturally open 1♠. Partner raises to two and, remembering the earlier hand, you invite with 3♠. Partner passes and tables

♠ 8 6 4 3   ♡ K Q 7 6   ◇ Q 5 2   ♣ 8 4.

Despite the favorable location of the opponents' cards you go down one, losing two clubs and one trick in each of the other suits. Partner, who has been sympathetic until now, bursts out with "Can't you ever make the right deci-
44

sion?" Although you can usually hold your own in a post-mortem, this time you find yourself unable to reply.

The remainder of the session seems to drag on forever, and the spark has definitely left your partnership. You check your scores and find you are two points below average, which hasn't happened in more than a year. You leave the club soon thereafter, but not soon enough to avoid all the "What happened to the champs? They not only didn't win – they were under average." And the "Thanks for giving the rest of us a chance."

As you are driving home in complete silence, you remark to partner: "Well, we'll get them next week."

"Gee, I don't think I can make it," he says. "I've got some shopping to do."

Lying awake in bed that night, you think about the three fateful boards. It doesn't seem you did anything terrible, yet in each situation your decision led to the wrong contract. Is there any solution to the problem?

All beginning books on bidding advocate light opening bids when partner is a passed hand. However, they are deficient in describing how to respond while allowing for the light opener. Fortunately, one man saw the problem and saw fit to propose a solution.

Doug Drury realized that a problem would occur when the passed hand had a good fit for the suit opened as well as a maximum in high cards for the pass. Such a hand would call for a raise to the three-level, but this could get the partnership too high if the opening bid was minimum. Drury's solution was for responder to bid 2♣ after a third or fourth-seat 1♡ or 1♠ opening bid when holding a hand that he would like to jump raise to 3♡ or 3♠. Note that this applies only to major suit opening bids, which are more likely to be shaded and involve more worry about missing game. *[Doug felt that an opening bid of 1♢ or 1♠ showed either a good hand or a good suit.]*

Now the major-suit opener clarifies the nature of his bid. If his opening bid was light or shaded, he rebids 2♢ which means his hand is minimum enough so that game is unlikely. He not only bids 2♢ when he doesn't hold an opening bid, but also when he holds minimums that have no chance for game.

When the opening bidder is interested in game, he usually bids something other than 2♢. He can show a second suit, rebid his major with a six-carder or bid notrump with a good balanced hand. These are not forcing to game, but allow the Drury bidder to bid game with a maximum.

Now let's look at some hands for opener to rebid after he has heard a Drury 2♣ bid from his partner. The bidding proceeds:

PARTNER	YOU
Pass	1♡
2♣	?

1) ♠ A 6   ♡ A K 9 8 6 4   ♢ Q 8   ♣ 9 4 2.

Bid 2♡. This shows a sound opening bid and a six-card suit and it is forcing.

2) ♠ 8 5   ♡ A K 10 6 2   ♢ K J 4   ♣ 8 7 6.

Bid 2♢. You are not interested in game opposite a passed hand.

3)   ♠ K 5   ♡ K Q 8 7 2   ◊ Q 6 3   ♣ A J 8.

Bid 2 NT. You intend to play 3 NT or 4♡.

4)   ♠ J 8   ♡ K Q J 6   ◊ A Q 6 4   ♣ 8 7 2.

Bid 2 ◊. Even though you have a full opening bid, game is very unlikely from your point of view.

5)   ♠ A   ♡ K Q 9 4 2   ◊ A 6 4   ♣ K Q 8 6.

Bid 3♣. You expect to play in 4♡, but show your clubs since 6♣ is still possible.

Now let's see how the use of Drury could have saved the day on the three problem hands from the duplicate game:

YOU	PARTNER
♠ A 8 7 5	♠ K Q J 10
♡ K 9 4 2	♡ J 8 5
◊ 8 6	◊ A J 7 2
♣ K 7 3	♣ 9 4
Pass	1♠
2♣	2◊
2♠	Pass

YOU	PARTNER
♠ K 6 5 4	♠ A J 9 7 3
♡ A 8 7 3	♡ 4
◊ 9 2	◊ A 7 5 4
♣ K 6 3	♣ Q J 8
Pass	1♠
2♣	2◊
2♠	3♣
3♡	3♠
4♠	Pass

Partner should not be tempted to jump rebid 3◊ even though he is " all there." A jump shift by opener suggests slam with the right values opposite. Remember the opener *usually* rebids something other than 2◊ when he is interested in game. The 3♣ call over 2♠ (which could have been passed) indicated that he is interested in a game and 2◊ was a natural call.

YOU	PARTNER
♠ K Q 7 5 2	♠ 8 6 4 3
♡ 4	♡ K Q 7 6
◊ A 8 7 3	◊ Q 5 2
♣ Q J 6	♣ 8 4
—	Pass
1♠	2♣
Pass	

Another benefit of Drury is that some sequences are clarified which otherwise might be ambiguous. Some of these are:

1)   Pass   1 ♡
                            3 ♡

This has the same meaning as 1 ♡ – 4 ♡ by an unpassed hand (five trumps, a singleton or void, and not many high card points). Or it shows a hand containing a lot of trumps such as

                ♠ 8 6 3   ♡ K Q J 4 2   ◇ K 10 7   ♣ 6 4.

2)   Pass   1 ♡
                            4 ♡

This does not exist unless responder regularly overlooks a king when sorting his hand the first time.

3)   Pass   1 ♡
                            2 ♡

The range for this bid is narrowed when playing Drury, since some maximum raises are worth 2 ♣.

4)   Pass   1 ♠
                            2 ◇   2 ♡
                            2 ♠   Pass

2 ◇ denies three trumps, since with three you would bid Drury, so the bid of 2 ♠ shows a preference, not a true raise.

5)   Pass   1 ♠
                            3 ♣

The way the convention was originally written, all jumps by a passed hand were preemptive. However, there have been alternative methods tried – some partnerships play this as a splinter bid, others use it to show the hand "Standard" bidders would have when they responded 2 ♣ followed by 3 ♣. Partnerships who guarantee a fit when they bid 2 ♣ generally use the jump to show a club suit.

What should you do when playing against a pair who uses Drury? In the sequence

                            Pass   1 ♡
                            2 ♣   2 ◇

both the 2 ♣ bid and the 2 ◇ bid are artificial, so a double of either shows length and strength in that suit. This can help partner with his opening lead – it can even allow him to compete on hands where it might otherwise have been difficult to enter the auction. Also, if you wish to make a takeout double of spades after Pass–1 ♠–2 ♣, cuebid 2 ♠, since the double shows clubs.

After a slow start, the popularity of Drury has increased greatly in recent years. It is especially valuable at matchpoints where lead-directing opening bids in third seat can be very advantageous. The benefits of Drury are important enough to appeal to any partnership. The most important are the ability to determine a possible light opening bid while remaining at the two-level and the ability to clarify other auctions.

Now, armed with your knowledge of Drury, you can avoid the guesses that led to the worry that your partner really was going shopping for a new partner.

♧ _____ ♧

Reverse Drury

For those of us who believe in the principle of "fast arrival," the concepts governing opener's rebids with Drury were illogical. With fast arrival, once we find a trump fit and are forced to a certain level, the weakest action is bidding the trump suit at the level forced to. Yet after

Pass	1 ♠
2 ♣	

standard Drury calls for a 2 ◇ rebid when opener is minimum, while a 2 ♠ bid promises a goodish hand and is forcing.

Therefore, most Drury followers in 1985 use what is referred to as "Reverse Drury." Opener returns to the trump suit with no game interest, so 2 ◇ promises a decent opener. The bid does not guarantee a diamond suit, each of the following should rebid 2 ◇ after

Pass	1 ♠
2 ♣	

1) ♠ A 10 7 4 3   ♡ J 3   ◇ 9 4   ♣ A K 7 5

2) ♠ K Q J 6 3   ♡ A K 10   ◇ 3 2   ♣ 10 7 4

3) ♠ A J 8 6 4 3   ♡ K 7 4   ◇ Q J   ♣ J 6

All in between hands which are too good to give up on game by rebidding 2 ♠, but don't want to get to the three level opposite a minimum, each of these hands should quit if responder can't do more than rebid 2 ♠.

2 Way Drury
(2 ◇ = 4 + Card Drury)

One reason why Drury is considered desirable is that you give up so little — merely the ability to bid 2 ♣ naturally as a passed hand. Holding

♠ A 6   ♡ A 7   ◇ 9 4 3   ♣ Q 8 6 4 3 2

we must respond 1 NT playing Eastern Scientific. This forcing in principle but can be passed if opener has a balanced minimum.

Well, if we can accept the loss of a passed-hand 2♣ response, can't we live without 2♢ as well? In fact, as rare as a passed-hand 2♣ bid is, a natural 2♢ response must be rarer still for those of us who open 2♢ as a weak two-bid.

What should this show?

Pass   Pass   1♠   Pass
2♢

How about a Drury bid guaranteeing 4+ trumps? That way we can distinguish a passed hand like

♠ 10 8 3   ♡ A Q 6 5   ♢ 9 5   ♣ K J 6 3

from

♠ A Q 10 6   ♡ A 7 3 2   ♢ 8 3 2   ♣ 6 4.

This will be most helpful for opener holding a hand like

♠ J 7 4 3 2   ♡ K 4   ♢ A Q J 7 4   ♣ 8.

If partner has only three trumps, the future of this hand is doubtful. Even 3♠ could be too high. However if partner promises 4+ trumps, we can confidently jump to 4♠. The ninth trump makes all the difference.

Try these hands now, using 2-way reverse Drury. In each case, state what you would bid opposite

a) 2♣, 3-card Drury and
b) 2♢, 4+ -card Drury.

You have opened 1♠ in third seat

1)   ♠ Q 10 7 4 3   ♡ A J 9 7 4   ♢ K 5   ♣ 7

a) Bid 2♡ over 2♣. Game is possible, but partner has to have the right hand. If partner can say only 2♠, call it a day.

b) Bid 4♠. It is hard to imagine a good passed hand with four trumps that won't give you some play for game, so don't tell the opponents about your hearts. Game is excellent opposite

♠ K J 8 2   ♡ 3 2   ♢ A 8 7   ♣ 9 8 6 5,

and partner surely has more than that.

2)   ♠ K J 8 6 5   ♡ Q 7 4   ♢ A J 6 3   ♣ 8

a) Rebid 2♠, the least encouraging action. With only three trumps opposite, chances for game are almost nil.

b) Bid 3♢. A waiting bid that shows a full opener. With the knowledge of four trumps opposite, you can afford to make the more encouraging rebid since partner's extra trump will be very helpful in covering your fourth diamond as well as eventually drawing trumps.

Limit Raises

For many years in this country it was standard for jumps by responder to be forcing to game. Although this style was simple and worked well on game-going hands, it caused problems on invitational hands of 10–12 point strength. For example, your partner opens 1♡ and you hold

♠ A 6 4   ♡ A Q 10 5   ◊ 8 6 4 3   ♣ 5 2.

You are too strong for 2♡, and not good enough for a forcing 3♡ bid. The "solution" was to make a "2½" raise, which you did by bidding 2◊ and then raising hearts. Nobody was happy about bidding those emaciated diamonds, which would be likely to mislead partner, but that was the "book" way to handle this hand.

English bridge players never had a problem with these hands. They bid 3♡ over 1♡ as an invitational raise, which opener could pass with a dead-minimum hand. If they held an extra king or so, they used 3 NT or 4 of a minor as a conventional forcing raise. These bids gave up little and avoided all of the problems of the 2½ raise.

Inevitably, limit raises broke through in this country. An observer at tournaments in 1985 would probably find about 75% of the duplicate players using limit raises, and among top players the figure would probably be closer to 90%.

A limit raise in a major suit shows at least four-card support, and 10–12 points including distribution. The requirement of four-card support should be adhered to even if the partnership is employing five-card major openings. With three-card support, responder should go ahead with a 2½ raise, or for those partnerships playing 1 NT forcing, responder can bid 1 NT followed by a jump raise.

Here are some other examples of limit raises after 1♡:

1) ♠ A 6   2) ♠ 9   3) ♠ K 5 4
    ♡ Q 9 5 3   ♡ J 10 6 3   ♡ A Q 8 7 3
    ◊ K 8 6 4   ◊ A 8 7 4 3   ◊ J 6
    ♣ J 3 2   ♣ Q J 5   ♣ 8 6 4

What does opener do after the limit raise? He will usually pass with a minimum or carry on to game with some extra values. Not much extra is needed though, since with the promise of four card support by responder, even a minimum hand with distributional values is sufficient for game because of extra flexibility provided by the presence of a ninth trump. Thus with

♠ Q J 10 6 4   ♡ 9   ◊ A 6 5 4   ♣ A 7 3,

bid 4♠ after 1♠–3♠, which will be virtually laydown opposite even a minimum like

♠ K 9 7 3   ♡ J 10 7 4   ◊ 9 2   ♣ K Q 5.

Occasionally, opener will have a strong enough hand to visualize slam. He can then cuebid to discover if responder's hand is suitable for slam. Since responder has less than an opening bid, though, it would be most unlikely for opener to have a slam try, unless he is very distributional.

Try these hands after 1♠–3♠:

1)   ♠ A Q 6 5 4   ♡ Q 9 4   ◊ Q 5   ♣ K 7 4

Pass. This is just a minimum balanced hand.

2)   ♠ A J 6 5 4   ♡ 8   ◊ A J 10 5 3   ♣ 9 2

Bid 4♠. Although the opening bid would not be popular with all, bidding game is now automatic. Opposite a fair hand with 4 trumps, you should have very few losers.

3)   ♠ A K 8 7 4 3   ♡ 9   ◊ A 10   ♣ A 5 3 2

Bid 4♠. Chances for slam are now excellent. Just look at those controls.

4)   ♠ A J 7 4 2   ♡ K J 4   ◊ A Q   ♣ Q J 5

Bid 4♠ or even 3 NT. You have lots of points, but your controls and distribution are mediocre. It is hard to picture any limit raise which offers even a 50–50 play for slam.

Limit raises in the minor suits have also been adopted by many players. The strength shown is about the same as in the majors, but there are some differences. The bid denies a four-card major, and five-card support is therefore very common, although four and six trumps are possible holdings. Here are some examples of limit raises in the minors: After 1◊, *bid 3◊* on

1) ♠ K 8 7	2) ♠ J 3	3) ♠ 8 4
♡ 8 4	♡ 10 6 5	♡ A 5
◊ K 9 6 5 3	◊ A Q J 7	◊ A J 7 6 3 2
♣ A 4 3	♣ K 9 6 4	♣ 10 8 7

After a limit raise in his minor, opener will pass with a minimum and try for game with a little extra. However, rather than five of a minor, the game that is first considered is 3 NT. For that reason, the high card content of a minor-suit limit raise is usually a little better than in the majors.

Opener bids 3 NT with more than a minimum and stoppers in each of the other suits, or cuebids stoppers up the line if one or more stoppers are missing. The bidding then proceeds intelligently. If 3 NT must be bypassed, a bid of 4♣ or 4◊ (the agreed minor) is not forcing.

Try rebidding with these after your opening bid of 1♣ has been raised to 3♣.

1)   ♠ A Q 6   ♡ 9 4   ◊ A J 5   ♣ A Q 7 4 3

Bid 3◊. If partner bids 3♡, you will have an easy 3 NT bid. You are strong enough to play 5♣ if partner has no heart stopper.

2)   ♠ A 6   ♡ K Q 7 5   ◊ 10 4   ♣ A J 8 7 4

Bid 3♡. This shows a heart stopper while denying a diamond stopper.

3)   ♠ 8 7 5 3   ♡ K Q 4   ◊ A 6   ♣ K 10 8 4

Pass. This is just a minimum opening bid.

4)   ♠ A 8 6   ♡ A 5 3 2   ◊ –   ♣ K J 8 7 4 3

Bid 3♡. You have no intention of playing 3 NT, since this hand will play beautifully in clubs. Despite the minimum point count, slam is very possible. Even if partner has wasted diamond strength, 6♣ would be cold opposite a hand like

         ♠ 9 4   ♡ K 6   ◊ K 8 7 4   ♣ A 10 6 5 2.

A splinter bid of 4◊ would also be just fine.

    When playing jump raises as limit, another bid is needed to show the forcing raise, particularly in the majors. Most players use 3 NT as the major suit forcing raise, although 2 NT also has its followers. In the minors, some players use inverted minors, while a fair number do not have any direct forcing raise, but cope by using 4th suit forcing. Splinter bids are also used, particularly after a major-suit opening.

    Limit raises are commonly played in competition also, and they are theoretically sound here. In fact, some players who normally play the jump raise as forcing use limit raises after an overcall since there is no reasonable second choice with a hand like

         ♠ A 6   ♡ A Q 8 5   ◊ 8 6 4 3   ♣ 10 7 4

after 1♡ –2◊ –?

    There is also a limit raise available after the opponents interfere with a takeout double. The most popular limit raise here is 2 NT, since 3 of the agreed trump suit is played as a weak distributional raise. Therefore, after 1♡ –Dbl., *bid 3♡* on

         ♠ 8 6   ♡ K Q 7 4   ◊ 10 7 3   ♣ 9 7 4 3,

and *2 NT* on

         ♠ A 6   ♡ K Q 7 4   ◊ J 7 3 2   ♣ 9 7 4.

Using 2 NT as a limit raise in such cases is referred to as "Jordan," and is also used with the minors by some players. With a game-forcing raise, *bid 3 NT* after 1♡ –Dbl. This frees the redouble for good hands which do not have trump support, although three-card support is possible.

52

Passed hand bidding is not affected by limit raises since

Pass	Pass	1♡	Pass
3♡			

has always been a limit raise. Those of us who use Drury usually show our maximum passed hands with support by bidding 2♣. Some experienced players play

Pass	Pass	1♡	1♠
3♡			

as somewhat preemptive, since the true limit raise can be shown in this situation by a 2♠ cuebid.

Limit raises can also be made opposite overcalls, but the modern expert trend is to use the jump raise as preemptive, cuebidding with the true limit raise. Therefore, after

1♢	1♡	1♠	?

bid 3♡ with

♠ 10 7 4   ♡ K J 6 3   ♢ 9   ♣ 10 7 4 3 2,

and 2♠ with

♠ K 7 4   ♡ K J 6 3   ♢ 9 4   ♣ K 10 7 4.

There is another convention which has acquired some popularity among top players. This is referred to as the "Mathe Asking Bid" and is employed after a major-suit limit raise. The cheapest bid after the limit raise asks responder for a singleton, which can be crucial to get to a "superfit" slam.

Here are all the responses to the Mathe Asking Bid.

After 1♡ – 3♡
      3♠
3 NT Spade singleton
4♣ Club singleton
4♢ Diamond singleton
4♡ No singleton

After 1♠ – 3♠
      3 NT
4♣ Club singleton
4♢ Diamond singleton
4♡ Heart singleton
4♠ No singleton

The reason for 3♠ being used instead of 3 NT after 1♡ – 3♡ is that otherwise there would be no way for responder to show a spade singleton without going past 4♡. This convention doesn't give up anything, since it is unlikely you would want to play 3 NT with a nine card (or more) major fit.

With these two hands, the bidding would go:

WEST	EAST
♠ 8	♠ A 10 6 5
♡ A K 9 6 5 3	♡ Q 10 7 4
◊ A K	◊ Q 7 3 2
♣ 10 6 5 4	♣ 8
1 ♡	3 ♡
3 ♠	4 ♣
4 NT	5 ◊
6 ♡	

West knows that he must have a super play for slam opposite a limit raise with 4 trumps, one ace and a singleton club.

Regardless of how you choose to embellish them, limit raises are definitely here to stay. They eliminate the gap problem hands that used to exist for which there was no good bid available. Even beginners can be taught the bid easily since what could be more natural than 1 ♡, Pass, 3 ♡ showing slightly more strength than 1 ♡, Pass, 2 ♡?

Question: I like to play limit raises in all suits. However, this leaves me without a forcing raise in the minors since I don't like to use Inverted Minors. Is there an answer?

Answer: Many players who use limit raises in the minors go without a direct forcing raise after 1 ♣ or 1 ◊. Instead, they improvise a bid on the first round like 1 ◊ over 1 ♣, and then give a strong raise on the next round. Although this gets the job done on some hands, it leaves much to be desired.

Some players use 2 NT as a forcing minor suit raise, but this gives up an important bid. My suggestion is to use the jump to 3 of the other minor as the forcing raise. These are bids which otherwise have limited utility. 1 ♣ - 3 ◊ and 1 ◊ - 3 ♣ therefore show 13–16 distributional points while denying a four-card major.

Cuebid – Limit Raise Or Better

How do you play an auction like

PARTNER	OPPONENT	YOU	
1 ♡	1 ♠	3 ♡	?

Twenty years ago the Standard answer would have been "forcing." Ten years ago, most people would have answered "invitational," meaning a limit raise. Today more and more pairs treat most jumps in competition as preemptive.

So let's assume that if we jump raise to 3♡ after an overcall, we have a weak hand with four trumps like

♠ 6 3   ♡ K J 9 4   ◇ 9 7 4 3   ♣ 6 5 3.

But what do we do with a limit raise like

♠ 6 3   ♡ K J 9 4   ◇ A Q 4 3   ♣ 6 5 3

or a forcing raise like

♠ A 3   ♡ K J 9 4   ◇ A Q 4 3   ♣ 6 5 3?

The answer is we cuebid 2♠, which partner Alerts as "a limit raise or better, saying nothing about spades."

Does this cuebid guarantee four trumps? No. Sometimes it's just not practical. Suppose you hold

♠ Q 6   ♡ A 7 4   ◇ A 5 3   ♣ J 9 7 4 2

after 1♡ by partner and a 2◇ overcall. If you couldn't bid 3◇ what would you do? If you bid 3♣, your chances of stopping in 3♡ opposite a minimum are about nil. You can't negative double with only two spades – partner might bury you in that suit.

On the other hand, one doesn't go out of one's way to cuebid with only three trumps, particularly three weak ones.

After 1♡ by partner, 2◇ by RHO, I would negative double with

♠ A Q 6 5   ♡ 10 7 4   ◇ A 3   ♣ 10 7 4 2

rather than bid 3◇. I can't get buried in spades, and hopefully the auction will remain under control. If the auction continues:

PARTNER	RHO	YOU	LHO
1♡	2◇	Dbl	3◇
Pass	Pass	?	

3♡ should show a three-card limit raise, since with all single raises you should have bid 2♡ earlier, even with spades. However, after

1♡	2◇	Dbl	4◇
5♣			

I will regret my decision. Any time you withhold major-suit support from your partner you shouldn't be surprised when the auction explodes in your face.

In case the auction remains competitive, I recommend having the understanding that we are in a "forcing pass" auction after our "limit raise or better" cuebid. Otherwise, after

1♡	1♠	2♠	4♠,

if a pass wasn't forcing, opener would have impossible problems! Therefore, we are forced to make the final bid or double in all such auctions.

If responder's cuebid shows exactly a limit raise, as it would if made by a passed hand, it would be reasonable for forcing passes to be in effect only when opener shows extra strength. However, this would be unwieldy after "limit raise or better."

Bidding a limit raise or better is easy enough, but if the partners aren't careful, the rest of the auction may leave much to be desired. For openers the key considerations to keep in mind are: (1) We're not in a game force. (2) Don't take unilateral actions unless you don't care whether responder has the limit or the forcing raise (rare).

For responder, the key to good contracts is: try to let opener know as soon as possible which type of raise you hold.

To understand these guidelines better, let's look at an auction which begins

<table>
<tr><td>1♠</td><td>2◇</td><td>3◇</td><td>Pass</td></tr>
<tr><td>?</td><td></td><td></td><td></td></tr>
</table>

Opener should:

1. Bid 3♠ holding

♠ A K J 4 2   ♡ K 6   ◇ J 7 4   ♣ 9 5 2

showing a minimum hand with no interest in game opposite a limit raise. Responder will bid again only with a forcing raise.

2. Bid 3♡ (game try +) with

♠ A Q 8 7 4   ♡ K Q 10 6   ◇ 6 4   ♣ Q 2

This game try doesn't promise hearts since there is no other game try available. It's also possible that opener wants to try for slam. 3♡ would certainly be the right bid with

♠ A K 6 5 4 2   ♡ A J 8   ◇ A 6   ♣ J 7.

Responder must be careful as to his choice of actions after the 3♡ game try. Holding a minimum limit raise like

♠ K 9 5 2   ♡ 9 7 4   ◇ A 7 5   ♣ K 9 3

responder signs off in 3♠. With a good limit raise responder can accept by bidding 4♠, but shouldn't jump to 4♠ with a good forcing raise, since opener can have a slam try. Responder should try to cuebid, which tells opener that we are willing to cooperate with a slam try, and we hold the "or better," as opposed to the limit raise.

If opener makes a bid like 4♣ or 4◇ after the 3◇ L.R.O.B., it is clear that he is hoping for slam. Responder must now limit his hand. Holding only a limit raise, he should invariably bid 4♠, even if he has a convenient cuebid. Remember, responder's normal range for the limit-raise-or-better cuebid is 11-16 distributional points. It's nice if you think your 12 points are attractive, but you're still down at the lower end of the spectrum.

The direct jump to 4♠ by opener is the area where most errors are made by lazy thinking. It's just so easy to do holding a hand like

♠ K Q 10 8 7 4   ♡ A 5   ◇ 9   ♣ A 8 4 3.

After all, we have only 13 HCP and partner has guaranteed only a game invitational raise. But partner *could* have a forcing raise! In fact, opener's hand is so good that even the perfect limit raise will produce slam!

♠ A 6 5 3   ♡ K 4 3   ◊ 8 7 4 2   ♣ K 2.

So opener shouldn't bid 4♠ with a hand with any slam interest. 4♠ should be bid only on a hand that is good enough to "shoot out" a game opposite a limit raise, but doesn't have enough high cards to warrant any interest in slam. Opposite a normal forcing raise

♠ Q J 10 7 4	♡ A 6 3	◊ 8	♣ A 10 7 4,
♠ Q 9 7 4 3 2	♡ K Q 5	◊ 9	♣ K J 3, and
♠ A K J 7 4	♡ 9 2	◊ 6 4	♣ K Q 8 5

all seem to qualify.

We've made it clear that responder must limit his hand as soon as possible in order to let opener know whether to expect a forcing raise, or *only* a limit raise. But there are exceptions to even good rules.

Look at these two hands after the auction.

1♠	2◊	3◊	Pass
4♣	Pass	?	

1.   ♠ K 10 8 6 4   ♡ A 7 4   ◊ 7 4 2   ♣ K 5

2.   ♠ K Q J 4   ♡ K J 7   ◊ Q J 6   ♣ J 6 5

At the time that we bid 3◊, we presumably intended to make a limit raise with (1) and a forcing raise with the second hand. But for slam purposes, the first hand is much better. If partner has

♠ A 9 5 4 3 2   ♡ 9   ◊ A 5   ♣ A 8 7 4,

we are cold for a slam opposite the first hand, but even 4♠ isn't cold opposite (2). So I would cuebid 4♡ on the first hand, even though I only have a limit raise (although this hand may be too good for a limit raise), but would show a minimum with the garbage in (2), even though I have a forcing raise.

Let's look at some examples of "Limit Raise or Better" auctions, some successful, some not. See if you can spot what went wrong in the bad auctions, while noting the difference in the good ones.

1.

♠ K Q 10 9 6	♠ A 8 5 4
♡ A 7 5	♡ 4
◊ 8	◊ A 7 4
♣ A 9 4 3	♣ K 8 6 5 2

WEST	NORTH	EAST	SOUTH
1♠	2♡	3♡	Pass
4♠	All Pass		

Although slams with 24 HCP are not usually easy to bid, 6♠ should have been reached. There were major errors, one by each player. East's mistake was the 3♡ bid. A better action was available. East should have made a splinter bid of 4♡, showing a game-forcing raise with a heart singleton or void, since it is a more precise description of the hand. West could now drive to slam via

1♠	2♡	4♡	Pass
5♣	Pass	5◇	Pass
5♡	Pass	6♣	Pass
6♠	All Pass		

However, West could have saved the day – the 4♠ bid was poor. West's hand was worth a lot more than 13 points – good trumps, good distribution, good controls. West should bid 4♣ over 3♡, showing slam interest opposite a suitable forcing raise. Slam was still biddable after East's failure to splinter, perhaps:

1♠	2♡	3♡	Pass
4♣	Pass	4◇	Pass
4♡	Pass	5♣	Pass
5◇	Pass	5♡	Pass
6♠	All Pass		

2.

♠ A 10 8 5	♠ K J
♡ 8 4	♡ A K 5
◇ A Q J 4	◇ K 9 8 3
♣ J 5 2	♣ K 7 4 3

1◇	1♡	2♡	Pass
3◇	Pass	3 NT	

It's clear that this auction was successful, since 3 NT is clearly the correct contract for East-West. But was it right for East with 17 HCP, to bid only 3 NT at his second turn? Yes, it certainly was. When West bid 3◇ over the "limit raise or better" 2♡, he said he had no interest in game opposite a limit raise. That was a fine example of limiting the hand – which is so crucial after a "limit raise or better" cuebid (not to mention many other auctions).

Most players would bid 2♠ over 2♡, but that would be an example of what I refer to as *advertising*. East denied four spades with the diamond raise of 2♡, just as 1◇ – Pass – 2◇ and 1◇ – Pass – 3◇ deny spades. If East has four spades after 1◇ – 1♡ –?, East must negative double first, before supporting opener's minor. Therefore there is no point in West showing the spades at this time. West's first duty must be to indicate the minimum opening bid.

Look how easy it was for East to give up on slam after West's 3◇ signoff. Would you be able to stop at 3 NT with East's hand after hearing a 2♠ rebid by West? Keep in mind that East's hand is so good that as little as

♠ A 6 4 3   ♡ 9 2   ◇ A 10 7 5 4 2   ♣ 8

in the West hand makes slam a virtual certainty – and it is safe to assume that West has more than an 8-count for the opening bid!

Remember, bidding can be defined as an exchange of relevant information. There are many times when you know where you are going, so you need not *advertise* to the opponents what you have in your hand.

Here are a few examples of this type of practicality.

1.   1 NT   Pass   ?

    ♠ 6 5   ♡ 8 4   ◊ A K Q J 6 4   ♣ 9 5 2

Any experienced player would bid 3 NT without showing the diamonds. You know you want to play 3 NT, so why stop off to tell the world that you have a diamond suit?

2.   1 ♡   Pass   2 ♡   Pass
               ?

    ♠ K 7   ♡ K J 10 9 7 4   ◊ 6   ♣ A K J 4

Is there any reason to show your clubs? Since you are on your way to 4 ♡ regardless of what partner has for the raise to 2 ♡, bidding clubs would only serve to help the opponents' defense. Of course it's possible that 6 ♡ would be a good contract. Partner might hold

    ♠ A 5 3   ♡ A 6 3 2   ◊ 10 8 7 4   ♣ 6 5

But it is silly to look for slam. There are many good raises that partner might hold where he will cooperate in your slam try and you will land in a poor 6 ♡ or an unnecessary 5 ♡.

3.   E-W: Vul.
          ♠ A K J 8 7 4   ♠ Q 9 6 3
          ♡ 6   ♡ 8 4
          ◊ Q 7 4   ◊ A K 9
          ♣ A J 5   ♣ K Q 8 3

          WEST   NORTH   EAST   SOUTH
          1♠   2♡   3♡   4♡
          4♠   All Pass

West criticized East for passing 4♠ with a maximum, and it is true that East had a lot more than promised. However, the blame must be taken by West. West argued that he could hardly pass 4♡ when he knew that 4♠ was cold. But that's exactly the point! A pass of 4♡ by West would be 100% forcing, as stated earlier. Therefore East would be forced to take action over 4♡ regardless of whether he had a forcing raise or a limit raise.

There were three options for West after 4♡ without going past 4♠.

1. *Forcing Pass.* This says that East is given the choice between bidding on and doubling. Presumably East should double with either an offensive minimum like

a.   ♠ Q 6 5 2   ♡ Q 8   ◊ K 8 6 3   ♣ K Q 3

or a maximum defensive hand like

b.   ♠ Q 6 5   ♡ K Q 4   ◊ 6 3   ♣ K Q 8 3 2

With a normal forcing raise like

c.   ♠ Q 10 6 5   ♡ 9 2   ◇ A K 8 3   ♣ K 9 2

or an attractive limit raise such as

d.   ♠ Q 10 3 2   ♡ 3 2   ◇ A K 10 9 2   ♣ 4 3

East should bid 4♠. Notice that West has no chance for slam opposite hand (a) and (b) and rates to go down at the five-level opposite either one. Whereas if East has hand (c) or (d) we are completely safe at the five level and have a very good play for 6♠.

2. *Double*. West has the opportunity to double 4♡ with a hand that has good defense and poor offense. This would suggest to East that it seemed right to defend 4♡ doubled since 4♠ was unlikely to make. West would double 4♡ holding

   ♠ A 8 7 4 2   ♡ K Q   ◇ 6 4 3   ♣ A 7 4 or

   ♠ 10 7 5 4 2   ♡ A Q   ◇ Q 6 3   ♣ A 9 2

where taking a sure plus vs. 4♡ is clearly better bridge than going down in 4♠, which would be the likely result opposite a lot of likely hands for East. Of course if East had a hand which was all offense and no defense like

   ♠ K Q J 9 3   ♡ 4   ◇ K 8 7 4 2   ♣ 8 6,

it would be clear for him to overrule and bid 4♠.

Clearly there are also some hands on which it is right for West to exercise the third option.

3. *Bid 4♠ over 4♡*. What hands fall into this category? Good question. The answer is the same hands that would have bid 4♠ even if South hadn't cramped the auction with the 4♡ bid. All of the following opening hands should bid 4♠ over 1♠ – 2♡ – 3♡ – 4♡:

   ♠ A K J 8 4 2   ♡ 9 2   ◇ Q J 6 3   ♣ 9,

   ♠ K J 10 8 7 4   ♡ K   ◇ Q 4   ♣ A 7 4 2, and

   ♠ J 10 8 7 4 2   ♡ A K   ◇ Q 10 6 5   ♣ J.

Please note that even opposite East's maximum of

   ♠ Q 9 6 3   ♡ 8 4   ◇ A K 9   ♣ K Q 8 3,

none of the above hands offers any play for slam, and even getting to 5 would be fatal on two of the three. So East was clearly correct to pass 4♠.

So, how should East-West have bid to get to the cold 6♠ after

WEST	NORTH	EAST	SOUTH
1♠	2♡	3♡	4♡
?			

with

♠ A K J 8 7 4	♠ Q 9 6 3
♡ 6	♡ 8 4
◇ Q 7 4	◇ A K 9
♣ A J 5	♣ K Q 8 3

Here is a good auction with the appropriate thoughts of each player.

WEST: *Pass.* "Let's hear what my partner wants to do now so I can decide whether to risk the five level. If partner doubles I'll know slam can't be good, so I'll bid 4♠ and take my sure vulnerable game. But if partner's hand is reasonable enough offensively for him to bid 4♠ rather than double, I can cuebid 5♣ in safety, knowing East cannot have a *disaster* hand."

EAST: *4♠.* "We must be cold for this with my hand, and I doubt that we can get 4♡ doubled for 700."

WEST: *5♣.* "I know it's safe to cuebid."

EAST: *5◇.* "I'm certainly willing to cooperate."

WEST: *5♡.* "I have a control in hearts, partner, don't worry about that. I don't want to commit us to 6♠. My 6-1-3-3 is not as good for slam purposes as 6-1-4-2 would be. I'm going to pass 5♠ if that's all you can do. Opposite something like

♠ Q 10 6 5 2   ♡ A 7   ◇ A K 3   ♣ 8 4 2

slam would have little play, and your bidding would certainly be correct."

EAST: *6♣.* "Partner, I'm glad to hear you have a heart control. I'm certainly interested in seven, which will be cold opposite

♠ A K 10 8 5 4   ♡ –   ◇ Q J 10 4   ♣ A J 4 or

♠ A K 8 7 4 2   ♡ A 5   ◇ Q 6 4   ♣ A 9.

My partners never seem to have the perfect hand, but there's no harm in trying."

WEST: *6♠.* "Enough is enough. Seven seems remote, and since I could have had first-round control of hearts for my 5♡ bid, any other call could risk an accident. I'm more than satisfied to get to a good small slam. Even if the grand has play, there will always be a good number of pairs that stop in game. In fact the first time we bid this hand we stopped in four because of my stupid premature 4♠ bid."

EAST: *Pass.* "Good auction, partner. It's nice to know that you at least get them correct the second time around."

Here is our good auction—the second time around.

WEST	NORTH	EAST	SOUTH
1♠	2♡	3♡	4♡
Pass	Pass	4♠	Pass
5♣	Pass	5◇	Pass
5♡	Pass	6♣	Pass
6♠	All Pass		

Jump Shifts

One of the most significant modern trends in bidding is the one toward practicality. Compare the list of conventions used by most players today with those generally in use 25 years ago.

1959	1984
penalty doubles	negative doubles
strong jump overcalls	weak jump overcalls
strong two-bids	weak two-bids
1 NT 16–18 or 16–19	1 NT 15–17
forcing jump raises	limit raises
3 NT 25–27	"Gambling" 3 NT
game forcing cuebid	Michaels, etc. – weak 2 suiters

Although not all these changes are dramatic, most are quite significant. You can also observe that in most cases the amount of strength needed to make a certain call is less in 1984 than in 1959. Using a bid to indicate a type of hand that occurs rarely is impractical, especially if there is another usage which occurs more often.

One bid that remains in limbo is the jump shift response to an opening one-bid. Most players continue to use this to show a powerhouse opposite partner's opening bid – a hand which clearly has enough for game and is suggesting the possibility of a slam. Others, however, have concluded that this very strong hand will occur only rarely, they feel the very good hand can still be handled with careful exploration. This is certainly analogous to the arguments presented by weak jump overcallers in arguing against the need for a strong jump overcall.

While the number of radicals who use 1 ◊ – Pass – 2 ♣ as a weak bid is still reasonably limited, many moderates and liberals have made a partial concession. 1 ◊ – Dbl – 2 ♣ is now almost universally played as preemptive. As for what the jump shift should be after an overcall, such as 1 ◊ –1 ♡ –2 ♠, the strong and weak camps both have a significant number of followers, although most top players use the weak approach. This is undoubtedly due to the fact that it is rare to have a strong jump shift response after your partner opens the bidding and an opponent overcalls.

Even in the treatment of passed hand jump shifts, opinion is now sharply divided. While the average players in general still use

Pass	Pass	1 ◊	Pass
2 ♡			

as something like

♠ J 6 4   ♡ K Q 7 4 3   ◊ 9 3   ♣ K Q 4,

many of the top players use 2♡ to show hearts and diamonds such as

♠ 8 4   ♡ Q J 7 4 3   ◊ A K 7 3   ♣9 2,

while others use the jumps for terrible hands, such as

♠ 9 4   ♡ K J 10 9 4 3   ◊ 10 7   ♣ 8 6 5.

We are going to take a detailed look at these treatments. In our study of strong jump shifts, we will see that the prevailing opinion on these hands has changed. Most experienced players would bid 2♡ over 1◊ with

♠ 8   ♡ A Q J 5 4   ◊ A K 8 7 5   ♣ 7 5,

but would bid only 1♡ with

♠ A K 7   ♡ Q 10 6 4 3   ◊ A   ♣ A Q 4 2!

Strong Jump Shifts

The concept of a strong jump shift is still the same: a very strong respond-ing hand that has enough for game and potential for slam. However, the requirement of 19 points as required in early Goren is no longer considered practical. A good player would jump shift over 1 ◊ with any of the following:

1) ♠ A K Q J 9 4 3
   ♡ K J 7
   ◊ 10 4
   ♣ 6

2) ♠ K J 8
   ♡ A Q J 10 6
   ◊ K 4
   ♣ K 7 5

3) ♠ A Q 10
   ♡ A 7
   ◊ 4 3
   ♣ K Q J 10 7 4

4) ♠ A Q 10 6 2
   ♡ A 7
   ◊ A Q 5 4
   ♣ 9 4

Notice that none of these hands contains 19 high card points, but they all have several things in common: good suits, good rebids, slam-try strength. The most important strong jump shifts are the ones where you wish to invite a slam if partner has the right minimum.

Hand (1) will next jump to 4♠. This shows a solid spade suit with not too much on the side. Partner need not worry about the quality of his spade support, but can simply look at the controls in the remainder of his hand. Partner will bid a slam with

♠ 7   ♡ A 10 6 2   ◊ A J 7 3 2   ♣ A 5 4,

and 6♠ will be virtually cold.

On hand (2) you will rebid in notrump. This shows a relatively balanced hand with scattered strength in addition to the good heart suit. You merely need to find partner with something like

♠ A 3 2   ♡ K 7   ◊ A Q 8 6 5 3   ♣ 8 4

to have an excellent try for slam.

Hand (3) will be handled similarly to (2). If you simply bull your way into slam, you deserve to find partner with a hand like

♠ K J 6   ♡ J 10 6 4   ◇ K J 7 2   ♣ A 5,

which is not my idea of a good slam.

The fourth hand which has a big diamond fit is also best pictured by jump-shifting. Compare

1◇ - 2♠   1◇ -1♠
3♣ - 3◇ with 2♣ - 3◇ even if your partnership treats the latter as forcing. Don't you have that leftover feeling? Couldn't you bid that way without the heart ace? Won't partner bid 3 NT on the latter auction with

♠ 9   ♡ K Q 10   ◇ K 9 7 3 2   ♣ A J 5 3?

While jump shifts are quite necessary with slam-invitational hands as above, it is not crucial with

♠ K Q J 10 7 6 5   ♡ A 4   ◇ A 5   ♣ A 3.

Now we are going to bid at least a small slam. There is nothing wrong with a 2♠ bid, but we are all right after 1♠. We will get to hear partner's natural rebid and can then make a forcing bid or two before taking charge and proceeding to a small or grand slam. Contrast this hand with the first three, none of which can make a slam if partner has an unsuitable opening bid.

The absolutely worst kind of hand to jump shift on is the hand with a lot of high cards but no idea as to what denomination is best for the final contract. With

♠ Q   ♡ A J 7 6   ◇ K Q J 4   ♣ A Q 3 2,

after partner opens 1♠, you need all the room in the world in order to probe for the correct contract. You might want to play a slam in any of the four suits or notrump, or even stop off in game opposite a hand with no good fit like

♠ A 8 7 5 4 2   ♡ K 4 3   ◇ A 2   ♣ J 5.

Once we have established that it is wrong to jump shift on hands with great flexibility (potential to play in many denominations), we are only one step away from playing Soloway Jump Shifts. Paul Soloway's concept is that you should not jump shift on a two- or three-suiter, so there are only three types of hands which constitute a strong jump shift: (1) one-suiters (not necessarily a solid suit); (2) the relatively balanced hand which will rebid in notrump; (3) and the hand with a big fit for partner's suit.

Therefore, if playing Soloway Jump Shifts,

1◇ -2♠
3♣ -3◇   shows four or more diamonds, not merely a preference with three, since you must have been planning to support diamonds all along. Since

1 ◊ – 2 ♠
2 NT – 3 ♣   does not exist as a natural bid (since we do not jump
shift with two-suiters), Soloway advocates treating this
as a "splinter" raise of opener's diamonds, pinpointing
a singleton club – a hand such as

♠ A K 8 7 4   ♡ K 7 4   ◊ K Q 6 5   ♣ 9.

This will allow opener to bid a slam with confidence with as little as

♠ J 6   ♡ A J   ◊ A J 7 4 3   ♣ J 8 6 4,

knowing of the perfect fit of the clubs. It is very significant to note that
although Soloway Jump Shifts are played by relatively few "average" players,
a great number of top players have adopted them.

Weak Jump Shifts

Let's look at the opposite extreme from the strong jump shift – the use
of a jump shift as a weak, preemptive bid.

How many times have you picked up a hand like

♠ 10 6 4   ♡ K J 9 7 4 3   ◊ 6 5 4   ♣ 8,

and heard your partner open 1 ♣? You hate to leave partner in 1 ♣ with a
singleton, and you do have a six-card major, so you bid 1 ♡. Partner now
jumps to 3 ♣. You can't possibly bid over this, so you pass and watch partner
go down with your 4-point dummy when he could have made a more modest
contract.

In addition to not being able to make 3 ♣, you may find you're cold for
4 ♡. This could happen when partner has something like

♠ A K   ♡ 10 6 5   ◊ A 8   ♣ A Q 7 6 4 3.

But if you try bidding over 3 ♣ next time, you deserve to find partner with

♠ A K Q   ♡ 2   ◊ 8 3   ♣ K Q J 7 5 3 2,

and your last chance for a plus score was 3 ♣.

You wouldn't be any better off even if your partner did something else
besides jump rebidding clubs opposite your

♠ 10 6 4   ♡ K J 9 7 6 3   ◊ 6 5 4   ♣ 8.

After 1 ♣ – 1 ♡, you would not be too well placed after any bid by partner
other than an unlikely heart raise or 1 NT.

Obviously, there is just no good answer for this kind of hand in Standard
American. But if we can jump to 2 ♡ over 1 ♣ preemptively, showing a hand
not good enough for a Standard minimum response but at least (usually) a
six card suit, we can leave everything to partner.

A weak jump response can be a slightly better hand at the 3-level. Bid
3 ♡ over 1 ♣ with

or
♠ 8   ♡ K Q J 10 7 4   ◇ 6 3 2   ♣ 8 6 4

♠ 4 2   ♡ Q J 10 8 7 5 4   ◇ Q 4   ♣ 6 3,

giving partner an immediate description of your modest hand. This may serve
to give the opponents difficulty when it is their hand. It also serves to warn
partner immediately about your lack of strength.

Should we make this bid if vulnerable? Sure, why not? We would like
to have a better suit when vul, but if the hand qualifies on other counts,
you might as well.

Playing weak jump responses also puts you in a nice position when the
bid doesn't come up. After   1♣ –1♡
                                   1♠ -2♡

opener can assume that responder has a fairly respectable hand, since he
must have been *too good for a weak jump shift*. Opener can now try for game
on a borderline hand, knowing that partner does not have a "dog."

To sum up, check out each of the following and decide which hands are
suitable for the weak jump shift. Partner has opened 1 ◇ in each case, with
neither side vulnerable.

1)   ♠ K Q 10 9 6   ♡ 7 5 2   ◇ 8 6 3   ♣ 8 4

Yes, bid 2 ♠. You'd like to have six, but this is the best way to tell partner
that you have a good suit and a rotten hand.

2)   ♠ 6 5 4   ♡ 8 7   ◇ 9 3   ♣ J 9 8 6 4 3

Pass. It is too dangerous to commit this hand to the 3-level.

3)   ♠ 8 6   ♡ A K 7 5 3 2   ◇ 9 4   ♣ 10 3 2

Bid 1 ♡. This is a reasonable hand. Partner will not be misled if you bid
and rebid hearts.

4)   ♠ 9   ♡ Q J 10 9 4   ◇ 8 5   ♣ J 10 7 4 3

Bid 2 ♡. Although it may seem wrong to emphasize hearts with a two-
suiter, how could you ever conduct an auction to show both suits but only
four points? 2 ♡ is the practical bid. If you get a convenient chance you will
then show your clubs.

How should you bid opposite a weak jump shift? Carefully! Partner has
warned you that his hand is really terrible, so you will probably find yourself
passing most of the time. Any minimum rebid by you should be regarded
as non-forcing and non-invitational. However, a 2 NT bid can be used as
an attempt to find out more about partner's hand – but there really isn't too
much to find out.

In competition, responder's jump shifts are played by increasing numbers
as preemptive. 1 ◇ –Dbl–2 ♡ is a typical auction. Because the opponent has
indicated length in hearts with his double, the requirements for the weak
jump shift are increased slightly to at least guarantee a good suit. Bid 2 ♡
over 1 ♣ –Pass, with

♠ Q 8 5   ♡ Q 8 7 4 3 2   ◇ 8 5   ♣ 9 6,

but pass after 1♣–Dbl. Remember that partner will get another turn when the opponents intervene, whereas passing after 1♣–Pass, may result in partner never getting a second chance.

A smaller group of traditionalists uses 1♣–Dbl–2♡ (or similar) to be a "good" invitational hand, such as

♠ 8 5 3   ♡ K Q J 10 7 4   ◇ K 4   ♣ 8 5,

or even a forcing hand, with another king. This can be indicated on the convention card.

Since strong jump shifts are unlikely after an opponent's overcall, there is a trend toward the use of weak jump shifts over this form of competition. If you don't bid 3♣ with

♠ 8 5 4   ♡ 10 7   ◇ 3 2   ♣ K Q J 10 7 4

after 1◇ –1♠ –? you will either have to go to the two-level on a six count, or risk never showing your clubs at all. Remember that you are not severly inconvenienced if using preemptive jump shifts here. If you are fortunate enough to pick up a strong jump shift; just bid your suit and cuebid at your next turn. Going slowly on big hands to discover information is a cornerstone of good bidding.

Weak jump shifts are also used today opposite overcalls. If you play

LHO	Partner	RHO	You
1◇	1♡	Pass	1♠

as a forcing bid, then 2♠ is unnecessary to show a very good hand. But with

♠ Q J 10 9 4 3   ♡ 8 5   ◇ 4   ♣ Q 10 7 3,

you'd like to mention your spades without encouraging partner, and you'd also like to make it difficult for opener to rebid. Since there is also a good case for the jump shift response to indicate an intermediate or very good hand, especially with new suits not being forcing, you had better get around to discussing this with your partners.

Another matter that definitely must be discussed by all good partnerships is the meaning of jump shifts by passed hands, with or without competition. Is

You	LHO	Partner	RHO
Pass	Pass	1◇	Pass
2♠			

a strong bid or a weak bid? Is it forcing? Does it promise a fit for opener's suit? Is there any difference if the auction went

Pass	Pass	1♡	Pass
3◇,			

and the shift was *into* a minor instead of from a minor to a major?

Another noteworthy jump shift situation has evolved from one segment of the forcing 1 NT group. With 1 NT forcing, the two-over-one is normally played as game forcing except when responder rebids his suit, such as

$$1\spadesuit - 2\diamond$$
$$2\heartsuit - 3\diamond.$$

Some of us prefer to use the 2 over 1 as completely game forcing, so as not to distort our bidding for the infrequent classes of hands where responder is planning only to invite. Therefore, since we use

$$1\spadesuit - 2\diamond$$
$$2\heartsuit - 3\diamond$$

as game forcing, we need a way to distinguish the invitational

♠ 8 4   ♡ 7 5   ◇ K Q J 7 4 3   ♣ A 5 2

hand from the near hopeless

♠ 8 4   ♡ 7 5   ◇ K Q J 7 4 3   ♣ 6 5 2

sort. What's the answer?

$$1\spadesuit - 1\,NT$$
$$2\heartsuit - 3\diamond$$

becomes invitational, while $1\spadesuit - 3\diamond$ is our old friend, the weak jump shift response.

Our last jump shift auction stems from the Drury Convention. If

$$Pass - 1\heartsuit$$
$$2\clubsuit$$

shows 3+ hearts and 10+ points using Drury, then we need some other way to show clubs. Therefore, we bid 3♣ as the only direct way to show clubs, not really weak nor strong. At times, even the lowly club suit has its day.

We have seen that the jump shift is no longer a straightforward proposition. Partnerships that wish to be thorough must discuss a great number of auctions involving jump shifts. I will conclude with a list of the type of auctions that should be discussed by a pair aiming for proficiency. Those aiming for greatness will probably want to include a few more.

WHAT DO THESE BIDS MEAN?

1)	Opponent	Opponent	
	—	1♡	Pass	2♠ ?
2)	—	1◇	Dbl	2♡ ?
3)	—	1◇	1♡	3♣ ?
4)	Pass	Pass	Pass	1◇
	Pass	2♠ ?		
5)	1♣	1♡	Pass	3◇ ?
6)	—	Pass	Pass	1♣
	1♡	2♠ ?		
7)	—	Pass	Pass	1♡
	Pass	3♣ ?		

Jacoby Transfers

Because it is usually advantageous for the stronger hand to be declarer, auctions such as 1 NT - 2 ♠, 1 NT - 3 ♡, or 1 NT - 4 ♡ often result in contracts being played from the "wrong side." With the notrump bidder as dummy, the opening lead comes through opener's strength. The defenders' task is eased by being able to view the honor cards in dummy.

However, transfer bids eliminate this problem. Responder accomplishes the transfer by bidding the suit below his real suit, showing a suit at least five cards long. Opener then completes the transfer by bidding the cheapest suit as requested. The following are all examples of transfer bids:

1 NT - 2 ◇	2 NT - 3 ♡	1 NT - 2 ♡	2 NT - 3 ◇
2 ♡	3 ♠	2 ♠	3 ♡

In each case, responder has shown at least a five-card suit, but the opener has now been assured of becoming the declarer in the likely occurrence of the hand being played in responder's long suit.

Another advantage of transfer bids is that it facilitates responder's handling of two-suited hands. Picture a hand like

♠ A Q 7 6 3   ♡ K   ◇ 8 5   ♣ K J 7 4 3.

Without transfers, you would bid 3 ♣ over partner's 1 NT, and over a rebid of 3 NT you would then have to guess whether or not to risk going past 3 NT to show your club suit.

With transfers, on the other hand, you can have your cake and eat it too. The auction would go

1 NT - 2 ♡
2 ♠ - 3 ♣

and opener would be well positioned to select the correct strain.

Now that we've examined the advantages of transfer bids, let's take a look at the way responder rebids after making the transfer.

After 1 NT - 2 ◇, showing 5 hearts, responder can make any of the following calls:

Pass – no game interest.

2 ♠ – at least four spades, game interest.

2 NT – invitational to 3 NT or 4 ♡, but can be passed.

3 ♣, 3 ◇ – at least four cards in suit bid, forcing to game.

3 ♡ – invitational to 4 ♡ based on six-card suit.

3 NT – choice of games (3 NT or 4 ♡), shows five hearts.

4 ♣ – Gerber.

4 ♡ – six or more hearts, signoff.

4 NT – slam try, invites 6 ♡ or 6 NT, but can be passed – not Blackwood.

There is not universal agreement as to the meaning of all bids involved in Jacoby Transfers. I will try to present the most popular methods here. Other interpretations will be provided as well. Each partnership that decides to play Jacoby Transfers must discuss the various sequences to insure that both partners are on the same wavelength.

Try these examples to test your understanding of responder's rebids. We will assume in this series that 1 NT shows 15-17 high card points. This seems to be the most popular range in use today, having replaced the old standby 16-18. Of course, you can use Jacoby regardless of the point count shown by 1 NT – you merely adjust accordingly. Now, holding each of the following hands, what do you do after the auction has proceeded

1 NT   2♡
2♠   ?

1.   ♠ J 10 7 4 3   ♡ 9   ◇ Q J 7 5 2   ♣ 8 4

Pass. Partner may like diamonds better than spades, but you can't afford to bid your diamonds to find out, since 3 ◇ is forcing.

2.   ♠ K J 8 7 4   ♡ A 8 3   ◇ K 7 4   ♣ A 4

Bid 4 NT. Slam is certainly possible, but it would be rash to commit this hand to the six level. Partner can bid slam in either spades or NT, or he can pass with a minimum hand.

3.   ♠ K Q 10 9 7 4   ♡ 8   ◇ Q 5 4 3   ♣ 9 4

Bid 4♠. You are willing to shoot out a spade game, so bid it. Showing your diamonds will only serve to provide information to the opening leader.

4.   ♠ Q J 10 7 4   ♡ K Q 5   ◇ 6 3   ♣ 9 4 3

Bid 2 NT. Game is still possible, but you are not strong enough to force. This invitational bid preserves all your options, and, if partner is forced to pass, hopefully there will be eight tricks in notrump.

Although the responder usually is in charge, opener must cooperate in order for the partnership to reach the correct final contract. He must analyze the sequence produced by his partner as to strength and distribution and decide whether his assistance is being requested. If the answer is yes, opener will then look at the strength and distribution in his own hand in order to take the correct action.

What do you do as opener in each of the following?

5.   1 NT   2♡
                    2♠   3♣
                    ?

          ♠ A 5   ♡ K J 9 4   ◇ A J 9 4   ♣ A 6 2

Bid 3 NT. Although you have a maximum, you don't have a good fit for either of your partner's suits. All you can do is bid the obvious game with your good stoppers in the red suits.

6.	1 NT	2 ♡
	2 ♠	4 ♠
	?	

♠ A 7 5   ♡ K J 9 3   ◇ A Q 10   ♣ K 8 4

Pass. Partner wishes to play in game and has precluded any thoughts of slam. On this auction it is safe to pass without looking at your hand.

7.	1 NT	2 ♡
	2 ♠	3 NT
	?	

♠ 10 4 3   ♡ A K 10 6   ◇ A J 10 7   ♣ K 5

Bid 4 ♠. Your partner has five spades and enough to be in game. With three spades and a ruffing value in clubs, you should prefer to play in partner's major. If one of your small hearts was a club, there would be a division among experts as to whether or not to bid. The weak spades and 3-4-3-3 distribution argue for a pass while the knowledge of the eight-card major suit fit suggests 4 ♠.

Occasionally opener will hear his partner transfer into a major suit for which opener has a terrific fit and a maximum in point count as well. Although partner can have a Yarborough, it is correct to show your super-hand to partner. Some players jump to identify this hand, others bid the suit of which they have a doubleton to provide partner with extra information. Therefore, with

♠ A Q J 7   ♡ K 9 4   ◇ A 10 6 3   ♣ K 5,

after 1 NT - 2 ♡, you should bid either 3 ♠ or 3 ♣, depending on how you and your partner have agreed to play this. The three-level is high enough, though, since partner may have

♠ 9 8 6 4 3   ♡ 7   ◇ 9 4 2   ♣ 8 7 4 3.

At this point, we have a sufficient knowledge of Jacoby Transfers to carry us through the basic transfer auctions. It is especially important to understand these well. Many players continually mess up these auctions because they have failed to master the meanings of responder's rebids.

However, we are far from through with our study of transfer auctions. We must examine the Stayman auctions that relate to Jacoby, see how other notrump auctions are affected by the use of Jacoby Transfers, and discuss transfers to minor suits. We also must consider our options when the opponents interfere.

We continue our study of Jacoby Transfers by examining some sequences which are affected by the use of transfer bids. We will begin by considering several hands where the correct bidding sequence is not immediately obvious.

In all examples, assume partner has opened 1 NT (15-17 HCP):

1.   ♠ K J 6 4 3   ♡ A 10 8 5   ◊ K 3   ♣ 9 2

Bid 2♣. If partner bids a major, you have an easy jump to game. If partner bids 2◊, you jump to 3♠. This must show four hearts along with your five spades, since otherwise why would you use Stayman?

2.   ♠ J 10 7 4   ♡ 10 8 5 3 2   ◊ 9   ♣ J 5 4

Bid 2♣. Rather than transferring to hearts and giving up the chance to play in spades, start with 2♣. You will be content if partner bids 2 of a major, and over 2◊ you will bid 2♡. Without Jacoby, that bid would be invitational to game promising five hearts – but you can't have that hand since you would have transferred to 2♡ and then invited with 2 NT. When you bid 2♡, partner will usually pass, but can bid 2♠ with three good spades and a doubleton heart, since you are promising four + spades.

3.   ♠ Q 10 6 4 3   ♡ A 5   ◊ J 7 4 3   ♣ K J

Bid 2♡, then 3 NT. After transferring to spades, don't bid 3◊ to show your other suit. You don't want to play in 5◊, do you? Bidding a second suit should show a very unbalanced hand or slam possibilities. With this hand rebid 3 NT, just as if the hand were 5-3-3-2.

4.   ♠ Q J 7 4 3   ♡ K 9 8 5 4   ◊ 5 4   ♣ 8

You would like to show both majors with some interest in game if partner has the right hand. You can accomplish this by the following sequence:

                1 NT   2◊
                2♡   2♠

This shows a limited 4-5 or 5-5, since with a better 5-5 you would transfer to spades and then force to game by bidding 3♡, and with a better 4-5 you would start with Stayman and jump.

5.   ♠ A 4 2   ♡ K 10 7 4   ◊ 9   ♣ A Q J 6 3

Start with 2♣ hoping partner will respond 2♡. You next bid 3♣ to show a good club suit, some slam interest, and very often a four-card major on the side. Although a cuebid or club raise is a strong possibility, your partner can sign off with an unsuitable hand.

6.   ♠ 10 9 8 7   ♡ J 10 9 3   ◊ –   ♣ 9 8 6 4 3

Bid 2♣. If your diamonds and clubs were reversed, you could easily bid Stayman and then pass the response. However, since you really don't want to put down this dummy in 1 NT, bid 2♣ anyway. There will be no problem if partner has been dealt a major. Over 2◊ bid 2♡, just as in hand #2. Partner is only allowed to pass or bid 2♠, so nothing too terrible can happen.

7.   ♠ J 8 4   ♡ K Q 9 5   ◊ 6 4   ♣ 10 7 5 4

You will pass 1 NT of course, but fourth hand now balances with 2◊, which comes back around to you. Since you don't want to sell out to 2◊, bid 2♡. Since you didn't transfer, partner knows you don't have five hearts, so if he has a doubleton heart he can convert to 2♠, 2 NT, or 3♣.

8. ♠ 8   ♡ J 8 4 3   ◊ 5 4   ♣ Q 10 9 7 6 4

Bid 3♣. It isn't practical to bid 2♣, since you won't be in a position to sign off unless partner bids 2♡. A 3♣ rebid would be forcing, showing a hand like #5. Therefore, be practical and jump to 3♣ immediately to sign off. This also makes life more difficult for the opponents.

Four-Suit Transfers

Although everyone who plays Jacoby Transfers uses the transfers into major suits, many players today are also using transfers into the minor suits. This method is referred to as four-suit Jacoby and is especially popular in the Northeast.

With four-suit Jacoby, responder bids 2♠ as a transfer to clubs, and 2 NT as a transfer to diamonds.

Notice that this method provides for an in-between bid in each case. This comes in very handy. Opener now has an option after the minor suit transfer. He can either bid the minor that responder has shown, or can make the cheapest bid. The method most commonly used is that the in-between (cheapest) bid is the more encouraging, although it can just as easily be played the other way. Thus with

♠ A 5   ♡ A 6 4   ◊ K J 7 2   ♣ A 10 8 5

rebid 2 NT after 1 NT – 2♠ showing clubs, or 3♣ after 1 NT – 2 NT promising diamonds. On the other hand, with

♠ K J 6 5   ♡ A Q J 5   ◊ K 5   ♣ J 9 4

make the more discouraging rebid of 3♣ after 1 NT – 2♠ or 3◊ after 1 NT – 2 NT.

What type of hand will responder have for the minor suit transfer? He will always have six or more trumps, except when he is very strong and contemplating slam. His strength can be almost anything at all – a signoff and hand with no game aspirations, a hand worth inviting to game, or a hand that might produce slam. The only type of hand where it is unnecessary to transfer holding a long minor suit is a hand that definitely wants to play 3 NT, something like

♠ K 7 4   ♡ 8 5   ◊ A Q J 7 4 3   ♣ 6 4.

Try these responding hands after partner opens 1 NT. Plan your rebid as well.

1. ♠ Q 6   ♡ 10 9 4   ◊ J 10 9 8 5 3   ♣ 6 3

Bid 2 NT. If partner bids 3◊, you will pass. If partner encourages with 3♣, you will sign off in 3◊.

2. ♠ A 5 3   ♡ 9 4   ◊ K 10 9 8 4 2   ♣ 10 8

Bid 2 NT. If partner rejects with 3◊, you will pass. You are hoping that he encourages by bidding 3♣ and then you will bid a hopeful 3 NT.

3.   ♠ K Q 6   ♡ A 8 7   ◊ 4   ♣ A 10 9 4 3 2

Bid 2 ♣. You intend to play at least 3 NT, but 6 ♣ is quite likely. If partner can bid 2 NT showing a fit in clubs and a good notrump, you will be on your way.

4.   ♠ K Q 6 4   ♡ 7   ◊ 9 4   ♣ A Q 9 6 5 3

Bid 2 ♣, then bid 3 ♠ naturally to show a game-going two-suiter. Hearing partner's opinion after 2 ♣ may be very helpful, since even a grand slam may be there opposite a perfecto like

♠ A J 7 3   ♡ A 6 3   ◊ A 5 2   ♣ K 8 4.

Although we have decided the in-between bid is the more encouraging action for opener, it would be worthwhile to consider what criteria opener uses to make his decision. The most important is the fit he has for responder's suit. In fact, opener is advised to assume that responder has the invitational-type hand, in which case what is most needed is a high trump honor, preferably with some length.

The secondary factors are controls, stoppers, point count, and distribution, in order of importance. Since responder is hoping to take nine fast tricks in 3 NT, aces, kings, and number of stoppers have extra significance.

Practice rebidding with these hands after partner has responded 2 NT to 1 NT, promising a long diamond suit.

1.   ♠ A 7 4 3   ♡ Q 10 8 6   ◊ K Q 6   ♣ A 5

Bid 3 ♣. You only have 15 points, but your diamond fit is magnificent and you have stoppers in every suit. Partner merely needs six diamonds to the ace and a black king for 3 NT. If partner signs off in 3 ◊, you will pass because partner could have

♠ 9 5   ♡ 7 3 2   ◊ J 10 9 8 5 4 3   ♣ 8.

2.   ♠ K J 7 4   ♡ A K 5   ◊ J 5   ♣ K Q 9 8

Bid 3 ◊. Your diamond fit is very poor, both in quality and quantity, and that is most important. Your 17 points and double stoppers won't help in 3 NT if partner has a normal hand like

♠ Q 10 5   ♡ 6   ◊ K Q 10 9 7 4   ♣ J 5 4.

3.   ♠ A K 6   ♡ A J 8   ◊ 10 7 5 4   ♣ A 3 2

Bid 3 ♣. You would like to have a diamond honor, but your four-card length is practically as good for 3 NT. If partner has A 9 8 6 3 2 in diamonds, you rate to make 3 NT even if he has nothing else.

One adjustment is necessary with four-suit Jacoby. Since 1 NT – 2 NT promises diamonds, we have to find another way to invite to 3 NT with balanced nine-point hands. Therefore we must bid

1 NT	2 ♣
2 any	2 NT

on these. Opener should alert the 2♣ as not guaranteeing a major suit, as it would in standard.

Also with four-suit Jacoby, there is no natural meaning for a direct three-level response to 1 NT. Here are two methods I have seen used.

First, a three-level bid is a three-suited hand intending to force to game. Responder jumps to three of the short suit, which promises a singleton or void there and serves to pinpoint the danger suit for 3 NT. Thus after 1 NT, responder would jump to 3♣ with

♠ K Q 7 5   ♡ A 10 6 4   ◇ Q 10 8 7 5   ♣ –,

and 3♡ with

♠ Q 10 6   ♡ 8   ◇ K J 7 4 2   ♣ A Q 6 5.

The bidding then proceeds naturally until game or slam is reached.

The other meaning for a three-level response is to show an excellent suit with a slam-try hand. With all of the following hands you would bid three of your long suit after 1 NT, inviting partner to cuebid toward slam with appropriate hands containing controls and winners.

♠ K Q J 8 7 4	♡ K 6 3	◇ K 5 4	♣ 9
♠ K 6	♡ A 5 4	◇ A Q J 7 4 3	♣ 10 3
♠ 10 9 3	♡ A K Q J 8 4	◇ 7	♣ K 6 3

What happens when the opponents have the nerve to interfere with our transfer fun? If the opponents make a bid or double after partner opens 1 NT, all transfer bids are off and you revert to standard methods.

If the interference occurs after the transfer bid has already been made, this provides your side with options. After 1 NT–Pass–2◇–Dbl, opener will redouble with four or five diamonds hoping responder can sit for it. With fewer diamonds and only two hearts, opener should pass to warn partner about his inadequate number of trumps. For opener to accept the transfer, he merely needs three or more trumps. Even a jump is permitted with the right hand.

If the belated interference takes the form of an overcall, opener will tend to let it come around to partner to see what he has in mind. After 1 NT–Pass–2◇–2♠, opener doubles with superb spades, bids 3♡ with a good heart hand, and passes with all other hands.

Also it is advisable not to be overly concerned about having opener play the hand after an interfering overcall. Thus after

1 NT	Pass	2◇	2♠
Pass	Pass	?	

responder should bid a competitive 3♡ with

♠ 10 4   ♡ K J 8 6 4 3   ◇ 5 4   ♣ J 10 6

and 4♡ with

♠ 9   ♡ A Q J 8 7 4   ◇ Q 10 5   ♣ 9 7 4.

With a good hand, he can bid a second suit if he has one.

One convention that grew out of Jacoby and has become useful for notrump bidding on certain hands is Minor Suit Stayman. A response of 2♦ to 1 NT asks partner to bid a four-card (or longer) minor if he had one, just like Stayman asks for a four-card major. If opener has a four-card minor, he bids it; if not, he says 2 NT.

When do you use the 2♦ response? Minor Suit Stayman, like most conventions, has several treatments currently in practice. Here I will give one of the most popular ones. Of course, when playing Minor Suit Stayman, you can't also play transfers to the minor suits.

In this method, 2♦ is bid on three different types of hands:
1) a minor two-suiter (5–5 or 6–5) with any strength range
2) a signoff hand in diamonds (6+)
3) a fairly balanced two-suiter in the minors (4–4 or 5–4) with no singleton or void and 14+ HCP.

The weak hands take care of themselves. After responding 2♦ to 1 NT, opener will bid either 2 NT, 3♣, or 3◇. With

$$♠ 9 \qquad ♡ Q 8 4 \qquad ◇ J 10 9 7 4 3 \qquad ♣ 10 7 3,$$

responder would bid 3◇ over 2 NT or 3♣ and pass if partner unexpectedly bids 3◇. With

$$♠ J 4 \qquad ♡ 8 \qquad ◇ Q 10 7 4 2 \qquad ♣ J 9 8 6 5,$$

you would pass if opener rebid 3♣ or 3◇, and bid 3♣ over 2 NT to show the weak two-suiter.

With the game forcing hands, responder rebids 3♡ or 3♠ to show a singleton or void there with game forcing strength, or will rebid 3 NT with the good balanced hands (logically). The reason that more strength is needed with the balanced hands is that responder should bid 3 NT directly with something like

$$♠ K 4 \qquad ♡ 9 5 \qquad ◇ K J 7 4 \qquad ♣ A J 5 4 3.$$

Try these problems now to practice Minor Suit Stayman. In each, you hold

$$♠ A K 4 3 \qquad ♡ 9 6 5 4 \qquad ◇ A 4 \qquad ♣ K Q J$$

and have opened 1 NT and rebid 2 NT after 2♦ to deny four or more cards in either minor. What would you bid now based on partner's rebid?

1. Partner bids 3♣. Pass. Partner is showing a terrible hand with at least 5–5 in the minors. All you are asked to do is take a preference. Remember, partner could have a 0–3–5–5 hand without a face card.
2. Partner bids 3♡. Bid 4 NT. We're off to the races. Partner has a game forcing hand with heart shortness. He must have the ♣A and good diamonds – how else could he have forced to game? If partner has a heart void, 7♣ is not out of the question.
4. Partner bids 3♠. Bid 3 NT. There still could be a slam, but for the moment all we can do is show our spade stoppers.

5. Partner bids 3 NT. Bid 4♣. Partner's bidding shows a mild slam try. We have a maximum with three nice clubs. From our failure to bid 3♣ earlier, partner will not be misled about our club length. We can still sign off a 4 NT if necessary.

Jacoby Transfers are also commonly played after a 2 NT opening or after a 2 NT rebid following a 2♣ opening bid. In fact, a higher percentage of players use Jacoby here, since it is clear that transfers are even more necessary when the strength is so concentrated in one hand. Also, with less room to maneuver, how else can you get to exactly 3♠ with

♠ 9 7 6 5 4 2   ♡ 10 7 3   ◇ 8   ♣ 9 5 4

after your partner opens with 2 NT? Partner still has the option to jump to 4♠ with something like

♠ A K 8 3   ♡ A 4   ◇ A J 7 3   ♣ K Q 8.

Also after a 2 NT opening bid, 3♣ is widely played as Minor Suit Stayman while four-suit Jacoby is used only after 1 NT. One of the reasons for this is that it would be necessary to play 2 NT–3 NT as a transfer bid forcing opener to bid. How many of your regular partners would be sure to remember that this auction was a transfer?

There is also no reason not to use transfers after an auction like

2♣   2◇
3 NT

since we still want opener to be declarer. This is true only when the response to 2♣ is 2◇. After

2♣   2♠
2 NT   3♡

it is quite clear that responder is not trying to force opener to bid the spades that responder has already bid, but simply showing a heart suit on the side.

No discussion of transfer bids could be considered thorough without including a word about Texas Transfers. These are direct transfers to the four-level on hands which usually belong in game but have no slam potential. Using Texas gives us one additional sequence: since 1 NT–4◇ forces opener to bid 4♡ with no option,

1 NT   2◇
2♡   4♡

can now be treated as a mild slam try.

Why isn't Texas used by nearly as many players as Jacoby? One problem is that 1 NT–4♡ doesn't sound like a request for partner to bid something. Many famous players have suffered disasters because their partner forgot Texas. You really haven't lived until you have played 4♡ with

DUMMY	DECLARER
♠ A K 6	♠ Q J 10 9 7 6
♡ Q 5	♡ 8
◇ K J 7 4	◇ A Q 9 3
♣ K 10 5 4	♣ 8 7

Here are a few other transfer auctions which your partnership must be prepared for. Have you discussed them?

1.   1 NT   2♡
             2♠   4◇

2.   1 NT   2♡
             2♠   3♣
             3♡

3.   1 NT   2◇
             2♡   3♣
             3♡

4.   1 NT   2◇
             2♡   3♣
             4♡

On the first auction, 3◇ would be game forcing, so why is responder bidding 4◇? How about

♠ A Q 8 6 4 3   ♡ K 7 4   ◇ 9   ♣ K 8 5?

If opener has strength outside of diamonds, slam could be on opposite as little as

♠ K 5 2   ♡ Q J 10 4   ◇ A 8 7   ♣ A J 4.

But you'd better stay low opposite

♠ J 5   ♡ A Q 8 3   ◇ A K 7   ♣ Q J 7 4.

Also, wouldn't it be lovely to get to 6♣ on

♠ 7 5   ♡ A J 3   ◇ A 8 5   ♣ A Q J 9 4

and find that it·was the only slam that made! On auction 2, some players would call 3♡ an advanced cuebid in support of one of responder's suits. Since game considerations should come before those of slam, I believe that responder should assume that 3♡ promises heart strength and shows concern about diamonds. If opener is making an advance cuebid in support of clubs, it will be easy for him to clarify later on. I don't believe that 3♡ should ever be an advanced cuebid in support of spades. I would always prefer to bid 3♠ over 3♣ to set the trump suit immediately.

Auctions 3 and 4 go together. What's the difference between them? Since 3♣ is game forcing, 3♡ should be more encouraging than 4♡, since it leaves more room for cuebidding. A reasonable alternative would be to play the jump to game as showing particularly good trumps – values which are hard to cuebid. Once again, almost any method is reasonable, assuming that the partnership understanding is firmly established.

After a 1 NT Overcall. One very obvious trend regarding transfers is their use after a notrump overcall. If you think about it, it is hard to think of a single theoretical objection to this concept. As long as the partnership can remember they are using transfers here, they don't even have to discuss methods! Just bid the same as you would if partner opened 1 NT. And what would you bid after 1 ♡ –1 NT–Pass, holding:

♠ 9   ♡ J 10 9 8 7 4   ◇ 8 6 4   ♣ 10 7 5?

Now you can transfer to the opponent's suit and leave partner there!

Transfers after notrump overcalls are even more clear-cut after your side makes a 2 NT overcall of a weak two-bid, since there is so little bidding room below 3 NT. Let's face it, do you play an auction like 2 ♠ –2 NT–Pass–3 ♡ as forcing? Do your favorite partners play it the same way? Are you sure? Are you sure enough to bid 3 ♡ on a very good hand since you believe it is forcing? Should it be forcing? Who knows? But there is no problem whatsoever when using transfers.

When I wrote about Jacoby Transfers in 1978 in *The Bulletin*, few pairs used them after NT overcalls. Now almost every convention card that you encounter has "front of card" written in for the section on NT overcalls.

Question: **I play 4-suit transfers, but seem to have trouble with hands containing both minors. Is there a way to overcome this short of switching to Minor Suit Stayman (2 ♠)?**

Answer: Sure, just use three level responses to identify minor suit hands. The following structure seems reasonable.

3 ♣, 3 ◇   5 in suit bid, 4 in other minor slam try
3 ♡, 3 ♠   0–1 in suit bid (splinter), 5–5 in minors, 8 + high card points

Question: **You suggest**

1 NT   2 ♣
2 ◇   3 ♡

to show a hand like

♠ A K 6 5   ♡ K J 8 4 3   ◇ 9 2   ♣ 8 4.

Won't the "wrong hand" now be declarer in 4 ♡?

Answer: Yes, you bring up a good point. For this reason, many experienced players use the Smolen convention. Over 1 NT and 2 NT openings, responder now bids his four-card suit at the three-level, so opener will always be declarer if the 5–3 fit is played. This is clearly a desirable convention as long as both players remember it.

Question: **If playing Texas transfers, what is the difference between**

1 NT   2 ♡
2 ♠   4 ♠

and

1 NT   4 ♡
4 ♠?

Answer: Since the second auction is a forced signoff for opener, the first one is usually played as a mild slam try with a balanced hand, perhaps

♠ A J 8 6 4 2   ♡ A 6 3   ◇ K 8   ♣ Q 2.

Of course, you could agree to invert the meanings of the two. Also since

1 NT	4♡
4♠	4 NT

is readily available for Blackwood (RKC if used), then

1 NT	2♡
2♠	4♣

is not needed as Gerber, and is freed for something else (perhaps a 6‑3‑3‑1 splinter like 4♢).

Question: **You wrote that**

1 NT	2♣
Any	3♣

is strong, forcing and natural. Are there some players who use it as a signoff?

Answer. Yes, there is a significant number who do. This is one of those auctions that must be discussed. I once lost a Swiss team when two expert teammates had a misunderstanding and played a laydown slam in a partscore!

Advanced Jacoby

Fit Bids After Notrump Openings

Playing Jacoby transfers you hold:

♠ 9   ♡ Q 7 5 4 2   ◇ A J 9 3   ♣ 9 5 4

and hear your partner open 1 NT. Before bidding 2◇, you correctly consider what you will do after partner completes the transfer. Although you could have transferred holding much less, you are not strong enough to take another bid. Of course, if partner can jump to 3♡ to show a maximum with four hearts, you can bid a game.

As expected, partner makes the usual 2♡ response. You pass and are astounded to see partner taking 12 tricks. You were "lucky" that both red-suit finesses worked and that partner's hand contained only one wasted point opposite your singleton. On the other hand, partner's shape was 3‑4‑3‑3 and contained only 15 HCP. The exact hand was

♠ J 7 4   ♡ A J 10 6   ◇ Q 10 5   ♣ A K 6

What went wrong?

The problem was that your hand would almost always have a play for game opposite a strong notrump that contained four hearts. Even if partner had wasted spade cards in a hand such as

♠ K J 5 2   ♡ A J 10 3   ♢ Q 6   ♣ A J 3,

game would be good. Your singleton and five trumps give this hand great potential if you have a nine-card fit with the notrumper. As I've said before, the ninth trump is the most underrated concept in bridge.

It would be nice if we could bid Stayman first to see if partner holds four, but even if you weren't using Jacoby Transfers, Stayman would not be the solution here since we would be very awkwardly placed if partner should bid 2♠.

Is there an answer then? Sure! With a little imagination, there always is. If it is crucial for us to know whether opener has four (or conceivably five) of the major transferred to, let's force partner to reveal that fact.

After 1 NT–2♢, all non maximums with 4+ hearts bid 3♡. If opener has a maximum with 4+ hearts he can still bid a doubleton (*Bulletin*, Feb. 82) *en passant*. If opener has no doubleton he can bid 2 NT with the maximum.

Does getting to the three-level with a minimum 15–17 notrump opposite a possible yarborough scare you? This is really the same question we raised when I advocated bidding 3♢ over partner's 1♡ bid, holding

♠ 9 4   ♡ Q J 10 6   ♢ 9 7 4 3 2   ♣ 8 5.

After hearing from many readers regarding the 3♣ and 3♢ responses to one of a major, I know that some of you have overcome your fears and are venturing to the three-level when assured of a 9+ card fit – which is all I'm advocating now; it is so important to distinguish how many trumps partner has that we won't be overly concerned about the three level. In fact, there may be several occasions where we get to the three level after a four-card jump and go minus, but do very well since the opponents are cold for game!

Therefore every time we transfer to a major after a 1 NT opening, if opener merely completes the transfer at the two-level, we can be sure the notrumper lacks four trumps. Not only can this prove vital to responder in deciding whether to try for game, but it can also be critical in evaluating slam possibilities.

Here is the schedule of rebids for opener after 1 NT–2♡.

2♠ = two or three spades, any strength
2 NT = four spades, 4-3-3-3, maximum
3♣ = four or more spades, doubleton club, maximum
3♢ = four or more spades, doubleton diamond, maximum
3♡ = four or more spades, doubleton heart, maximum
3♠ = four or more spades, non-maximum.

Obviously, the same principles apply after 1 NT–2♢.

By the way, does everyone know how to "retransfer" to arrange for opener to be declarer as intended, after opener has preaccepted? Responder simply rebids the *suit below* once again. This time opener must obey orders and *accept the transfer*.

Retransfers do not necessarily signal the end of the auction. Holding

♠ A K J 6 5   ♡ 4   ◇ 8 7 3   ♣ A 7 4 2

after 1 NT-2♡

3◇, first bid 3♡ to get the stronger hand to be declarer, then bid 4♣ to show your slam ambitions.

There is no way to retransfer at the three level after 1 NT-2♡

3♡. For that reason, some players bid 2 NT with the one-under preacceptance as well as a 4-3-3-3 super maximum.

Do we use the same structure after 2 NT openings? The answer is a definite yes and no. We don't *always* jump with four trumps, since the jump is now to the four level. However, if we do have a super maximum we can preaccept with a doubleton in case this will be of value for slam exploration. Therefore after 2 NT (20-21)-3◇, opener should bid 3♣ with

♠ A 7   ♡ A K 8 3   ◇ A 9 4   ♣ A J 10 6,

but only 3♡ with

♠ K J 5   ♡ A 9 4 2   ◇ K J 7   ♣ A K J.

We'll conclude this section with a few spectacular illustrations of what is possible with our mandatory four-card jumps and doubleton-showing fit bids.

1)	♠ K 8 6 2	♠ Q J 7 6 4 3
	♡ A J 6 2	♡ 8
	◇ A 7	◇ 8 6 4 2
	♣ K Q 5	♣ 5 3
	1 NT	2♡
	3◇	3♡
	3♠	4♠
2)	♠ Q 7 4 2	♠ 8
	♡ Q J 9 5	♡ K 10 8 4 3
	◇ K 2	◇ Q 9 6 5 4
	♣ A K 5	♣ 9 3
	1 NT	2◇
	3♡	4♡
3)	♠ A 10 6 5	♠ K 8 7 4 3 2
	♡ A Q 6	♡ 8
	◇ A Q 7 3	◇ 9
	♣ A 7	♣ K 10 6 4 2
	2 NT	3♡
	4♣	4♡
	4♠	4 NT
	5♣	7♠

If you decide to try these fit bids, remember that they are all Alertable. Even 1 NT-2♡-2♠ is Alertable, since 2♠ indicates fewer than four spades.

Five-Card Stayman

One of the most interesting and controversial areas in bridge is that of BID-DING STYLE. Should new suits be forcing opposite an overcall? What is the right suit to open holding 5–5 in the black suits? Should responder go up the line in response to a 1♣ opening bid holding a weak hand with diamonds and a major?

For each of the above questions, there are two distinct schools of thought, and partisans tend to have very strong opinions. For the record, my strong preferences are No, 1♠, and No.

Another topic with more than one answer is: What is the correct opening bid holding the values for a 1 NT opening with a balanced hand which contains a five-card major?

Would you open 1♡ or 1 NT with

♠ Q 10 4   ♡ A Q 10 6 3   ◇ K J 5   ♣ K J ?

Would it make a difference if your majors were reversed? Does your favorite partner agree with you? What would you rebid after a 1♠ response if you opened 1♡?

When this subject arises in a beginner or intermediate class, I strongly urge my students to open 1 NT, which is usually not their inclination. After opening 1♡ an inexperienced player is bound to have serious rebidding headaches with the aforementioned hand.

How do experts feel about the notrump versus major question? They can be divided into three camps. A small number "always" opens the major suit, in fear of missing a 5–3, or even a 5–4, major-suit fit. A significant number goes to the other extreme, and "always" opens 1 NT, willing to play in notrump rather than the major as long as they can let partner know about their strength and balanced distribution.

A good number of experts doesn't have a fixed rule on the subject, preferring to use their judgment to decide which way to go. They'd probably open 1♠ with

♠ K Q J 10 8   ♡ A 4   ◇ A Q 4   ♣ 10 6 3

because of the good suit, while preferring 1 NT with a hand like

♠ J 8 6 4 3   ♡ K Q 10   ◇ A Q   ♣ K J 9,

which looks "notrumpish" because of the tenaces.

My partnerships prefer to open 1 NT whenever we can. Accordingly we risk losing 5–3 fits when responder has a game-going hand like

♠ K Q 5   ♡ A Q 6   ◇ 9 3   ♣ 8 7 4 3 2.

Normal Stayman wouldn't solve the problem since we could hardly raise opener's major on three – sometimes he is only dealt jack fourth!

Puppet Stayman is a possible solution, since provisions are made for opener to distinguish between four- and five-card majors. But this would necessitate some major changes in our notrump structure, which we are unwilling to make. That's how we came up with **Five-Card Stayman**.

We needed an idle bid for this maneuver, and in our structure it was the 3♣ response. We didn't need this to show clubs since we use a 2♠ response as a transfer to clubs.

This worked very simply. After 1 NT – Pass – 3♣ – Pass, opener bid a five-card major if he had one. Failing that, 3 NT.

What kind of hands did we use Five-Card Stayman on? At first, it was only game-going hands with one or two three-card majors. Usually responder had a singleton or doubleton somewhere; we were satisfied to raise to 3 NT with a flat 3 – 3 – 3 – 4 type.

Then one day we were playing IMPS and I picked up

♠ J 6 5 3   ♡ J 7 6 2   ◇ A K 3   ♣ K 5.

Partner opened 1 NT and I didn't really want to bid 2♣ and risk playing 4♠ opposite

♠ 10 8 7 4   ♡ K Q 3   ◇ Q J 9   ♣ A Q J.

On the other hand, a direct 3 NT bid would not be too bright if partner held

♠ K Q 10 4 2   ♡ K Q 5   ◇ 10 6   ♣ A J 3.

We would be cold for 4♠, but 3 NT would have no play on a diamond lead. So I tried 3♣. Partner rebid 3 NT holding

♠ A K Q 8   ♡ A 10 9   ◇ Q J 7 6   ♣ 6 3.

This made on a heart lead, so we only lost one IMP vs. our opponents' 420 in spades. We would have gone down on a club lead, and clearly were in the wrong spot.

Partner agreed that it was reasonable to use Five-Card Stayman with weak four-card majors and good hands, but it was unfortunate that we couldn't find a desirable 4 – 4 fit when opener had a strong four-card major. And then we saw the answer – have opener treat a strong four-card major the same as if he had five!

So finally we had come full circle. Responder can bid 3♣ with both three-card and four-card majors. Opener would show a major not only with five, but also with a very strong four-bagger.

Nothing complicated was involved, and no other bids were affected.

How did it work out? Just fine. Here are a few examples of the convention at work:

	WEST	EAST	WEST	EAST
1.	♠ A K J 9	♠ Q 10 6	1 NT	3♣
	♡ K 6 5	♡ A 10 4	3♠	4♠
	◇ 6 3	◇ A 4		
	♣ K Q J 10	♣ 9 6 4 3 2		
2.	♠ Q J 9	♠ A K 7	1 NT	3♣
	♡ K 8 6 4 3	♡ 10 9 7 5	3♡	4♡
	◇ A 5	◇ 6 4 3		
	♣ A Q 7	♣ K J 3		

3.	♠ A J 7 3	♠ 9 6 4 2	1 NT	3 ♣
	♡ K Q J	♡ 10 7 5 3	3 NT	
	◇ Q 7 5	◇ A K J		
	♣ K 10 6	♣ A J		
4.	♠ K Q 6	♠ A J 9	1 NT	3 ♣
	♡ A 9 5 4 2	♡ K Q 10	3 ♡	4 ♡
	◇ 8 4 3	◇ 9		
	♣ A Q	♣ 10 7 6 4 3 2		
5.	♠ K J 7	♠ A Q 10	1 NT	3 ♣
	♡ A 10 6 4 3	♡ 7 5	3 ♡	3 NT
	◇ A Q	◇ 8 6 4 3		
	♣ Q 4 3	♣ A J 10 9		

But trouble was just around the corner. What should I respond to 1 NT when I was interested in both majors, seeking five or strong four in one, but any four in the other? Picture

♠ A Q 7 4   ♡ K 10 6   ◇ 8   ♣ J 9 7 4 2 or

♠ K Q 10 4   ♡ 9 7 4 3   ◇ A Q   ♣ 10 7 4.

Presumably I would have to respond 2♣, thereby throwing away the advantages of five-card Stayman.

However, this time Puppet Stayman was the solution. With Puppet Stayman over 2 NT, a response of 3♣ asks for five- *or* four-card majors. Opener rebids three of his major holding five, 3◇ with one or more four-card majors, and only rebids 3 NT lacking either of the above. Responder can still direct the NT to opener's side, since his rebid of three in a major denies four there and promises four in the other one. With two four-card majors responder bids four of a minor, and opener places the contract in his major.

Finally the quest was ended. Although this structure may seem complicated, it really was easy after a little practice. We preferred to keep our modification that very strong four-card majors be treated as five, but otherwise 1 NT – 3♣ for us is the equivalent to Puppet Stayman over 2 NT.

Observe how easily we handle the problem hands mentioned earlier. With both

♠ A Q 7 4   ♡ K 10 6   ◇ 8   ♣ J 9 7 4 2 and

♠ K Q 10 4   ♡ 9 7 4 3   ◇ A Q   ♣ 10 7 4

we respond 3♣ to 1 NT. We pass 3 NT, raise three of a major to four, and bid 3♡ over 3◇, showing a willingness only to play in spades opposite a fair to poor four-card major.

Do we ever bid 2♣ any more? Sure, it is still needed with weak or invitational hands, as well as 5–4's, etc.

It may have taken a while, but for those who like to open 1 NT with imperfect hands to avoid rebid problems, we are now in a much stronger position to judge when to retreat from NT into a desirable major suit contract.

Gambling 3 NT

The Gambling 3 NT convention is an opening bid of 3 NT based on a long solid minor suit, usually with a weak hand. It serves partly as a preemptive bid – a very effective one since the opponents have to come in at the four level. In addition, by describing your hand to partner, he is in a very good position to judge where the hand should play, even if the opponents compete.

What exactly are the requirements for a Gambling 3 NT bid? Everyone agrees that you must have a solid minor suit, usually seven cards long containing the A – K – Q and possibly the J. However, when it comes to the amount of outside strength held by the 3 NT bidder, there are three distinct schools of thought.

(1) The so-called gamblers comprise the first group. They play that opener promises *no* outside ace or king, therefore probably no outside stopper. In fact, they may not have any honor outside their suit! Of course, their partners do not often pass 3 NT.

(2) Players in the next group agree to have one stopper outside the minor suit, possibly two when vulnerable. A typical hand might be something like

♠ K J 5   ♡ 9 4   ◇ 8   ♣ A K Q 10 7 6 5

nonvulnerable, with the ♡K substituted for the nine when vulnerable.

(3) Those in the third group don't seem to be gambling too much. They have two or three stoppers on the side, possibly a hand which rates to make 3 NT even if partner has nothing. A typical hand would be

♠ K 5 3   ♡ 8   ◇ A 7   ♣ A K Q 10 6 4 2

It is true, of course, that just like those who use strong jump overcalls, followers of the very strong Gambling 3 NT will seldom see their bid occur.

Which Style?

If you took a survey among followers of the Gambling 3 NT convention as to which style they prefer as far as outside stoppers go, most would admit a preference to have at least one outside stopper. Their reason would be one of security, preferring not to "gamble" excessively. In reality, the situation is not the way it appears to be. If playing that 3 NT shows at least one stopper (2) or at least two stoppers (3), responder would presumably pass 3 NT holding

♠ K 6 4 2   ♡ 10 7   ◇ 8 5 2   ♣ A 8 6 3.

Since partner may have

♠ A 5	♡ 9 4	◇ A K Q J 7 4 3	♣ 7 2,
♠ 8 3	♡ A 6	◇ A K Q 7 6 4 3	♣ K 5,
♠ Q J 7	♡ Q	◇ A K Q J 9 6 3	♣ K 5, or
♠ A	♡ Q 4	◇ A K Q J 10 6 3	♣ K Q 7

for his 3 NT bid, these are the groups that are really gambling. They are hoping that opener has a heart stopper or that the opponents will not lead the suit.

On the other hand, look at how easy the "nothing outside" group has it. They will pass 3 NT only with something like

♠ A 6 3 2	♡ A 5	◇ Q 10 6 4	♣ 9 3 2 or
♠ K Q 7 4 2	♡ A Q 4	◇ K 10 6 2	♣ 8 or
♠ K J 5	♡ A 7 2	◇ A 10 6 4	♣ 8 3 2.

Remember, just because partner has opened with a bid of game, you don't have to play it there. 3 NT is really just a fancy preempt; it is perfectly all right to play in a part score if responder knows that game is not a good bet. Ah, there's the rub – responder can never judge the situation if partner has some stoppers, since there is no way for him to know where they are. However if opener denies stoppers, responder is very well placed. With stoppers in all suits, he passes; otherwise, he runs as fast as he can!

Another reason why it is clearly preferable to play 3 NT as a solid suit and nothing else is an argument similar to the one which has resulted in most players using weak jump overcalls. When playing weak jump overcalls, you still have an adequate way of bidding the intermediate hands like

♠ A Q J 8 6 3   ♡ K 7 4   ◇ K 3   ♣ 9 2,

and the strong jump overcalls like

♠ A K Q 10 7 4   ♡ K 5   ◇ A J 3   ♣ 6 2.

However, if playing intermediate jump overcalls or strong jump overcalls, there is no efficient way to effectively bid

♠ K Q 10 9 4 2   ♡ 9 3   ◇ 10 9 8 2   ♣ 8

after the opponents open the bidding.

If playing that Gambling 3 NT shows nothing outside (1), you can still bid hands like

♠ K J 4	♡ 9 6	◇ A K Q 10 7 4 3	♣ 8 or
♠ K 6	♡ A 7 4	◇ A K Q 10 7 4 3	♣ 8

effectively after opening 1 ◇ since good hands usually take care of themselves. However, if you can't open 3 NT with

♠ 9 4   ♡ 8   ◊ A K Q 10 8 4 3   ♣ 9 3 2,

how in the world are you going to describe this hand to partner? Most players consider this hand too strong to open 3 ◊, but not strong enough to open 1 ◊.

Responses to Gambling 3 NT

Let's examine the responses to a Gambling 3 NT opener. We will assume you are playing the sensible way, promising no ace or king outside with a solid 7-card suit (possibly 8-card). For those who insist on having a stopper or two outside, we will also make some mention of how the responses are affected by that, although many of the responses are not affected by the style of the bid.

4♣ says, "Let's play a partscore at the 4-level; I'm running in fear from 3 NT." Opener is expected to convert to diamonds if that is his suit, and the assumption is that the final contract must either be in notrump or in opener's suit. (The one exception is if responder immediately bids four of a major over 3 NT.)

4◊ is usually played as asking opener to bid a singleton if he has one. Opener rebids as follows:

4♡ = heart singleton
4♠ = spade singleton
4 NT = minor suit singleton
5♣ = no singleton

Why would responder want to know if partner has a singleton? Picture the following hand:

♠ A K Q 4   ♡ 8 4   ◊ A K Q 5   ♣ 8 6 4.

When partner opens 3 NT, you want to play in 5♣ or 6♣, depending on whether or not partner has a singleton heart. So you bid 4◊. If partner bids 4♡, you confidently jump to 6♣. Over any other response, you will sign off in 5♣.

What happens if opener has a void, which is possible, although unlikely? Opener rebids as if he had a singleton for the time being, and listens to what responder does. If responder signs off, it means that opener's short suit was opposite responder's strength. Therefore, opener accepts the signoff, since the void will not be helpful. If responder jumps to six opposite the alleged singleton, opener can go all the way since he must have the right shortness.

4♡ and 4♠ are signoffs in responder's long suit. These are commands for the opener to pass. Responder would need a hand like

♠ K Q J 10 7 4 3   ♡ K Q 5   ◊ K   ♣ 8 4

to make this bid.

4 NT is invitational to slam. It basically says that the partnership has 11 tricks with opener's long suit. It asks opener to go on with an extra trick. Responder would bid 4 NT with a hand like

♠ A 6 4 3   ♡ A K 7 5   ◇ A 10 3   ♣ 8 4,

expecting opener to bid a slam with

♠ 8 5   ♡ 10   ◇ 7 4   ♣ A K Q 10 9 7 5 2 or

♠ Q 10 7   ♡ 9 8   ◇ 6   ♣ A K Q J 7 6 5.

Opener, of course, passes with a minimum.

5♣ says that responder would like to play in game in opener's minor. Opener will pass 5♣ or bid 5◇ if that is his suit.

5◇ is also a signoff by responder, and means that he knows that opener has diamonds and wants to play game from his side. A typical hand would be

♠ A Q 5 4   ♡ K Q 10 6 5   ◇ 9 4 3   ♣ K.

5 NT is a grand slam try. It says that responder has no losers outside the trump suit, but is void in trumps and is afraid of a trump loser. He is asking if opener's long suit is "completely" solid. Opener bids 7♣ or 7◇ if his suit is A–K–Q–J–x–x–x or A–K–Q–x–x–x–x–x. With A–K–Q–x–x–x–x he signs off in 6 of his suit. This hand can hardly play in notrump when responder is void in opener's long minor suit.

6♣ and 6◇ are signoffs saying that responder wants to play a slam in opener's minor. If opener hears a 6♣ bid, he should correct to diamonds if that happens to be his long suit. Although responder will usually want to play from his side, he may hold

♠ A K Q 8 6   ♡ A K 8 7 4 3   ◇ 8   ♣ 9

and honestly not be able to identify the suit.

Now that we understand the philosophy behind the "correct" style of using the "Gambling" 3 NT and have learned the responses, we are on our way toward efficiently employing this device. Next we will test ourselves on a few examples and then learn what to do if the opponents have the audacity to use our bid against us.

The following are examples of responding to the "weak" Gambling 3 NT bid:

1.   ♠ 8 7   ♡ 9   ◇ K Q J 9 6 4   ♣ 10 7 5 3

Bid 5♣. Of course you don't expect to make it, but it should be a good sacrifice against four of a major, which the opponents are surely about to bid.

2.   ♠ K Q 6 5   ♡ K Q 6 5 4 3   ◇ K Q 4   ♣ –

Bid 4♣. You can't honestly say that you are thrilled to hear partner's 3 NT bid, but at least you know where not to play. 3 NT won't make, and 4♡ is a big underdog, even if partner has a few hearts. Playing in your void is hardly appetizing, but at least partner will have good support!

3.   ♠ Q 7   ♡ A Q 7 3   ◇ A J 10 9   ♣ 9 6 4

Bid 4♣. If partner has three spades to the jack, you will certainly make 3 NT, and if he has three small spades you might luck out, but the odds are against you. You also don't rate to make 5♣. Take your probable plus score in 4♣, since you figure to find a 10th trick somewhere.

4.   ♠ A K Q 10 2   ♡ A Q 10 6   ◊ K 8   ♣ 6 4

Bid 6♣. Played from your side this is the kind of dream contract that gets a chuckle from everyone when the analysts talk about the perfect contract that couldn't possibly be reached. Yet with Gambling 3 NT, there's nothing to it.

For those who stubbornly still wish to play Gambling 3 NT promising at least one outside stopper, a few of the responses are changed. Here are the ones which are different from those previously stated in the "weak" opening 3 NT:

4◊ – Some continue to play that this asks for a singleton; others play that this asks opener to cuebid where his outside strength is. This also can be used as Blackwood, and I've even heard about some people who use this to ask for opener's better major. Partnership agreement is certainly necessary!

4 NT – This is played either as Blackwood or as a slam invitation. If Blackwood, some believe in cuebidding where the other ace is, some only count the number of aces held outside the long suit (since opener always has the ace of his suit), while others prefer the "normal" responding method of the total number of aces.

Question: **Does vulnerability affect the Gambling 3 NT at all?**

Answer: It doesn't as far as I'm concerned. I never mind risking the 4 level with seven sure trump tricks. However some conservative players would avoid a 3 NT opening with

♠ 8 6   ♡ 6 4   ◊ 5 3   ♣ A K Q 10 8 5 2

when vulnerable, for fear of going for 800.

Question: **Is Gambling 3 NT a bid which should be preferred at matchpoints vs. IMPs or vice versa?**

Answer: If you use Gambling 3 NT as a precise, well-defined bid with nothing on the side, partner will be able to put you into the right contract consistently, and that's good at any form of scoring. Possibly because of the word "gambling" in the name of the convention, people have gotten the idea that this is a very risky proposition where everyone must hold their breath as the opening lead is being made. I hope you have seen that this need not be the case.

Question: **Does position at the table affect the bid?**

Answer: Although some would say that in third or fourth position it shows a better hand and commands responder to pass, there is really no necessity for this. You might want to open 3 NT on

♠ J 6 2   ♡ 10   ◊ 9 6   ♣ A K Q J 10 6 4

even in fourth seat in case partner had a hand like

♠ A 7 4   ♡ A 8 6 3   ◊ Q 10 7 3   ♣ 9 3.

Even if partner had

♠ K 10 9 4   ♡ 8 6 5 3   ◊ A 8 4 2   ♣ 3,

you might make 4♣ and he couldn't have less. Certainly in third seat, it is even more crucial to preempt.

Question: **What happens when we get doubled in 3 NT?**

Answer: Since opener has described his hand, responder is the captain. If he wishes to play 3 NT doubled or redoubled, then opener must go along with that decision. Of course, responder will only do so with three sure stoppers in the other suits. Can you picture yourself sitting comfortably for 3 NT doubled when you've shown one stopper and partner is guessing where it is, with a wrong guess resulting in going for a number?

Incidentally, if you elect to play Gambling 3 NT, then a 2♣ opening bid followed by 3 NT shows 25–27 high card points.

If you do decide to play Gambling 3 NT showing nothing outside, there is a nice way to bid the hand with two stoppers. With

♠ K 10 6   ♡ Q   ◇ A K Q 10 7 4 3   ♣ A 5,

you open 1◇. If partner makes the likely response of 1♡, you jump to 3 NT. This shows a long diamond suit with an unbalanced hand having no interest in any other suit. Although there is some gambling here since partner may have four small hearts, you are probably on very secure ground. You should be aware though, that on an auction like

1◇	1♡
3 NT	Pass,

a heart lead very often hits the weak spot of the partnership. By the way, the 3 NT rebid should be alerted.

One last thought about playing Gambling 3 NT – if the opponents interfere after you open 3 NT, just sit there. Remember, after preempting you are out of the picture – and 3 NT is still a preempt.

Defense Against Gambling 3 NT

1. First of all, always find out how much outside strength is promised by the 3 NT bid.
2. A double of 3 NT shows a good hand. You may have a fairly balanced hand, or you may not; you don't have too many choices.
3. If you do have an offensive hand, particularly with both majors, many good players use *Ripstra* here – they bid their better minor asking partner to choose a major. So with something like

   ♠ K Q 6 5 4   ♡ K J 10 8 7   ◇ A Q 5   ♣ –

   bid 4◇ and partner will bid his longer major, but with

   ♠ 8 7   ♡ 9   ◇ K J 10 8 7 4 3   ♣ 6 5 4,

   he can bid 5◇.
4. With a nice long major suit, such as

   ♠ Q J 10 4   ♡ K Q J 10 7 4 3   ◇ A   ♣ 6,

bid your suit. Presumably your suit wouldn't be completely solid, since you would then want to defend 3 NT, possibly doubled.

5. If you are on a lead against 3 NT, it is good to lead an ace. This will enable you to get a look at dummy to find the opponents' weak spot, if any. At matchpoints it will also help to keep down the overtricks, if you can't beat the contract. Of course, leading an ace will probably not enable you to beat 3 NT against readers of this book, who probably won't be gambling, but it is a good policy, particularly against those whose 3 NT bid promises some stoppers, and responder may be gambling as to where they are.

"Gambling 3 NT" is a convention which has been unfortunately labeled. If played correctly, there is even less "gambling" than in the usual 3 NT contracts where you are "gambling" that the key suit splits well, or that a key finesse will work. Do you think that more people would play it if we renamed it "Sure Thing 3 NT"?

♠   ♠

Flannery 2 ◇

WEST	EAST
♠ A 10 8 4	♠ J 7 6 3
♡ A J 9 6 5	♡ Q
◇ A 6 5	◇ 8 3
♣ 4	♣ A K 9 6 3 2

WEST	EAST
1 ♡	2 ♣
2 ♡	3 ♣
Pass	

Two good players had this auction in a Swiss team event. With the cards lying well they made 3 ♣. However, at the other table their opponents bid and made 4 ♣. What went wrong? East could hardly be blamed for rebidding his six-card suit, and West was not strong enough to reverse into spades or bid again over 3 ♣. Was it wrong for West to open the bidding in his longest suit?

Bridge theorists have long disputed the correct opening bid with a minimum hand containing four spades and five hearts. Although the quality of the suits is relevant, generally the four-card majorites open 1 ♠ while those preferring five-card majors bid 1 ♡. Neither choice is perfect. Opening 1 ♠ on the hand above would work, but there are a great many other hands where it wouldn't. A common problem occurs when responder holds three of each major and prefers opener's first suit.

To avoid the four spade, five-heart dilemma on hands not strong enough to reverse, Bill Flannery proposed the following solution; use an artificial bid – 2 ◊ – to identify this hand (weak two-bidders are the first to admit that 2 ◊ is not effective as a preempt anyway).

The responder to a Flannery 2 ◊ knows opener has four spades, five hearts and 11 to 15 high card points. (Notice that such a hand is not strong enough to open 1 ♡ and reverse into spades.) Responder can place the contract, make an invitational jump in one of the majors or investigate further as the range between opener's minimum and maximum can be as much as an ace. The responses to 2 ◊ are easy to remember and are played by a majority of adherents of the convention:

Pass	Long diamonds and a weak misfit hand.
2♡, 2♠	Signoffs. May or may not be good trump support.
2 NT	Strong unlimited response, forcing to game. It may be the beginning of a slam try, and it asks opener to describe his minor suit distribution.
3♣	Natural, not forcing*.
3◊	Natural and invitational*.
3♡, 3♠	Invitational.
3 NT	Signoff.
4♣, 4◊	Transfers to 4♡ and 4♠, respectively, to allow opener to play the hand.
4♡, 4♠	Signoffs. No slam interest. Can be bid preemptively on a weak hand with good distribution.

* 3♣ and 3 ◊ responses may also ask the opener to rebid 3 NT with one of the top three honors in the suit bid. Reponder may use these bids to learn whether his own suit is solidified for notrump play, i.e. ♠ A x ♡ x x ◊ K x x ♣ A K x x x x – bid 3♣ over 2 ◊ to ask for ♣Q. With ♠ x x ♡ x x ◊ A Q J x x x ♣ A x x, bid 3 ◊ over 2 ◊ to ask for ◊K.

Note that for the most part responder is "captain" as opener's hand is a known quantity.

Your partner has opened 2 ◊, Flannery. What do you respond with these hands?

1. ♠ K 7 2
   ♡ 4
   ◊ J 8 6 2
   ♣ A 8 6 5 3

   Answer: 2♠
   Should be a reasonable contract, particularly if you avoid a trump lead.

2. ♠ 8 6 3
   ♡ 7 2
   ◊ Q J 10 9 8 4
   ♣ Q 7

   Answer: Pass
   Your side has seven cards in each major suit, but your hand is worth four tricks in diamonds. How else can you get to 2 ◊ from partner's side?

3. ♠ 7 2
   ♡ A 5 3
   ◊ K J 6 2
   ♣ K 8 4 3

   Answer: 3 ♡
   You want partner to bid game with a maximum and pass with a minimum.

4. ♠ 6 3
   ♡ Q J 10 7 6
   ◊ 4
   ♣ 9 8 6 3 2

   Answer: 4 ♡
   You may not make it, but the opponents can surely do well in diamonds if given the chance.

5. ♠ A Q 7 6 3   Answer: 2 NT
   ♡ K 8   Slam is possible – particularly if partner is short in
   ◊ 5 3 2   diamonds. If partner is *void* in diamonds you may
   ♣ K Q 7   even make a grand slam.

If responder bids 2 NT over 2 ◊, opener bids his minor suit distribution, i.e.
3 ♣ shows three clubs and one diamond.
3 ◊ shows three diamonds and one club.
3 ♡ shows two diamonds, two clubs, minimum hand.
3 ♠ shows two diamonds, two clubs, maximum hand.
3 NT shows two diamonds, two clubs, minor suit stoppers.
4 ♣ shows four clubs and no diamonds.
4 ◊ shows four diamonds and no clubs.

Note how natural most of these are. This is one reason for the growing popularity of the convention. It is fun to play and effective, comes up reasonably often and is not difficult to remember.

You hold:

♠ K Q 8 6 4 2   ♡ A J   ◊ 6   ♣ 8 7 5 3

Partner opens 2 ◊, Flannery. You suspect that 4 ♠ will be the final contract, but slam is possible if partner is short in clubs, so you try 2 NT. Partner bids 3 ◊! You now know that he holds a singleton club, so you can use Blackwood because you should be safe at 5 ♠ if partner has only one ace. But partner responds 5 ♡. You bid 6 ♠ as partner needs a red king for his opening bid. Partner apologetically tables this dummy:

♠ A 10 5 3   ♡ K 8 7 6 3   ◊ A 10 4   ♣ 6

True, he doesn't have much of an opening bid – but it is enough for you to score up a slam – on a total of 21 high-card points. It is most unlikely that slam would be reached by normal methods, whether the 11-count hand is opened or passed.

What happens if the opponents intervene? All bids retain their original meaning, although 3 ♡ or 3 ♠ become less invitational after a three-level overcall. Responder may double for penalties, needing only a good holding in the opponents' trump suit.

One of the reasons Flannery has become popular with five-card majorities is that it makes life easier for responder when he contemplates a 1 ♠ response to partner's 1 ♡ opening bid. With Flannery responder no longer need bid 1 ♠ with a bad four-card suit, for if opener has four spades he will be planning to reverse. When you play Flannery, a 1 ♠ bid over 1 ♡ shows a five-card suit or a very good four-card holding, so opener can raise freely with three trumps – knowing his partner will not have to struggle with such a trump suit as J x x x opposite Q x x. And for those playing forcing 1 NT – no more problems on

♠ Q J x x   ♡ A J x x x   ◊ A J   ♣ x x

when you have to rebid after 1 ♡ – 1 NT.

When the Opponents Bid Flannery: You know opener has a minimum opening bid so game is possible for your side. However, you must proceed carefully since your partner may be broke and you're forced to start your sortie at the two-level. Most top players agree on the meaning of these actions:

Double	Good hand, a strong notrump
2♡	Three-suiter, short in hearts
2♠	Natural
2 NT	Minors
3♣, 3◇	Natural

A word about your opening leads vs. Flannery auctions. As we saw earlier, responder is usually planning on doing some ruffing, so a trump lead often can be the killer.

Flannery 2◇ has become one of the most popular of modern conventions. It efficiently deals with the problem of what to do with a minimum opening bid in a hand that contains four spades and five hearts, yet it does not impose a complicated set of responses to be memorized. Most of its partisans have found the bid preemptive yet constructive, fun and easy yet efficient and sound.

♠ ♠

Weak Two-Bids

Without doubt, two of the most popular modern conventions are negative doubles and weak two-bids. Although negative doubles are played by most duplicate players, often chaos and disaster result when inexperienced players use and misuse this call. Weak two-bids, on the other hand, are much easier for even novice players to comprehend. Although any convention can be potential dynamite in the hands of an inexperienced player, the weak two involves far fewer concepts to be understood than many other conventions. Weak twos have filtered down to many social and rubber bridge games. It has therefore joined Stayman and Blackwood as a "universally played" convention.

What is a weak two-bid?

Let's approach it by comparing it with some known entities, the three-bid and the one-bid. Your normal all-American 3♠ bid looks something like

♠ K Q J 10 7 4 3   ♡ 8 2   ◇ 9 5   ♣ 8 5.

Take away one spade and resurrect it as an honor in another suit and you have a solid weak two-bid of

♠ K Q J 10 7 4   ♡ K 8   ◇ 9 5 2   ♣ 8 5.

Replace one more spade with another honor, and you have your "normal" minimum one-bid of

♠ K Q J 10 7   ♡ K 8   ◇ 9 4 2   ♣ A 8 5.

The progression from 3 to 2 to 1 sees a constant decrease in the length of the trump suit with a corresponding increase in the strength of the hand.

The purpose of the weak two-bid is twofold, just like the opening three-bid. It describes your hand to partner so he can judge the limits of the deal. It also serves as a barricade against the opponents, making it difficult for them to judge what their combined assets are, since they are forced to attempt to exchange information at a higher level.

What is the general description of the weak two-bid?

It shows a good six-card suit in a hand not good enough to open a one-bid, normally 7–10 high card points. Other popular ranges are 6–11, 5–11, or even 6–12, although 12 high card points and a good 6–card suit would invariably suggest a one-bid.

What is a "good suit"?

A good rule of thumb is to have either two of the top three honors, or three of the top five. By these criteria the minimum "good suits" are K–Q–8–6–5–3 or Q–J–10–5–4–2. Experienced players will sometimes stretch this a little to include A–J–9–5–4–2 or so, but you get the idea we have in mind—suits that have "body."

How does vulnerability affect weak two-bids?

Just like three-bids, vulnerability must have some effect on preempts because you are contracting for tricks that you are not always going to take. The main relevance of being vulnerable is to ensure that your suit requirements are solidly met. With a suit like K–Q–J–10–9–4, I would make a weak two-bid at any vulnerability, confident because of my solid suit.

Is position relevant for weak two-bids?

Yes, very definitely! First and second seats are similar—you should have a disciplined two-bid in either case. This is especially true in second seat, where the probability of the hand "belonging" to the opponents is not too great.

Of course, in fourth seat you have the alternative of throwing in the hand, so you open only when you think your side can get a plus score. A 2♠ opener in fourth seat is preferred to a 2♦ or 2♥ opener because the opponents might outbid you for the partscore if they have the spade suit. 2♠ in fourth seat should show about 9–12 HCP, but 2♦ or 2♥ should show 10–13 – a minimum one-bid.

In third position, though, things are quite different. Since you are weak and your partner is a passed hand, it is very likely that the hand belongs to the opponents. Also, fourth-hand, who presumably has most of that side's assets, is about to begin describing his hand. This is the time to be frisky. Five-card suits are just fine, particularly at favorable vulnerability. Suits like K-Q-J-6-5, A-K-10-9-4, A-Q-J-4-3, and K-J-10-9-4 afford some safety, and bids on such suits make it more difficult for the opponents to exchange information. It is also less risky to deceive partner as he is a passed hand and will probably be out of the picture. This author has found flexible third-seat weak twos to be constant winners at IMPs as well as matchpoints.

In what suits are weak two-bids available?

Any suit other than clubs is possible, since 2♣ must be reserved for very big hands. Most duplicate players use weak two-bids in the majors, but some use 2♦ as something else. There are two reasons for this: First, there are other popular and useful 2♦ bids such as Flannery, Roman, Precision, etc. Second, many players believe that 2♦ is too insignificant a bid to serve as a preempt. In my experience, however, the weak 2♦ bid has served very well as a barricade for the opponents and is a good descriptive bid for partner.

What distributional requirements go along with weak twos?

As was stated earlier, the suit should be six cards long, not seven and not five (except sometimes in third seat). There should not be a four-card major on the side, since you might very well preempt your side out of a makable game there. In fact, some authorities believe you should not have *any* four-card suit on the side. This gives the hand more playing strength than partner would expect from a weak two-bid. While others believe that this is being overly rigid, it certainly is a valid point.

Also, some authorities recommend not opening a weak two with three cards in a major, since you are playable there. Going this far, however, would tend to result in such limited use of the weak two that you would be virtually wasting the bid's use. Once again, though, in third seat, anything goes.

Then there's the problem of voids. This can also be a factor which can cause partner to "improperly" evaluate the hand. Hands with six-card suits and voids have so much potential in the other two suits that it is wrong to open 2♥ on something like

♠ J 6 4   ♥ K Q 10 7 4 3   ♦ K 8 5 3   ♣ –.

If partner is short in hearts with length and moderate values in spades or diamonds, you could find yourself going down in 2♡ when cold for 4♠ or 5♢. In third seat, though, most would agree that you shouldn't worry about such things. Singletons, however, are just fine, in any seat, particularly when you are 6-3-3-1.

Another situation to avoid—don't open a weak two with a lot of strength on the side. With

♠ K Q 10 6 4 3   ♡ K 9 5   ◊ Q J 4   ♣ 5,

a weak two-bid is not recommended. Partner could never picture that with

♠ J 5   ♡ A 10 7 4   ◊ A 10 8 5   ♣ 8 7 4,

you could produce 10 or 11 tricks. I suggest opening 1♠ with the hand in question, but for those who cannot bear a one-bid on only 11 highs and 1½ quick tricks, passing is more reasonable than 2♠.

We have been thorough in our discussion of weak two-bids because so many misuse the bid. Even the record of our top players in World Championship matches is full of weak twos that were undisciplined and led to disasters.

Let's apply our weak two-bid criteria on the following problems. We are using weak twos in diamonds, hearts, and spades and neither side is vulnerable. Consider each in the various positions so we can understand the differences between them.

Should we open a weak two-bid on these hands? Use a "☑" for yes, and "☐" for no.

		1st	2nd	3rd	4th
1.	♠ K 6 ♡ 9 4 ◊ K Q J 10 6 2 ♣ 9 8 5	☐	☐	☐	☐
2.	♠ A Q 9 8 6 2 ♡ Q 7 4 3 ◊ J 10 4 ♣ —	☐	☐	☐	☐
3.	♠ A 5 ♡ K J 7 4 3 2 ◊ K 9 4 ♣ 6 5	☐	☐	☐	☐
4.	♠ K Q J 10 6 5 ♡ 9 ◊ 8 7 4 3 ♣ 7 2	☐	☐	☐	☐
5.	♠ K 7 4 ♡ K Q J 10 6 ◊ J 10 5 4 ♣ 8	☐	☐	☐	☐

Answers:

		1st	2nd	3rd	4th
1.	♠ K 6 ♡ 9 4 ◇ K Q J 10 6 2 ♣ 9 8 5	✓	✓	✓	✗
2.	♠ A Q 9 8 6 2 ♡ Q 7 4 3 ◇ J 10 4 ♣ –	✗	✗	✓	✓
3.	♠ A 5 ♡ K J 7 4 3 2 ◇ K 9 4 ♣ 6 5	✗	✗	✓	✓
4.	♠ K Q J 10 6 5 ♡ 9 ◇ 8 7 4 3 ♣ 7 2	✓	✓	✓	✗
5.	♠ K 7 4 ♡ K Q J 10 6 ◇ J 10 5 4 ♣ 8	✗	✗	✓	✓

1) This is a classic weak two, but with no defense. Don't bother in fourth seat.
2) Do not distort opposite an unpassed hand with a void and four-card major, but once partner has passed, go for a partscore.
3) Open 1 except in third or fourth seat. You have too much outside and not enough inside.
4) With all the strength concentrated in spades, ignore the four small diamonds. In fourth seat, pass it out since your side is outgunned.
5) Don't open 2♡ with a five-card suit in first or second, but it is often the best action in third or fourth seat.

Now that we are familiar with the requirements and criteria for opening a weak two-bid, we must keep in mind that there are other considerations as well. Sometimes it will be partner who opens the weak two-bid; at other times it will be the opponents.

Our major concern here will be: how do we respond to partner's weak two-bid? There are various ways, but we'll start with the "standard" methods. Assuming that partner has opened 2♡, here's a list of possible responses with their meanings:

2♠, 3♣, 3◇ – Forcing bids with very good hands and good suits, but lacking heart support.

2 NT – Asks opener to further describe his hand. Based on a good hand for responder, usually with some kind of heart fit.

3♡ – A competitive effort, noninvitational. Responder is increasing the preempt.

3 NT – A conclusion by responder. He would usually have a long solid minor to run. Opener must pass.

4♡ – Another conclusion. Responder has a good hand and expects to make game, or has a poor distributional hand and is willing to sacrifice in 4♡, doubled if necessary.

Try the following responding hands with partner opening 2♠ in first seat. Assume that neither side is vulnerable and that your right-hand opponent passes. What is your action?

1.   ♠ A 6   ♡ K J 4 3   ◇ A 6 5   ♣ K 9 4 2

Bid 2 NT. You don't know if you want to be in a notrump game, a spade game or a spade partial. Partner will bid 3♠ with a minimum and 3♠ or 3◇ or 3♡ with an outside feature and a *good* weak two-bid. You will then be in a better position to make a final decision.

2.   ♠ A 10 6   ♡ 7 4 2   ◇ A 6 5 4 3   ♣ 8 6

Bid 3♠. You don't really know whether or not the opponents can make a game, but they certainly can make a three-level partscore. Don't greedily hope to buy the hand in 2♠ – it's too much to hope for.

3.   ♠ 6   ♡ K J 6   ◇ K Q 7 3   ♣ K Q 6 5 4

Pass. It is conceivable that you have a game, but you need a perfect maximum from partner – like

          ♠ K Q J 10 7 4   ♡ 8 4   ◇ 9 5   ♣ A 7 2

and some good breaks as well. This isn't worth trying for, so take your plus score in 2♠.

4.   ♠ K 7 4   ♡ 9 3   ◇ A K J 7 4   ♣ A 5 3

Bid 4♠. Game must have play opposite these controls – no need to beat around the bush.

5.   ♠ 8   ♡ 9   ◇ A K J 7 4 2   ♣ A K J 6 5

Bid 3◇. You may not be able to make game, but you must try. You'll show your clubs later, looking for a fit somewhere.

6.   ♠ 7   ♡ K 9   ◇ K 8 7   ♣ A K Q 10 8 6 4

Bid 3 NT. A good example of the rare 3 NT response. You have no interest in spades, but notrump from your side should be just fine.

7.   ♠ K J 8 6   ♡ 9 8   ◇ 10 7 6 4 3   ♣ 8 5

Bid 4♠. You have no defense at all, so preempt to the limit and sock it to them.

The 2 NT response to a weak two-bid is played by some as asking for a feature, but another very popular convention is *Ogust.* Using Ogust 2 NT responses, opener describes his two-bid more completely with the following step rebids:

3♣	= bad hand, bad suit
3♢	= bad hand, good suit
3♡	= good hand, bad suit
3♠	= good hand, good suit
3 NT	= solid suit (A K Q or better)

The 3 NT response is also commonly used with "feature" responses. What is a good suit? This question is certainly partly subjective. A reasonable rule of thumb is a suit that will play for one loser opposite a small doubleton, K–Q–J–x–x–x or A–J–10–x–x–x or better. As far as the "good hand" requirement goes, we're looking in general for the upper half of the 6–11 or 7–10 point structure. Of course, we must consider vulnerability as well. Some hands might be considered good nonvulnerable, but nothing special if vulnerable.

Let's learn some more about weak two-bid auctions by answering some often-asked questions.

Question: **What does this auction mean when using Ogust or feature responses?**

| 2♠ | 2 NT |
| 3(♣, ♢, ♡) | 3 NT |

Answer: Responder thinks 3 NT is the right spot, but can be overruled. If he was sure 3 NT was right, he would have bid a direct 3 NT.

Question: **What does a jump shift response by responder mean? (2♠–Pass–4♢)**

Answer: A few play this as a splinter bid, but this has limited usefulness. Some players prefer to use it as an asking bid, checking on opener's diamonds when there is a possibility of slam.

Question: **Since third seat weak two's can be quite different, are there any inferences we should be aware of after one player has passed?**

Answer: Yes, there are several. After Pass–Pass–2♠–Pass, for example, the dealer can still use 2 NT to try for game, but he would rarely do so. However, it wouldn't be at all surprising to see dealer try for game on this auction.

| Pass | Pass | 1♠ | Pass |
| 1 NT | Pass | 2♠ | Pass |

Third seat is marked with six spades, yet didn't open a weak two-bid. Therefore, he must have a respectable hand in high cards, with some game interest. Regardless of whether you would open

♠ K Q J 10 6 4   ♡ 4 3 2   ♢ A   ♣ 8 7 4

with 1♠ or 2♠ in first seat, open 2♠ in third seat, since game is quite remote unless your partner regularly passes opening bids.

Also, if a player passes and then overcalls in a suit that he could have opened a weak two, you should play him for a five-card suit, since it is most unlikely that he has six when he didn't open a weak two-bid. This negative inference will vary somewhat depending on the discipline and rigidity of your partner.

This concludes our discussion of responding to weak twos in non-competitive auctions. We still must consider competitive decisions after partner opens a weak two, as well as how to compete when the other side makes the bid.

We continue our study of weak two-bids by learning how to offset competitive bidding by the opponents. Let's begin by observing the effect of an opponent's overcall on our weak two-bid auction.

Immediate Overcalls

Assume that partner opened 2♡ and RHO overcalled 2♠. Here is the meaning of the actions available to the responder.

2 NT. Unaffected by the overcall. It has the same meaning as 2 NT in a noncompetitive auction.

3♣, 3♢. These new suits should be treated as non-forcing in competition. They suggest a misfit for opener's suit, with responder holding a very fine suit of his own. Opener may bid again with a suitable hand.

3♠. A cuebid of the opponent's suit can be used in many ways. In the sequence 2♡ - 2♠ - 3♠ it could ask opener to bid notrump with a stopper in the opponent's suit. 3♠ could be the start of a slam try auction, although this would occur quite infrequently. 3♠ could even be used to ask partner to choose between the unbid suits. A practical use would be to indicate a raise to game in opener's suit based on high cards, so that partner will be *in the picture* if the opponents sacrifice. Consequently, after 2♡ - 2♠ - 4♡ - 4♠, the 2♡ bidder would be *out of the picture* and would always pass. The 4♡ bid did *not* ask for his cooperation. However, after 2♡ - 2♠ - 3♠ - 4♠, opener, still in the picture, could bid 5♡, double, or pass. Responder's 3♠ showed a strong heart raise and set up a forcing situation, so the hand probably "belongs" to the heart team.

3 NT. The end of the auction, what else?

4♣, 4♢. Presumably the same as 2♡ - Pass - 4♣ or 4♢.

4♡. Responder is willing to play 4♡, whatever his motives, and *opener is barred.*

Double. Last, but certainly not least. This is a *plain ordinary penalty double,* though you won't get the right hand for it very often. You could arrange to play the double as negative or "card-showing," but this would be the case *only* with a very specific understanding.

The Opponent Doubles

What if the opponent interferes with a takeout double instead of an overcall? Well, we're ready for that, too. Take a look at these responses after the auction begins 2♠ - Dbl - ?

2 NT. Unaffected by the double. It has the same meaning as 2 NT in a noncompetitive auction.

3♣, 3♢, 3♡. Lead directing and forcing back to opener's suit if necessary. When second hand makes a takeout double, fourth hand will usually be declarer, causing the weak two-bidder to be on lead. Helping partner with his "blind" opening lead is always a good idea. These new suit bids may or may not be based on a hand with true support. Bid 3 ◇ after 2 ♠ – Double with

♠ 10 7 4	♡ 8 6 3	◇ K Q J 5	♣ Q 7 4 or
♠ 6 2	♡ 10 4	◇ A Q J 9 7 2	♣ K 6 2.

In this way you secure the defense that will get your side off to a good start.

3 ♠. A normal competitive raise.

4 ♣, 4 ◇, 4 ♡. Since slam is so unlikely, these bids should be put to a practical use. Lead directing and forcing back to opener's suit seems pretty reasonable, with other possibilities suggesting themselves in a very sophisticated partnership. You can bid 4 ♡ after 2 ♠ – Dbl with

♠ J 7 4 3	♡ A Q 10 6 4	◇ 9 7 5 3	♣ –

so as to ensure a heart lead if the opponents bid 5 ♣.

Redouble. This action should be used in much the same way as the redouble after 1 ♠ – Dbl. It shows a good hand interested in defending. You might choose to redouble on other hands as well, but partner will assume that he can double the opponents if they land in a suit that he is prepared for. Redouble with

♠ 6 2	♡ K Q 9 4	◇ A Q J 8 5	♣ K 4,

so partner can double 3 ♣ with

♠ A Q 7 5 4 3	♡ 10 5	◇ 9 3	♣ Q J 7,

and you can handle the other suits.

Other Actions

Opponents may also make a nuisance of themselves later in the auction. Consider the following: 2 ♠ – Pass – 2 NT – 3 ♡. Responder has bid 2 NT asking opener about the quality of his two-bid. This is true regardless of whether 2 NT asks for a feature or is Ogust or something else. How do we defend against this?

(1) Double should presumably show good defense, probably with three-card length in the opponent's suit.

(2) Pass could then indicate a minimum.

(3) 3 ♠ or 3 NT, etc., should show a maximum. Obviously, other defenses are possible.

If the opponents interfere in a higher suit, such as 2 ♡ – Pass – 2 NT – 3 ♠, (1) double would again suggest defending, (2) pass would still be a minimum, and (3) any bid would signify a maximum.

Defending against Weak Two-Bids

We are now ready to discuss how to defend against the opponents' weak two-bids. It would be nice if the only weak two-bids allowed were our own, but life is not like that. Assume RHO opens 2♠. Here are all the actions you might take, with the appropriate meanings. Keep in mind that in general these actions mean the same as those you take over an opening one-bid. Do keep in mind, though, that you are a level higher.

The bidding has started, RHO: 2♠ YOU: ?

Double. Takeout, as usual. You should strive to act when you are short in the opponent's suit as it will be difficult for partner to act when he has length there. With a singleton spade you need about 12+ high card points to double in the direct seat. With a doubleton spade, you should have extra high cards to compensate.

2 NT. This shows an opening 1 NT bid or slightly better, with at least one spade stopper. Some less than expert players believe that 2 NT is "unusual" asking for minors, and it is possible to play it with that meaning, but it definitely is not Standard. Virtually no expert player treats 2 NT as unusual in this sequence.

3♣, 3♢, 3♡. These overcalls are almost always based on a six-card suit with at least opening bid strength.

3♠. The cuebid shows a very good hand. Among most of the top players, it is used only to signify a two-suited hand, one suit being the "other" major. It is possible to use the cuebid to show a specific two suits, such as the higher two unbid. It may be very helpful for partner to know immediately what your suits are, but if you have a very good hand that is not two-suited or that has the "wrong" suits, you must find some other action.

3 NT. This is a natural bid, but it may very well be an unbalanced hand. You would certainly bid 3 NT over 2♠ with

♠ A Q 4   ♡ K 4   ♢ A K Q 10 7 4   ♣ K 6,

and you might even have a singleton someplace. If you have a balanced 25 count you have to double 2♠ first and then bid 3 NT. This lets partner know you were willing to hear a suit from him.

4♣, 4♢, 4♡. Regardless of how you treat a jump overcall after an opposing one-bid, jump overcalls after a weak-two show very good hands. There is little point in preempting after an opponent preempts, as the partner of the opener is in such a good position to make a decision. 4♣ and 4♢ are not forcing, but they show very good one-suited hands unsuitable to any other action. You would bid 4♢ over 2♠ with

♠ 9   ♡ A   ♢ K Q J 10 7 4 3   ♣ K J 8 6,

for example.

4♠. Believe it or not, some players have assigned a meaning to the jump cuebid. This shows a terrific minor two-suiter. Because we have a way to bid this hand type, the non-jump cuebid guarantees the other major, plus a minor, ala Michaels.

4 NT. Most would treat this as Blackwood, although admittedly it would not come up very often. Some would prefer to play 4 NT as a natural bid, with a hand like

♠ A 4   ♡ A 7   ◇ A 9   ♣ A K Q J 8 4 3,

where there is no convenient way to make a slam try.

We will now wrap up our discussion of bidding over an opponent's weak 2 ♠ opener by answering some relevant oft-asked questions.

Question: **Does any great change occur against weak twos in the balancing seat vs. direct seat actions? For example: 2 ♠, Pass, Pass, ? compared to 2 ♠, ?.**

Answer: There are certainly some differences. Fourth hand does not require as much to act, since the opponents have stopped at a low level. However, the responder to the weak two-bid may pass a good hand that has no fit, so discretion is still important. If you are short in the opponent's suit, you can certainly double without much. Partner may have spade length and a good hand and so be eager to pass for penalties.

Question: **If my partner doubles a weak two-bid, do I make the same response with**

♠ 6 5 4   ♡ A 10 7 5 2   ◇ K 6 3   ♣ 9 4

as I do with

♠ 6 5 4   ♡ 10 7 5 4 2   ◇ 8 6 3   ♣ 9 4 ?

Answer: Yes. Playing Standard, you have no choice but to respond 3 ♡ with each. However, if you use a variation of lebensohl here, you can have your cake and eat it. Using lebensohl, you would bid an encouraging 3 ♡ with the first hand, and a discouraging 2 NT then 3 ♡ with the second.

Question: **If my partner overcalls 2 NT over a weak 2 ♠, and I bid 3 ♡, will he pass thinking I have**

♠ 8   ♡ K 10 7 4 3 2   ◇ 9 4 2   ♣ 10 7 5

or go to game somewhere which would be correct if I had

♠ 8   ♡ K 10 7 4 3   ◇ A 7 5   ♣ K 6 5 3 ?

Answer: Good question. I would guess that in Standard, 3 ♡ is a "go get the coffee" signoff. You must cuebid with the second hand, but that does not describe your fifth heart. What's the answer so that you can bid the second hand more effectively? Use transfer bids, so your partner won't have to guess your intentions. By transferring via 3 ◇ to 3 ♡, you are then in a nice position to pass with the first hand, and continue with 3 NT on the second, giving partner a choice of game contracts.

Question: **If I overcall a weak two-bid and my partner responds with another suit, is this forcing?**

Answer: It would be quite impractical to stop below game after an auction like 2 ♠ – 3 ♣ – Pass – 3 ♡, so we say that new suits are definitely forcing by an unpassed hand after partner has overcalled a weak two-bid.

Now try this quiz on weak two-bids. There are 25 questions altogether, so each correct answer is worth four points. At the end you will be able to grade yourself on your overall knowledge of weak two-bids.

The quiz is separated by topics to allow the reader to zero in on individual strengths and weaknesses. Assume you are playing matchpoints and everyone plays weak two-bids in diamonds, hearts, and spades. Okay, let's go!

Part I — Opening a weak two-bid

You are in first seat, both vulnerable. Do you open a weak two-bid?

1. ♠ K Q J 10 7 4   ♡ 8   ◇ A J 10   ♣ 9 7 4

2. ♠ 7 4 3   ♡ 10   ◇ K Q J 10 7 3   ♣ 8 5 4

3. ♠ K 9 7 5 4 3   ♡ 8   ◇ Q 8 7   ♣ Q J 5

4. ♠ K Q 7 5   ♡ Q J 6 4 3 2   ◇ 7 4   ♣ 8

5. ♠ 10 6   ♡ K Q J 10 7 4 3   ◇ 6 5 4   ♣ 7

Part II — Responding to a weak two-bid

With neither side vulnerable, the bidding has proceeded:

PARTNER	RHO	YOU
2♡	Pass	?

What do you do?

6.   ♠ A K J 6 5   ♡ 8   ◇ K 7 4   ♣ J 6 5 4

7.   ♠ 9 5 4   ♡ 8   ◇ Q 7 5   ♣ A K J 10 6 3

8.   ♠ K 5   ♡ –   ◇ Q J 5   ♣ A K Q J 10 7 4 2

9.   ♠ A J 4   ♡ 8 2   ◇ A 6 5 4   ♣ A Q 7 4

10.   ♠ K Q 6 5   ♡ 8   ◇ K Q 6 3   ♣ K Q 4 3

With opponents vulnerable, the bidding has proceeded:

PARTNER	RHO	YOU
2♡	3♣	?

What action do you take?

11.   ♠ A 7 4   ♡ K 9 3   ◇ A 7 4 3   ♣ 8 6 5

12.   ♠ 8   ♡ A J 6 5   ◇ J 10 7 4 3 2   ♣ 9 4

13.   ♠ K J 7 4   ♡ J 5   ◇ K 10 6   ♣ J 10 4 3

Part III – Opponents open a weak two-bid

Your side is vulnerable and the bidding has proceeded:

	RHO	YOU
	2◇	?

What action do you take?

14. ♠ 9   ♡ A J 7 4   ◇ K J 9 4   ♣ A Q 7 5

15. ♠ A Q 10 7 5   ♡ K Q 9 7 4   ◇ 8   ♣ A 10

16. ♠ 9   ♡ A K 8 7 4 3   ◇ A 7   ♣ K Q 10 3

17. ♠ A 6   ♡ K   ◇ Q 7 4   ♣ A K Q 8 4 3 2

18. ♠ A 10 8 4   ♡ A 10 9 3   ◇ –   ♣ J 10 9 4 3

19. ♠ A Q 7 4   ♡ 8   ◇ 6 2   ♣ A Q 8 6 4 3

With both vulnerable, the bidding has proceeded:

LHO	PARTNER	RHO	YOU
2♠	Pass	Pass	?

What action do you take?

20. ♠ K Q 10   ♡ A 8   ◇ A 10 6 3   ♣ J 10 9 5

21. ♠ 4   ♡ A Q 10 5   ◇ K 10 9 3 2   ♣ 10 7 4

22. ♠ K J 7 5 2   ♡ 10   ◇ A J 7 6 2   ♣ A K

Part IV – Partner doubles a weak two-bid

Assume neither side is vulnerable, the bidding has proceeded:

LHO	PARTNER	RHO	YOU
2♡	Dbl	Pass	?

What action do you take?

23. ♠ A K 5 4 3   ♡ 10 8 7   ◇ 9   ♣ 7 6 5 3

24. ♠ A Q 7   ♡ 5 4   ◇ A 10 7 4   ♣ K 8 7 5

25. ♠ A 6   ♡ 9 8 7 4 3   ◇ 5 4 3 2   ♣ 8 3

ANSWERS TO WEAK TWO-BID QUIZ
Part I – Do you open a weak two-bid?

1) No. This hand is clearly too good. You would have opened 1♠ if you had never heard of a weak two-bid. So 1♠ it is.

2) Yes, bid 2◇. This is just what they had in mind when Howard Schenken and company first thought up weak two-bids. You have a gorgeous suit, but without the weak two-bid you would have to pass. (Remember, an opening three-bid shows seven cards in the suit.) If you passed since you were vulnerable and had nothing outside, you are part chicken.

3) No. Pass. Your point count is fine for a weak two, but your suit is not nearly good enough. Also, your considerable outside strength could cause partner to misjudge the hand. There is no big hurry when you hold the spade suit.

4) No. Pass. If partner has four or more spades, you could easily miss a nice spade fit by preempting in hearts.

5) No. A weak two-bid shows six-cards in the suit, not seven. This is a classical 3♡ bid. If you opened 2♡ since you were afraid to open 3♡, you could audition for the part of the Cowardly Lion.

Part II – Partner opens a weak two-bid

6) Pass. You have an opening bid with nice spades, but partner has less than an opening bid and the hand is a misfit. If you pass smoothly, the opponents may balance.

7) Pass. 3♣ may be a better contract than 2♡, but the bid is forcing. Be practical.

8) 3 NT. Isn't this where you want to play opposite a long, strong heart suit and a weak hand?

9) 2 NT. If partner has a maximum weak-two, you'll try game based on your three aces.

10) Pass. Game is much against the odds since you rate not to make it even if partner has the K-Q-J-sixth and an ace.

11) Bid 3♡. Compete gently for the partscore.

12) Bid 5♡. You know 4♡ will fetch 4♠ from the opponents. Let's see how well they'll judge the hand at the five-level. In a competitive auction, even a raise to the five-level is preemptive, not invitational.

13) Pass. What's the problem?

Part III – Opponents open a weak two-bid

14) Pass. The best bet for this hand is defending against diamonds, even at this vulnerability. Of course, you hope partner can reopen with a double.

15) Bid 3◇. The cuebid of an opponent's preempt shows a two-suiter. You are willing to play four of partner's better major.

16) Bid 3♡. The jump overcall of a preempt is always intermediate, regardless of how you use a jump overcall of a one-bid. Doubling 2◊ would encourage partner to bid spades, and who needs that?

17) Bid 3 NT. The failure to double suggests you do not want to hear partner's longest suit.

18) Double. It would be more comfortable to double 1◊ or to have more high card points, but it is a cardinal rule among good players that the person who is short in the opponent's suit must be the one to act. Anyway, wouldn't you rather have exciting shape, good spots, and aces than a dull hand with lots of high cards?

19) Bid 3♣. Spades may well be the best contract, but double is out of the question holding a singleton heart. Also, we may still be able to get to spades if we belong there.

20) Bid 2 NT. A 2 NT overcall usually shows about 16–19, but in the balancing seat a little leeway is necessary.

21) Double. Chances are excellent that partner is sitting with a spade stack to collect a number. If partner has a modest hand we still rate to survive.

22) Pass. Where are we going? Take your plus score.

Part IV – Partner doubles a weak two-bid

23) Bid 3♠. You would bid 2♠ on

♠ J 9 6 3   ♡ 8 7 4 3   ◊ 6 3   ♣ 10 7 3.

24) Bid 3♡. Cuebid on the way to game. You will raise partner's suit to game, even spades.

25) Bid 3◊. Remember, the double is takeout, not optional. If you play lebensohl here (definitely recommended), your correct bid is 2 NT to show a bad hand.

Okay, score it up. How did you do. Here's a reasonable way to rate your bidding:

88+ – Expert knowledge of weak twos.

76-84 – Although you play weak twos, you're not weak on the subject.

64-72 – I've seen worse.

52-60 – At least you got more right than wrong.

0-48 – It is still legal to play strong twos, but what will you do if they open a weak two against you?

Bergen - Cohen Two-Bids – Circa 1984

Note: The presentation of weak two-bids just concluded has been written from the "Standard" point of view. However, any presentation by Marty Bergen on weak two-bids would be remiss if it omitted an explanation of his style of weak two-bids, which led to the infamous "Marty Bergen" rule that was passed at the San Antonio Nationals in March; 1984.

At that time, the Board of Directors ruled that "a weak two-bid, by part-nership agreement, with either fewer than five high card points or a suit of fewer than five cards of the suit bid is defined as a Convention. This convention is barred at all ACBL events."

Marty Bergen and Larry Cohen have had great success since they began playing regularly in late 1982 with a very aggressive style featuring a constant barrage of preemption. They believe it is good bridge to open 2♡ at favorable vulnerability in third seat with all of the following:

♠ 8 5	♡ Q J 10 9 6	◇ 8 4 3	♣ 9 5 2,
♠ 9	♡ J 10 9 5 3	◇ Q J 10 6	♣ 8 7 4

or even

♠ 9 4   ♡ K Q J 10   ◇ 9 4   ♣ 9 7 5 3 2.

The bridge community may have looked askance at these actions, but their remarkable success could not be ignored, particularly in the Fall Nationals in Miami, 1983, when Bergen-Cohen won the Life Master's Men's Pairs and the Blue Ribbon Pairs back to back.

Right or wrong, it is no longer possible to open weak two-bids with those hands by partnership agreement, since they fail to meet the "5 and 5" rule, in fact, more normal weak two-bids, such as

♠ 9 5   ♡ K J 10 9 6 3   ◇ 10 9 8 6   ♣ 8

are not even allowed in the Spingold and Vanderbilt.

Undaunted, Marty and Larry continued their string of successes in 1984, capped by their victory in the Spingold. Here are their "secrets."

Bergen-Cohen Agreements

Length. Five-card suits are possible at any time, particularly with good suits. In fact in first or third seat with favorable vulnerability, we are much more likely to have five than six; we will usually open three when holding a six-card suit in those situations! Bad six-card suits are always possible, and even bad five-card suits are okay with the right position and vulnerability.

Vulnerability. From the point of view of aggressiveness;

Fav   Neither   Both   Unfav

Although this is obvious, it is a much more crucial determining factor for us than for most experts, many of whom are very disciplined, regardless of vulnerability.

Position

3rd   First   Second

Again, while this is true for most, our degree of variance is far greater than others. Of course, in 4th seat, we are normal, since we can pass with nothing.

Side four-card suits, even majors, as well as voids. These don't bother us very much, particularly if the main suit is good.

♠ 8 4   ♡ Q 7 5 3   ♢ K Q J 10 6 4   ♣ 8

looks like a weak two in diamonds to us, hearts not withstanding.

♠ A 6 3   ♡ Q J 10 9 7 4   ♢ 8 6 4 3   ♣ –

would be a normal weak two-bid in hearts. On the other hand, we are not total madmen.

♠ K Q 10 3   ♡ J 8 6 4 3 2   ♢ 8   ♣ 5 3

would only be considered in third seat.

Two-suiters. Describing

♠ 8   ♡ 6 4   ♢ K Q J 10 6   ♣ Q J 10 7 5

by opening with 2 ♢ for the preemptive effect, with a club bid to follow, makes sense to us. By the way, if partner inquires with 2 NT, we jump to the four level to show the second suit.

Side strength. Like all experienced players, we prefer our strength to be in our long suit. However, we are willing to preempt with outside strength when the hand (and/or vulnerability) is otherwise suitable. We would open 2 ♡ with

♠ K 7 4   ♡ Q J 10 9 6 3   ♢ K 4   ♣ 8 2,

and at first seat with favorable vulnerability 2 ♢ on

♠ 6 3   ♡ K 5   ♢ Q J 10 9 7   ♣ K 8 5 4

is correct as we strive to disrupt the opponents.

Holding standard weak two-bids. Many of these get opened with three, especially (1) with good suits and minimum hands, therefore little side strength; (2) Nonvulnerable, particularly favorable; (3) Third seat or first seat – in second we will usually open a quiet two.

Two of that suit is not available. When our suit is clubs, or 2 ♢ doesn't show diamonds, we will tend to open three as opposed to passing. Again we prefer good suits, minimum hands, favorable vulnerability, and an odd numbered seat. The ACBL may not allow us to open 2 ♢ with

♠ 8   ♡ 6 4   ♢ Q J 10 9 7 6   ♣ 10 9 5 4,

but it is still Kosher to open 3 ♢ (based on the open-mindedness that board members are famous for, I sincerely hope that this is still true when you read this).

Theory of "one more." I frequently subscribe to the theory of "one more," meaning I like to open and preempt *one* more than the field on close decisions (for me), since I believe that the majority of players are too conservative. Thus if it is normal to open 2 ♡ with

♠ 8   ♡ Q J 10 9 7 4   ♢ K 5 4   ♣ 8 6 2,

I open 3. Instead of passing with

♠ A K 10 6   ♡ 8 4   ♢ K J 10 8   ♣ 9 4 3,

I open. Instead of 3♣ with

♠ Q J 10 9 7 5 2　　♡ 9　　◊ J 10 8 5　　♣ 9,

I open 4♠.

Responses to Weak Two-Bids

We use Ogust to inquire about both suit quality and overall strength. Vulnerability and position are definitely taken into account by us in responding to Ogust. After opening 2♡ as the dealer at favorable vulnerabilty with

♠ 8　　♡ Q J 10 9 6　　◊ A J 9 3　　♣ 7 4 3,

I would respond 3♠ (good hand, good suit) to the Ogust inquiry, since my expected value is so low here. However, with second seat and unfavorable vulnerability, I might even rebid 3♣ (bad hand, bad suit), since I only have a five-card suit and I'm expected to be respectable in this situation.

We use new suits as nonforcing corrections, which I feel so strong about that I would play them even if our weak two-bids were disciplined. Having to languish in 2♠ when partner opens that and I hold

♠ —　　♡ 6 4 3　　◊ Q J 10 8　　♣ A K Q 9 4 3

is not for me. New suits may be bid on a fair hand, opener should tend to raise with a fit.

Jumps are forcing, and 2 NT followed by a new suit is natural and invitational. Our constructive bidding is not as accurate after natural two-bids as when playing transfer preempts, but we do well enough. Of course most of the time it is the opponents' hand, so we can sit back and relax, supporting, of course, when we hold adequate trumps.

Since our third seat weak two-bids may be awful five-card suits nonvulnerable, and we open the bidding very light, we use 2 NT as a rescue, not as a try for game. With

♠ —		♠ K Q 9 4 3
♡ A 9 4 3		♡ 8
◊ A 8 6 5	opposite	◊ J 7 4 3
♣ 10 9 6 4 2		♣ 8 5 3

we would bid

Pass	2♠
2 NT	3◊
Pass	

Of course we use Key Card 4♣ with big hands, although we usually first try 2 NT to get the flavor of the hand. That way we can try for slam without getting past game if the strength needed is not present. A recent example (west deals, neither vulnerable)

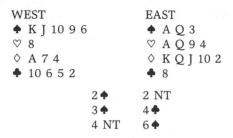

WEST	EAST
♠ K J 10 9 6	♠ A Q 3
♡ 8	♡ A Q 9 4
◊ A 7 4	◊ K Q J 10 2
♣ 10 6 5 2	♣ 8

2♠	2 NT
3♠	4♣
4 NT	6♠

3♠ showed a good hand and good suit, and although slam was very unlikely, responder had nothing to lose by bidding 2 NT on the way to 4♠. After the most encouraging response, he could try 4♣ and when opener obliged with 4 NT (2 Key Cards, no queen) slam had to be a good bet, at worst on the heart finesse.

Another small wrinkle, after

2♠	2 NT
3 NT	

showing a solid suit by opener (although I can't remember when we last had one) 4♣ asks for length, 4◊ showing the expected 5, while 4♡ guarantees six.

Our most interesting responses are transfers after the opponents' double, beginning with 2 NT. We don't need 2 NT any more as a game try, we redouble with game interest. Why do we transfer? We would like to be able to bid a long strong suit of our own, as well as make lead-directing raises. After 2♡ Dbl, we would bid 3♣ with

♠ A 7   ♡ J 7 5   ◊ K Q 10 9   ♣ 8 7 4 2

to get a diamond lead on the way to 3♡, as well as with

♠ A 6   ♡ 9   ◊ A Q J 10 9 7 2   ♣ 8 6 4

which is where we want to play. You would have to give up one or the other with Standard methods, since opener would not know whether to bid after

2♡	Dbl	3◊	Pass
?			

These transfer responses also help us on lead when partner raises. Since both 2♡–Dbl–3♡ (not a transfer) and 2♡–Dbl–3◊ are raises to 3♡, we can distinguish between hands with high honors in partner's suit, and those without them. Bid 3♡ after 2♡–Dbl with

♠ A 7 4 3   ♡ 10 8 5 4   ◊ Q 9 3   ♣ Q 8

but bid 3◊ holding

♠ 10 7 4 3   ♡ A 8 5 4   ◊ Q 9 3   ♣ Q 8.

Let's conclude by looking back at all the possible weak two-bids discussed earlier to see what the Bergen-Cohen action is (assume first seat, neither vulnerable):

1.   ♠ K Q J 10 7 4   ♡ K 8   ◇ 9 5 2   ♣ 8 5

Two spades, but I sure would prefer to be vulnerable. Otherwise we could miss a game since I have so much extra.

2.   ♠ J 6 4   ♡ K Q 10 7 4 3   ◇ K 8 5 3   ♣ —

One heart. Just too much playing strength. Our opening bid style is *light*, so we shouldn't get hung by partner.

3.   ♠ K Q 10 6 4 3   ♡ K 9 5   ◇ Q J 4   ♣ 5

An obvious 1 ♠ bid.

4.   ♠ K 6   ♡ 9 4   ◇ K Q J 10 6 2   ♣ 9 8 5.

Our first choice with this would be to open a transfer preempt of 2 N T to show a 3 ◇ opening, possibly very good, since we have room to learn more. Failing that I'd have the imperfect choice of 2 ◇ (if available) too chicken, or 3 ◇ could miss a game. But it is too late for this leopard to change spots, so I'd try 3 ◇.

5.   ♠ A Q 9 8 6 2   ♡ Q 7 4 3   ◇ J 10 4   ♣ —

1 ♠. Same comments as with hand (2).

6.   ♠ A 5   ♡ K J 7 4 3 2   ◇ K 9 4   ♣ 6 5

1 ♡, as would all normal people.

7.   ♠ K Q J 10 6 5   ♡ 9   ◇ 8 7 4 3   ♣ 7 2
3 ♠, very good suit, bad hand, therefore automatic.

8.   ♠ K 7 4   ♡ K Q J 10 6   ◇ J 10 5 4   ♣ 8
1 ♡, enough for a one-bid. But I would be even happier to not be dealt the spade K, then this would look exactly like my idea of a weak two-bid regardless of colors, including unfavorable.

9.   ♠ K Q J 10 6 4   ♡ 4 3 2   ◇ A   ♣ 8 7 4

1 ♠, but barely, since I have the two x – x – x suits. In second seat, two spades would be my choice.

        ♠ A Q 7 5 4 3   ♡ 10 5   ◇ 9 3   ♣ Q J 7

2 ♠ is fine.

10.   ♠ K Q J 10 7 4   ♡ 8   ◇ A J 10   ♣ 9 7 4

1 ♠, of course.

11.   ♠ 7 4 3   ♡ 10   ◇ K Q J 10 7 3   ♣ 8 5 4

3 ◇. Whether or not 2 ◇ was available, this would be our choice.

12.   ♠ K 9 7 5 4 3   ♡ 8   ◇ Q 8 7   ♣ Q J 5

2 ♠. I realize that this will offend many, but nonvulnerable, this is the way we bid.

13.   ♠ K Q 7 5   ♡ Q J 6 4 3 2   ◇ 7 4   ♣ 8

Pass. But that doesn't mean I like it.

14.   ♠ 10 6   ♡ K Q J 10 7 4 3   ◇ 6 5 4   ♣ 7

4♡, based on my theory of "one more."

Key Card 4♣
After Preempts

Everyone likes to preempt, but sometimes this creates a difficult problem for partner. Suppose you hold

     ♠ 8 6 5   ♡ 9   ◇ A K Q 5 4   ♣ A K J 7,

and hear your partner open 3♠ with both sides vulnerable. All partner needs for slam is seven spades to the A K, so you bid 4 NT. Fortunately you are playing Key Card Blackwood, where the king of trump is counted as an ace.

Unfortunately your partner holds

     ♠ Q J 10 9 7 4 3   ♡ K J 8   ◇ 7 3   ♣ 4,

and is set one trick in 5♠. Partner's 3♠ bid was beyond reproach, and certainly you were unlucky. If you had just raised to 4♠, you "know" that partner would have been dealt

     ♠ A K 10 9 7 4 3   ♡ 7 4 3   ◇ 3 2   ♣ 3,

with an easy slam there for the taking.

Cheer up, readers – help is on the way. It was not wrong to be interested in slam, nor was it wrong to want to know the number of key cards partner had. The problem was you had to get to the five level, which no longer is necessary.

The answer is to use 4♣ as the key card inquiry. This gives up 4♣ as a natural response to a preempt – but when was the last time you used such a response?

Key Card 4♣ can be used over both weak two-bids and three-bids. Key Card is still on after a weak-two if responder first bids 2 NT. Responder should be able to first inquire with 2 NT, then follow with 4♣ if slam is still possible.

The only exception to Key Card 4♣ is the obvious one – when the preempt is in clubs. Since 4♣ is needed as a natural bid, 4 ◇ is used as the Key Card bid.

We do *not* use the same Roman responses that are employed after 4 NT. The preempter's number of key cards is quite limited, so information about the trump queen is more essential.

Opener's Responses to Key Card 4♣

4♦	= 0 key cards
4♥	= 1 key card, no trump queen
4♠	= 1 key card with trump queen
4 NT	= 2 key cards, no trump queen
5♣	= 2 key cards with trump queen

We need go no further since three key cards are impossible for a preempt. Notice how routine our disaster hand would have been.

WEST	EAST
3♠	4♣
4♦	4♠

If opener had the two high trumps that responder was hoping for, we would bid

WEST	EAST
3♠	4♣
4 NT	6♠

Let's look at a few more hands.

1.

WEST	EAST
♠ K 4	♠ A Q J 4 2
♡ 8 5	♡ A 9 4 3
♦ A Q 9 8 6 5	♦ K 7 4
♣ 10 7 3	♣ A

WEST	EAST
2♦	2 NT
3♠	4♣
4♠	7♦

Responder is pleased when his 2 NT bid finds opener with a spade feature. Upon learning that opener has the A Q of trumps, he can bid the grand slam confidently.

2.

WEST	EAST
♠ 6	♠ A K 8 4
♡ 7 3 2	♡ A K 8
♦ 9	♦ K Q J 6
♣ A 10 9 8 7 6 4 3	♣ Q 5

WEST	EAST
4♣	4♦
4♠	5♣

Sure, Key Card 4♦ can even be used over 4♣ openings (but no further). If anyone knows another way to *intelligently* stop at 5♣ with these cards after opening 4♣, I'd love to hear it.

WEST	EAST
♠ 8 4	♠ A 3
♡ A 10 9 7 4 3 2	♡ K Q 5
◊ 7 3	◊ A K Q J 9
♣ A 5	♣ J 7 6

WEST	EAST
3 ♡	4 ♣
4 NT	7 NT

Responder would not be secure in bidding 4 NT over 3 ♡ – the five level is not necessarily safe. But it doesn't take courage to ask for aces when you can still stop in four of a major.

The merits of the convention are clear. It also is easy to remember and gives up practically nothing. Even the responses are simple.

For those who would like to know a little more about Key Card 4♣:

(1) Should you use Key Card 4♣ in competition? We do not, but it would not be absurd to do so.

(2) How does responder ask for kings after hearing a Key Card response to 4♣? Just as with Gerber, 5♣ would ask for the number of kings. Don't worry about how to ask for kings if opener rebids 5♣ (two key cards plus the queen) – he can't have any!

(3) What responses do you use to show voids by opener? If opener chooses to show a void, he jumps to his void with one key card, and bids 5 NT with two key cards. If opener jumps to five of his trump suit, he shows one key card with a club void.

(4) What does it mean if responder's rebid after Key Card 4♣ is 4 NT or four of a new suit? Natural signoff, just like Gerber.

♤   ♤

2♣: Strong, Artificial and Forcing

With the growing popularity of weak two-bids, the use of 2♣ as the "big bid" in the system has become "standard." The "Big Clubbers," who use 1♣ for their giant hands, make up the only significant group not playing this way today. There are still some duplicate players who persist with strong two-bids, but theirs is a vanishing breed.

What kinds of hands should be opened with 2♣?

These can be divided into two distinct classes. The first group is easier to handle. These are the very strong balanced hands. They begin at about 22 High Card Points (HCP), and the first rebid is expected to be in notrump. Here is a schedule for handling these balanced "giants".

Step 1. 20+-22 HCP–Open 2 NT
Step 2. 22+-24 HCP–Open 2♣, Rebid 2 NT
Step 3. 25-26 HCP–Open 3 NT
Step 4. 27-28 HCP–Open 2♣ Rebid 3 NT
Step 5. 29-30 HCP–Open 2♣, Rebid 4 NT
Step 6. 31+ –*Play Rubber Bridge!*

If the partnership uses an opening 3 NT for something special like Gambling 3 NT, Minor 4-Bid, Kantar 3 NT, etc., we modify the third, fourth and fifth steps so that:

Step 3. Special Conventional Bid
Step 4. 25-27
Step 5. 28-30

Other ranges remain unchanged.

Most 2♣ bids represent unbalanced hands, so-called "Strong Two-Bids." We used to open these hands by bidding two of our longest suit, but weak two-bids have changed all that. Now we don't get around to identifying our suit until it is time for our rebid.

There are five different types of unbalanced hands.

Type A–One-suiter. This type of hand has one long, dominant suit. The suit will have at least six cards and will be very strong. Here are some sample hands:

♠ A K Q J 7 4	♡ A K 6	◊ A 7 3	♣ 9
♠ A 5	♡ K Q J 10 8 6 3	◊ A Q 4	♣ A
♠ –	♡ A 5 4	◊ A K J 10 7 5 3 2	♣ A Q

Type B–Two-Suiter. True two-suiters contain at least five cards in each suit. Minor two-suiters are relatively rare for 2♣ openers as you would be required to have 10+ tricks in your own hand to have a forcing-to-game two-bid. Also, enemy preemption could make it very difficult for you to bid your suits at a sensible level. Here are some sample hands:

♠ A K J 10 7	♡ A 6	◊ A K Q 8 5	♣ 9
♠ A	♡ K Q J 7 4 3	◊ A K J 7 4	♣ 6
♠ A K J 7 4 3	♡ 6	◊ A	♣ A K 6 5 4.

Type C–One and one-half-Suiter. A hand-type that is a mutation of the first two is a hand like

♠ A 7   ♡ A K J 6 4 3   ◊ 7   ♣ A K 10 4,

6-4 being the normal shape. Such a hand has one dominant suit, but contains a second suit that could serve as a slam vehicle opposite moderate support and a few useful cards. Other sample hands of one and one-half suiters:

| ♠ A Q J 7 | ♡ 9 | ◊ A K | ♣ A K J 10 6 3 |
| ♠ K Q J 7 4 2 | ♡ A 6 | ◊ A K J 7 | ♣ A. |

Type D–Quasi-Notrump hands. These are still unbalanced hands, but ones that would not surprise anyone if they ended up in notrump, being only moderately unbalanced. Here are some sample hands:

♠ A J 7 4	♡ A Q	◇ A K J 7 4	♣ K J
♠ A K Q 10 5 3	♡ K 6	◇ A J 7	♣ A Q
♠ A Q 7	♡ K 10	◇ A K 8 7 4 3	♣ A Q.

Type E – Three-Suiters. These are undoubtedly the most difficult to bid. Picture a hand like

♠ A Q 7 4   ♡ 9   ◇ A K Q 6   ♣ A K Q 5.

After opening 2♣ and hearing partner bid 2◇, what suit do you show first? If you don't get supported after trying one suit, which of the other two should you try next? Also, if you do get supported, you must guess whether partner is raising on three or on four.

One good solution to this dilemma is to play "Roman 2◇." You open 2◇ on all three-suited "battleships" (17–24 HCP) – and it is relatively easy to identify your non-suit.

Some of those not willing to try this method rebid certain 4-4-4-1 hands in notrump as if they were balanced. With

♠ K Q 10 6   ♡ K   ◇ A Q J 7   ♣ A K J 8,

rebidding 2 NT after 2♣ – 2◇ is probably the best practical solution. Some other examples of difficult 2♣ opening three-suiters are:

| ♠ K J 10 6 | ♡ A Q 9 8 | ◇ A | ♠ A K Q J |
| ♠ A K J 7 | ♡ – | ◇ A K 10 4 | ♣ A K 7 5 2. |

Our other main consideration is the decision whether a hand is good enough for an opening 2♣ bid. Some textbooks recommend a table based on HCP. With a seven-card suit, you need 21 points; with a six-carder, 23 points, and with only a five-card suit, 25 HCP are required. In addition to being a bother to remember – points do not a strong two-bid make! Just as with overcalls, tricks and length are the keys, not points.

Here are some more practical guidelines concerning when you should open 2♣ instead of a one-bid. *Open 2♣* when:

1. You have more quick tricks than losers.

2. You are within one trick of game in your own hand.

3. You wouldn't merely be disappointed, you would be sick to your stomach if you opened a one-bid and partner passed!

In case some of these concepts are new, here is an explanation.

1. More quick tricks than losers.

♠ A K Q J 6   ♡ A K Q J 5   ◇ 8 4   ♣ 7

clearly is a three-loser hand, while it has four quick tricks in the two A–K's. Therefore, it is a proper 2♣ opening.

2. Almost game in your own hand. Major-suited hands with nine tricks like

♠ A K Q J 7 4   ♡ A K   ◇ A 6 3   ♣ 8 4

and minor-suited hands with 10 tricks like

♠ A K 8   ♡ 9   ◇ A K Q J 7 4 3   ♣ A 3

can be described as being within one trick of game in hand. These are suitable hands to open 2♣.

3. Don't open a one-bid if you would be ill if partner passes. If I opened 1♡ with

♠ A J 7   ♡ A J 8 6 4   ◊ A K J 7   ♣ K,

and everyone passed,, I would be very disappointed. But if partner could not respond, we probably don't have a game so playing 1♡ is as good as anything. With

♠ A J 10   ♡ A K Q J 8   ◊ K Q J 10   ♣ 8,

I would feel simply terrible to be left in 1♡, since partner would pass with

♠ 8 6 4   ♡ 9 3   ◊ A 8 7 4 3   ♣ 10 6 4

−and miss a probable slam in diamonds. The ♠K in partner's hand would probably be enough to make 4♡ −without another face card. Notice the two hands above have the same distribution and HCP. As Dorothy Hayden Truscott has said, "Points, shmoints."

We have taken a look at the opening 2♣ bid and have given some consideration to requirements for the bid. Next we will consider responder's actions. This will necessitate studying the three distinct styles of responding to 2♣. Eventually we will study complete auctions that commence with 2♣ and will offer bidding problems.

Now that our partner has opened 2♣ (strong, artificial and forcing), it is time for us to respond. There are three distinct schools of thought as to the best "style" of responding. I will present each of them.

1. 2◊ **Waiting Bid** − The waiting bid group has a significant following, particularly among top players. They believe there is no hurry for responder with a good hand, so they give opener a chance to bid his suit at a convenient level. Keeping the bidding low on good hands is one of the cornerstones of bidding, so that as much information as possible can be exchanged. As we saw, opener has many possible hand types, some of which require a lot of room to describe fully.

"2◊ Waiting" bidders describe their 2◊ response as "neutral" or "semi-automatic." They would not respond 2♠ over 2♣ with

♠ K 8 7 4 3   ♡ 8   ◊ A J 6 4   ♣ J 7 3,

even though the hand is obviously strong enough for a positive response. First of all, the spades are not strong enough to emphasize, at least not at this early stage. If partner rebids in notrump, it will be easy to show the spades, and if we are playing transfer bids, we can even arrange for partner to be declarer at a spade contract.

Waiting bidders are even fussier when it comes to positive responses in a minor suit. Since these responses kill the entire 2-level and part of the 3-level, they often result in the strong hand being preempted. The only reason for such an action would be a good hand with an excellent suit. Bid 3♣ over 2♣ with

♠ K 6   ◊ 9 4   ◊ 7 5 4   ♣ K Q J 7 4 2,

but make a "neutral" 2◊ bid with

♠ K 6 3   ♡ 9 4   ◊ J 5 4   ♣ K Q 7 4 2.

In order to respond two of a major over 2♣, two of the top three honors with at least a five-card suit and a positive response are required. Bid 2♡ over 2♣ on

♠ 9 4   ♡ K Q 10 7 4   ◇ A 5 4 3   ♣ 8 6,

but 2◇ is correct on

♠ 9 4   ♡ A 7 5 4 3   ◇ K Q 10 3   ♣ 8 2.

As far as a 2 NT response goes, "waiters" are in no hurry here as well. If the hand ends up in notrump, it is usually correct for the strong hand to play it. Therefore, this group would respond 2 NT only on a very nearly perfect notrump hand with all suits stopped and some tenaces. Respond 2 NT over 2♣ with

♠ K 6   ♡ Q 10 7 5   ◇ Q 9 3   ♣ K 10 7 4,

but "wait" (bid 2◇) with

♠ A 6 3   ♡ 9 5   ◇ A Q 4 3   ♣ 10 7 4 3.

For those who are aghast at these strong 2◇ responses, perhaps waiting responses are not for you. The theory however, is that there is plenty of time to catch up. Responder, may very well "never stop bidding" later on. He's simply in no hurry.

2. Step Responses—These bids say nothing about suit length by responder, but provide opener with the immediate knowledge of the number of aces and kings held by responder. Not all practitioners of step responses use the exact same responses, but here is one method.

The responses are based on the number of controls held by responder, since controls are so crucial for slam purposes. (A king counts as one control and each ace equals two controls.) The step responses to 2♣ are:

2◇ = 0 or 1 control, 0-4 HCP
2♡ = 0 or 1 control, 5+ HCP
2♠ = 2 controls
2 NT = 3 controls
3♣ = 4 controls
3◇ = 5+ controls

Notice that HCP are only relevant for the 2◇ and 2♡ bids. Not too many pairs use step responses, but such bids have a good deal of merit.

3. Natural Responses—This is the method used by most "average" duplicate players. Their 2◇ response is true negative. They strain to make an immediate positive response when the hand is good enough. How much strength is needed for a positive response? The general standard is roughly 1½ quick tricks or 8+ HCP.

Natural responders respond 2 NT with any balanced 8+ HCP, and bid a suit at the two or three level with a decent suit and decent hand. They bid 2♠ with

♠ K 10 7 4 2   ♡ K J 6 3   ◇ K 5   ♣ 8 4

or 3♣ on

♠ A 7   ♡ 6 5 4 3   ◇ 8 3   ♣ K Q 7 5 2.

When they do bid 2◇, they mean it.

Responses Above 3◇

We have seen the significant differences in the various responding methods. However, we have yet to discuss responses above 3◇. We will group these as follows:

3♡, 3♠

3 NT

4♣, 4◇

Responses above 4◇ are extremely rare.

Note that all of these bids are one more than would be necessary to indicate a positive response. They therefore must show something different, and presumably the suit jumps show very long suits.

Once again there is more than one point of view. One group feels these suit jumps show very good semi-solid suits, such as A Q J 10 6 4 or K Q J 10 7 5 2. If 3♡, 3♠, 4♣ and 4◇ show semi-solid suits, then 3 NT would designate a solid suit somewhere. Virtually everyone agrees 3 NT is such a space-consuming bid that it should be used only with a very rare, special type of hand. This segment of players would bid 3 NT with such a suit as A K Q J 7 3, A K Q 8 5 4 2, or A K Q J 6 4 2, regardless of which suit it is.

"That's fine if you pick up great suits after partner opens 2♣," says our doubting Thomas, "but we feel lucky to pick up any long suit, even a mediocre one." These play that a jump to 3♡ or 3♠ would be based on suits like K J 10 9 7 4, J 10 9 7 5 4 3, Q J 8 6 5 4 2 or Q J 10 9 6 5. This is a practical point of view since a long so-so suit must occur more often than a long excellent one after partner opens 2♣. Four of a minor is less likely to be bid since it goes past 3 NT, but that would promise a 7+ card suit, missing at least two honors.

3 NT is the system bid for either a solid or semi-solid suit somewhere, with clarification to follow. After a 3 NT response of either type, a 4♣ bid is used to ask for the particular suit. However, opener usually can identify the suit immediately since he usually has considerable strength in at least three suits.

Review Quiz

We have covered a lot of ground concerning 2♣ auctions. So far we have examined the 2♣ opening bid and the responses to it. Since the entire structure and subsequent auctions depend on the opening bid and the response, it seems worthwhile to stop for a review and a quiz at this point.

There will be 25 questions altogether. Readers may take credit for four points for each correct answer.

Opening 2♣ Bids – Yes or No

Do you open 2♣ on each of the following hands?

1. ♠ K Q J 10 6 4 3 2　　2. ♠ A K Q 10 4　　3. ♠ K 9 6 4 3
　　♡ 9　　　　　　　　　　♡ A K J 10 6　　　　♡ A Q 6
　　◊ K Q J 10　　　　　　◊ 8 6　　　　　　　　◊ A K Q 10
　　♣ –　　　　　　　　　♣ 9　　　　　　　　　♣ K

4. ♠ A　　　　　　　　5. ♠ K Q 10
　　♡ A Q　　　　　　　　♡ K Q J 10 6 4
　　◊ A Q 6 5　　　　　　◊ A K J 5
　　♣ A J 10 7 4 3　　　　♣ –

Rebidding After a 2♣ Opener

On each of these hands, you have opened 2♣ and have received a 2◊ response (negative or neutral). What would you rebid in each case? Be sure to think about hand types when you make your rebid.

What do you rebid after

YOU		PARTNER	
2♣	Pass	2◊	Pass
?			

6. ♠ A K J 4　　　7. ♠ A　　　　　　　8. ♠ A 4
　　♡ A K 6 4　　　　　♡ A K Q 8 5　　　　♡ K 10
　　◊ J 7 4　　　　　　◊ A 10 6 5 4 2　　　◊ A K 7
　　♣ A K　　　　　　　♣ A　　　　　　　　♣ A K Q J 6 4

　　　9. ♠ A Q 7 4　　　　　10. ♠ A Q
　　　　♡ A K Q 10　　　　　　♡ A K 10 6 4 3
　　　　◊ A K Q 7　　　　　　◊ A
　　　　♣ 8　　　　　　　　　♣ K Q 10 6

　　　11. ♠ 6　　　　　　　12. ♠ K Q
　　　　♡ A K　　　　　　　　♡ K Q 6
　　　　◊ A K J 10 8 7 4　　　◊ A K 9 8 6 4
　　　　♣ A Q J　　　　　　　♣ A J

Opening 2♣ Bids – Yes or No

1. NO. Although you have 10 sure tricks barring ruffs, it would be very misleading to open 2♣. Partner holding, for example,

　　♠ 8 7 5　　♡ A K 6 4　　◊ 8　　♣ A K 9 7 5

would have trouble picturing that there was no slam opposite a 2♣ bid followed by a spade rebid. Simply open 1♠ and await developments. Believe me, it won't be passed out!

2. YES. With four quick tricks and only three and one-half losers, you satisfy the quick trick guideline for a 2♣ opener. Since you rate to make a game in partner's longer major opposite a virtual yarborough, you are quite entitled to open a game-forcing bid. Although this hand contains only 17 HCP, it is a bonafide two-bid.

3. NO. 21 HCP notwithstanding, this is a 1♠ bid, that's all. You need some help from partner before you can anticipate making game. You need tricks as well as points when you open the bidding with a 2♣ bid.

4. NO. It isn't practical. This hand has enormous potential, as do all 6–4 hands with four aces. If your long suit were a major, you would be happy to open 2♣. However, on this hand, you would be forced to bid your suit at the three level. Opening 2♣ frequently loses too much bidding room on minor-suited hands. Instead open 1♣, planning to reverse with 2◊ and get your suits in cheaply.

5. YES. This hand has everything you need for a two-bid.

Rebidding After a 2♣ Opener

6. 2 NT. You would like to have a sure diamond stopper, but clearly you must identify this 2♣ bid as the *balanced* type. Partner can investigate for a major suit fit via Stayman.

7. 2♡. Although this *two-suiter* has more diamonds than hearts, it will be much easier to get in both suits starting with 2♡ rather than 3◊.

8. 3♣. Although the most likely game is 3 NT, the most likely slam is 6♣. You will rebid 3 NT next if possible, showing the *quasi-notrump* hand type.

9. 2♡. This is the deadly *three-suiter* hand, the most difficult type of 2♣ bid to describe. Since hearts is the cheapest suit over 2◊, you tend to start there when you lack a five-card suit. Fortunately your hearts are strong, so you won't have a problem until your next turn.

10. 2♡. *One and one-half suiters* provide an easy first rebid – you simply bid your long suit – but there may be problems at your next turn. For example, if partner rebids 3◊, will you rebid hearts or venture 4♣? In fact, even 3 NT might be right over 3◊ if partner has

♠ 8 7 4 3   ♡ 8   ◊ K Q 10 6 4   ♣ 9 7 2.

However, we don't have to cross that bridge yet.

11. 3◊. With a *one-suiter* hand, bid your suit. You probably will play this hand in 5◊, 6◊ or 7◊.

12. 2 NT. Although this may look like a *quasi-notrump* type of hand, it isn't strong enough to bid 3◊ then 3 NT. The practical solution is to rebid 2 NT, giving partner a chance to check out below game with no points. We don't really have a balanced hand, but by comparing this one with #8, we can see the need for not over-exciting partner.

For the next 13 questions, you are asked to respond to partner's 2♣ opening bid.

"Waiting Bids"

13. ♠ K 8 7 4 3
♡ 9
◊ A Q 7 4
♣ J 5 3

14. ♠ 9 4 3
♡ 8 6 4
◊ A J 5
♣ K Q 6 3

15. ♠ 8 5
♡ A Q J 9 6 3
◊ 9 6 4
♣ 8 7

16. ♠ A J 7 4
♡ 9 3
◊ J 7
♣ K J 8 6 4

17. ♠ A 8 7 4 3
♡ 8
◊ 6
♣ K Q 8 7 4 3

"Step Responses"

18. ♠ A 7 4 3
    ♥ Q 6
    ♦ A 9 6 3
    ♣ 7 4 2

19. ♠ K 10 9
    ♥ 8 5 4 3
    ♦ Q J 7
    ♣ 8 6 3

20. ♠ A K J 7 4 3
    ♥ 10 6 3
    ♦ 8 4 2
    ♣ 8

21. ♠ 9 4
    ♥ K Q 7 6 5
    ♦ K J 9 4 3 2
    ♣ −

"Natural Responses"

22. ♠ Q 10 6
    ♥ J 10 8 5
    ♦ Q 10 6
    ♣ Q J 3

23. ♠ A J 7 4 3
    ♥ A 6 2
    ♦ 9 4
    ♣ 8 7 5

24. ♠ K 8 6 3
    ♥ K 7
    ♦ K 5
    ♣ J 10 6 4 3

25. ♠ A K Q
    ♥ 8 7 4
    ♦ 9 6 3
    ♣ 8 4 3 2

Waiting Bids

13. 2♦. The spades are definitely not good enough to bid, so despite the two quick tricks, a "waiting bid" is called for. There is plenty of time later to show our strength.

14. 2♦. We can't bid 2 NT with stoppers in only two suits, so we'll just have to bide our time.

15. 2♥. With a very good suit, there's no time like the present. We want to tell partner that we may very well have THE suit to play this hand, even if he has length of his own.

16. 2♦. Once again, lacking a strong five-card major or six-card minor, wait patiently to show your strength. Let partner make his natural rebid at a convenient level.

17. 3♣. Enough is enough. We have two good suits, so start bidding them. Your next bid will be in spades, which will describe your hand nicely.

Step Responses

18. 3♣. This shows 4 controls, counting aces as 2, kings as 1. Partner will know immediately that you have a helpful hand for him.

19. 2♥. This is a semi-positive bid, showing fewer than two controls with at least 5 HCP. It is forcing to game, and assures partner that you have a little something.

20. 2 NT. This shows 3 controls, which is what you must show at your first turn. Your beautiful spade suit will have to wait.

21. 2♠. I agree that it would be more useful to bid your suits. That may be one reason that step responses are not universally played. The system says show your two controls now and worry later.

Natural Responses

22. 2 ◊ . You have the points and stoppers for 2 NT, but it can't be right to make a positive, encouraging response with zero quick tricks. "Points, schmoints"– remember that queens and jacks are overrated cards.

23. 2 ♠ . That's more like it. A decent five-card suit and two aces are more than enough for a natural bidder to make a positive response.

24. 2 NT. Bidding either spades or clubs would be emphasizing poor suits, and we can't bid 2 ◊ if partner will think that that denies a good responding hand. We are only slightly unbalanced, and if we land in notrump, we won't be embarrassed to have the lead come around to one of our king doubletons.

25. 2 ◊ . There just isn't any possible positive response for this hand. Any positive response would be an extreme distortion. You would prefer to be playing either "waiting bids" or "step responses" for this hand.

Well, how did you do? Are you ready to continue with the rest of 2 ♣ ? Next we will get into some actual auctions that will take us into responder's second bid of the auction as well as opener's third.

We are now ready to forge ahead with the subject of responder's rebid. We are also ready to begin studies of entire auctions.

Let's assume we are playing "Waiting Bid Responses," so responder may have a good hand. After 2 ♣ –2 ◊ , opener's rebid will result in our sequences taking dramatically different paths. So we will key our study of responder's rebids around opener's rebid.

2 ♣	2 ◊
2 ♡	?

The key to this auction is that a rebid of 3 ♣ by responder is a "double (or second) negative" showing a really horrible hand, roughly 0–4 HCP. The important corollary to this is that any other response guarantees some values and is game forcing. The 3 ♣ bid is Alertable.

Here is a run-through of responses.

2 ♠ – Suggests at least five spades, although it would certainly be correct on

♠ K Q J 7
♡ 6 4
◊ 9 7 3 2
♣ 8 6 5

The spade suit itself may be ragged. You would certainly make the 2 ♠ response on

♠ 10 7 4 3 2
♡ J 5
◊ K Q 8 7
♣ 9 2

2 NT. Although responder is not eager to become declarer, 2 NT is such a flexible action that it is frequently the most practical rebid. It shows scattered values, commits the partnership to game, keeps the bidding low, and avoids overemphasizing a particular suit.

3♣. As stated previously, this is responder's weakest action. It is completely artificial, saying nothing about clubs. If responder has a decent hand with clubs, it is just too bad – he cannot convey that message.

After responder's 3♣ denial, the auction could stop below game, depending on the follow-up. Both of the following auctions are possible:

2♣	2♦		2♣	2♦
2♥	3♣*		2♥	3♣*
3♥	?		3♦	3♥
			?	

*Alert

You must keep in mind that after responder's 3♣ response, opener will be assuming that partner has a virtual yarborough. Therefore with a little something, you must show a sign of life.
Holding:

♠ 9 7 6 3	after 2♣	2♦
♥ J 8 5	2♥	3♣*
◊ J 7 6 3	3◊	?
♣ 9 6		

you must jump to 4♥. Your red suit length and honors plus the doubleton club are more than enough to commit this hand to game opposite partner's two-bid.

3◊. Although this bid is very similar to a 2♠ rebid, there are some important differences. 3◊ takes up a lot more room, which is sufficient reason to think twice before making the bid. Also diamonds are "only" a minor, so mentioning diamonds cannot compare with the importance of the majors. Therefore with

♠ K 8
♥ 9 2
◊ K 10 7 4 2
♣ J 6 5 3

rebid 2 NT after

2♣	2◊
2♥	?

instead of 3◊.

3♥ The immediate raise is the most encouraging rebid that responder can make at this point. It shows a hand with a positive response to a strong 2♥ bid, at least 7+ distributional points or so. Responder should always have an outside control (ace, king, singleton or void).
Examples of 3♥ responses after opener rebids 2♥ are:

♠ A 7 4	♠ 10 6
♥ K 8 6 5	♥ Q 5 4
◊ 9 5 3	◊ A 7 4 3
♣ 8 6 4	♣ J 8 5 4

♠ A J 9 4
♡ 10 6 5 4
◊ K 7
♣ 10 6 5

What does responder do after

2♣	2◊
2♡	?

when he has heart support but not enough to give the encouraging raise to 3♡? We can examine and understand the alternatives if we consider the following examples.

1. ♠ A 6 5 3
♡ 10 9 4
◊ 8 7 5 3
♣ 9 4

2. ♠ 10 7 4 3
♡ K J 6 5
◊ 9 3
♣ 8 7 3

3. ♠ 9 4
♡ Q 5 4
◊ 8 7 6 5
♣ 9 7 4 3

4. ♠ 6 3 2
♡ 10 7 5
◊ 9 6 3 2
♣ 10 6 4

Example 1. Rebid 2 NT. This shows some values and is game forcing. You will support hearts next, showing about 5–7 support points. Partner will know that you are too good to double negative, but not good enough to raise hearts immediately.

Example 2. There is a special bid to show good trumps but no outside first or second-round control. A jump to game tells this story. When you bid 4♡ with this hand, partner will have a good picture of your hand.

Example 3. First give a double negative 3♣ bid, then jump to game. This will tell partner that you have an attractive yarborough with true trump support, and expect to contribute a trick or so to the cause.

Example 4. With this true yarborough, give a double negative and try to get out at 3♡. You will pass 3♡ if partner rebids the suit, or take a preference of 3♡ over 3◊.

3♠, 4♣, 4◊. These bids can all be lumped together since they mean the same thing. They are all splinter raises of hearts, showing at most a singleton in the suit bid. Responder should have four trumps but may have only three. The hand should have some values, but they need not be great. Examples of splinter responses after

2♣	2◊
2♡	

♠ 9
♡ K Q 7 4
◊ 10 6 5 4 2
♣ 8 7 5

♠ J 9 5 4
♡ A J 6
◊ Q 8 7 4 3
♣ 3

♠ A 8 7 4
♡ 10 9 6 5
♢ —
♣ 9 7 4 3 2

3 NT. This is a very rare bid, since you are preempting the 2♣ bidder and making it hard for partner to show the hand type. The 3 NT bid suggests a balanced hand with a lot of "soft" cards like queens and jacks. It is acceptable to rebid 3 NT with

♠ Q 7 5	♠ J 10 6 3
♡ 9 6 3	♡ 9 4
♢ Q J 6 4	♢ Q J 7
♣ Q 8 5	♣ Q 9 8 6

but I would not object if my partners never chose this action.

4♡. As we said before, this bid shows 4+ good trumps with nothing of value on the side.

Notrump Auctions

Now we will take a look at some of the notrump auctions that ensue after a 2♣ opening bid. In each case we will consider both the early auction and the possible followups.

2♣ 2♢
2 NT

Opener is showing a balanced 22–24, while responder could have almost anything. Responder can even pass here, since opener has limited his hand to one which needs some help to make game.

If responder takes a bid here, his rebids have the same meaning as responses to an opening 2 NT bid. 3♣ is Stayman, while 3♢ and 3♡ are Jacoby Transfers if the partnership employs this convention. Texas Transfers can also be used, although far more players use Jacoby.

Obviously, it is advantageous to use transfers after 2♣–2♢–2 NT–since opener's hand is so much stronger, you would prefer that hand to become declarer.

Most transfer enthusiasts would treat 3♣ as minor-suit Stayman, but all that must be remembered is that bids mean whatever they would after a 2 NT opening bid, keeping in mind that the 2♣ opener is a little stronger. 4 NT is a quantitative, invitational raise, while 4♣ would be Gerber. These strong responses are quite possible even after the 2♢ response, particularly among "waiting" bidders.

2♣ 2♢
3 NT

Opener's hand here is big enough to insist on game, so opener must have at least the equivalent of 25+ HCP. Once again, most of the responses are usually dominated by conventions. 4♣ is Stayman, 5♣ is Gerber (a jump in clubs over notrump), and 4 ◇ and 4 ♡ are treated as transfers by Jacoby enthusiasts. The response of 4 ♠ to 3 NT would presumably contain the same meaning as 3 ♠ after 2 ♣ – 2 ◇ – 2 NT.

$$2 ♣ \qquad 2 ♡$$
$$2 \text{ NT}$$

After a positive response, things are somewhat different. Opener would "never" need to jump to 3 NT even with 25–27 HCP, since the partnership is already in a game-forcing auction. Therefore, opener guarantees a balanced hand, but his point count ranges from a good 22 + on up. Stayman and transfers are off now. Responder's job is to bid naturally and explore for a playable trump suit for slam. Since the positive response of 2 ♡ shows at least a five-card suit, rebidding 3 ♡ would guarantee six, or at least a super five-card suit.

Should opener raise immediately with a balanced hand and 3-card support? There are good arguments for both sides of this question. By giving the immediate raise, you allow the trump suit to be set immediately – always a plus for slam exploration since cuebidding can be initiated. Those who prefer a 2 NT rebid argue that this allows responder to know that opener is balanced, since after 2 ♣ – 2 ♡ – 3 ♡ opener could have any distribution that included good heart support. Also, a direct raise would often set the 5–3 fit as trumps when there might be a desirable 4–4 fit which would play better in slam, and would never be found after the direct raise, since subsequent bids are cuebids.

$$2 ♣ \qquad 2 \text{ NT}$$
$$?$$

We have one more notrump auction to examine – when responder bids 2 NT directly after opener's 2 ♣ bid. 2 NT here shows a balanced positive response with scattered values. 3 ♣ by opener is now Stayman, but other suit bids are natural, looking for support. If opener has clubs, he must rebid 3 ♣ then 4 ♣. If a suit fit is established, cuebidding can then follow.

We have now discussed the various notrump auctions that may arise after 2 ♣, but since we haven't yet examined any actual hands, this would be a good time to do so.

Try the following, in which we'll assume that we're using Stayman, Gerber and Jacoby Transfers where appropriate.

$$2 ♣ \qquad 2 ◇$$
$$2 \text{ NT}$$

1. ♠ A Q 6 5
    ♡ 10 7 4
    ◇ 9 6 4
    ♣ J 5 3

2. ♠ 10 9 8 7 4
    ♡ 8
    ◇ 6 5 3
    ♣ 8 7 4 3

3. ♠ K 6
    ♡ Q 8 6 4 2
    ◇ K 10 8 5
    ♣ 9 3

$$2 \clubsuit \quad 2 \diamond$$
$$3 \text{ NT}$$

4. ♠ 8
   ♡ J 7 4
   ◊ K 10 8 7 6 5 3 2
   ♣ 8

5. ♠ K 8 6
   ♡ K 7 4
   ◊ 8 7 5 4 3
   ♣ 8 3

6. ♠ J 8 6 4 3
   ♡ 10 8 7 4
   ◊ 10 7 4 3
   ♣ —

$$2 \clubsuit \quad 2 \spadesuit$$
$$2 \text{ NT} \quad ?$$

7. ♠ K Q 7 4 3
   ♡ 8 6 4
   ◊ K 5
   ♣ 9 4 3

8. ♠ A K 9 7 6 5 4
   ♡ 8
   ◊ 10 6 4
   ♣ 7 5

9. ♠ A Q 6 5 3
   ♡ 9 2
   ◊ Q 7
   ♣ J 10 8 5

$$2 \clubsuit \quad 2 \text{ NT}$$
$$?$$

10. ♠ K 8 3
    ♡ A 6
    ◊ A K J 7 4
    ♣ A K Q

11. ♠ A K 7 4
    ♡ A Q 3
    ◊ A
    ♣ A Q 7 5 4

12. ♠ A K 6
    ♡ A Q 7
    ◊ K J 8 5
    ♣ A Q 4

Answers

1. Bid 3 NT. With about 30 points and your flat hand, notrump should do as well as a suit contract, so don't bother with Stayman.

2. Bid 3♡, transfer. You will then pass 3♠, which should be your best chance to go plus. Remember, partner can jump to 4♠ with a super hand.

3. Bid 3◊, transfer. After partner bids 3♡, you will bid 4◊ to show your second suit. (It is interesting that 4◊ will be your third consecutive diamond bid, yet the first one that really shows diamonds.) This hand may play game or slam in either diamonds, hearts or notrump.

4. Bid 5♣, Gerber. With the knowledge that partner has a balanced battleship, your hand becomes enormous also. If partner has four aces and at least one king, you'll bid a grand on your 4-count.

5. Bid 4 NT. You could show your diamonds by bidding 4♣ then 5◊, but the better practical solution is an invitational 4 NT. If partner has a suit-oriented hand, you will hear it mentioned over 4 NT, and you can then trot out your diamonds.

6. Bid 4♣. Although you can't be sure the hand will play better in a major, your club void and nine major-suit cards suggest that it's worth trying for. If partner responds 4◊, you will bid 4♠ to show five and hope for the best.

7. Bid 3 NT. You have a balanced positive response without anything great. The next move, if any, is up to partner.

8. Bid 3 ♠. You are presumably on your way to 6 ♠ or 7 ♠, but there's no hurry. Partner's reaction to 3 ♠ will be enlightening.

9. Bid 3 ♣. Your club suit isn't anything great, but it would be masterminding to conceal it. Partner could easily have something like

$$\spadesuit \text{ K 4} \quad \heartsuit \text{ A K 8 3} \quad \diamondsuit \text{ K 8 5} \quad \clubsuit \text{ A K Q 4,}$$

where 6 ♣ is definitely best.

10. 3 ◊. You may end up in 6 NT, but diamonds could prove to be your best friend on this hand.

11. 3 ♣. This is Stayman, as you check out a possible spade fit. If partner doesn't bid spades, you will follow with a natural 4 ♣ showing a real club suit.

12. Bid 3 NT. You have a minimum, balanced 2 ♣ bid, so you must limit your hand. Partner will be well placed to decide whether to go further.

We will now conclude our study of opening bids of 2 ♣. We will examine a few follow-up actions after the 2 ♣ opener and then finish with some competitive auctions.

| 2 ♣ | Pass | 2 ◊ | Pass |
| 3 ◊ | Pass | ? | |

Auctions where opener rebids in a minor at the three level are the most awkward of the 2 ♣ auctions. Responder has little room to maneuver, particularly with a balanced hand, when forced to make his second call at the three level.

Opener should embark on such auctions only when the hand is so strong that a one bid can't be risked. Even with a hand like

♠ A J 6 5
♡ A K J
◊ A K Q 5 4
♣ 8

it is probably better to open 1 ◊ and hope for another chance.

In order to fully appreciate the strangled nature of these auctions and to practice our rebids, try these deals after opener rebids 3 ◊ after getting a 2 ◊ response.

1. ♠ J 7 4
   ♡ 8 6 4
   ◊ 5 4 3
   ♣ 10 8 6 4

2. ♠ 10 6 5 3
   ♡ K Q J 4
   ◊ 9 3
   ♣ 5 4 3

3. ♠ Q 8 4
   ♡ Q 8 6 5
   ◊ 10 7 4
   ♣ Q 9 5

4. ♠ Q 8 6
   ♡ 10 7 4 2
   ◊ 9
   ♣ K Q J 8 5

5. ♠ 8
   ♡ K 9 4 3
   ◊ K 7 4 2
   ♣ 10 6 4 3

6. ♠ 9 6 4 3
   ♡ 9 3
   ◊ K Q 7
   ♣ 8 6 5 3

1. 3♡, double negative. Since 3 NT may be the only game, and it should not play from our side, we have to play 3♡ as a second negative to keep the bidding as low as possible. Of course this means we cannot show a heart suit at the three level, but there is no other practical solution.

2. 3♡ again. Although this is a respectable hand, a 3♡ double negative is the only possibility. You hope partner can bid 3♠ (which you will raise) or 3 NT.

3. 3 NT. You hate to have the big hand exposed, but you must make a more helpful bid for partner than a wishy-washy 3♡.

4. 4♣. You must show some life with this respectable hand and fine suit.

5. 4♠. Splinter. You have a superb hand in support of a strong two bid in diamonds. 4♠ cannot be a real suit, since any hand worth a jump here would have bid spades naturally in response to 2♣.

6. 4◇. You must show your excellent diamonds. If 3 NT is the best spot, it is just too bad.

A Jump by Opener

A jump by opener is very rare. Since an auction like 2♣–2◇–2♡ is forcing, 2♣–2◇–3♡ would be very unusual. What does it mean?

Since three-suited hands are so difficult to describe, you could play this as a kind of splinter bid, a big 4–1–4–4 like

♠ A K 7 4
♡ 8
◇ A K J 6
♣ A K Q J

However, most good players use the jump to show a solid suit with a "great" 2♣ bid, and to force responder to cuebid.

2♣	Pass	2◇	Pass
3♡	Pass	4♣	

This would show that responder had the ♣A. Responder can show kings and/or queens with subsequent cuebids.

2♣	Pass	2◇	Pass
4♣			

The only reason opener would take away all the partnership bidding room would be a minimum 2♣ bid based on distribution. This rare auction might indicate a hand like

♠ A K Q 10 6 5 4
♡ 8
◇ K Q J 6
♣ 9

It prevents responder from bidding too much with a smattering of kings and queens.

The Opponent Intervenes

So far the opponents have considerably stayed out of our way after we opened 2♣. However, matters may not always go smoothly. Let's see how we handle interference.

2♣   2◊   ?

This overcall has not inconvenienced us much as we are still at a low level. A double by responder is for penalties, showing good diamonds and a bad hand. A pass would tend to show a hand that would have made a 2◊ waiting bid. Responder should show a good suit if he has one, even if the hand is a little skimpy for a positive response.

The overcall also gives responder an opportunity to cuebid, showing a three-suiter short in the opponent's suit, with a hand that at least resembles a positive response.

2♣   Dbl.   ?

The opponent's double is a lead-director showing club length and strength. A redouble by responder suggests that the contract (2♣ doubled) is quite satisfactory. Otherwise responder would usually pass, since opener may have good enough clubs for a business redouble. Of course, with a very fine suit, responder should identify it.

2♣   Pass   2◊   3♣
?

A pass by opener here is quite forcing. In fact, after a 2♣ opening bid the opponents should never play an undoubled contract. Opener would usually pass with a balanced powerhouse, and his doubles are also penalty oriented. Holding one or two long suits, opener would usually show one of them here. This bid would also be forcing below the game level.

2♣   4♡   ?

This interference can't be ignored. Matters are quite complicated since opener could have many types of strong hands, and the opponent has left no room to identify the hand type. As responder is quite unlikely to have a lot of hearts, some good players use the double here to show a lack of values and to warn opener he can't expect much help. A pass would then be the encouraging call, suggesting that slam is quite likely. But it is wise to check with your partner before making any definite assumptions.

Summary on Handling Interference over 2♣

1. Passes by either player are forcing.

2. Redoubles are business.

3. Doubles at low levels are for penalties. Doubles at high levels say "beware of bidding on."

4. Bids show good suits, but may be lighter than usual.

5. Cuebids show shortness in opponent's suit, usually a three-suiter.

Partner opens 2♣ and RHO overcalls 2♠ with neither side vulnerable. What do you do with these holdings?

1. ♠ K J 6
   ♡ Q 10 5
   ◇ Q 7 4
   ♣ 10 6 5 4

2. ♠ 8 4
   ♡ 9
   ◇ 10 6 5 4
   ♣ K Q J 10 7 4

3. ♠ 9
   ♡ A 7 4 2
   ◇ K 8 6 4
   ♣ J 9 5 3

4. ♠ 7 2
   ♡ Q 8 5 4
   ◇ K 10 6
   ♣ Q 9 5 4

1. 2 NT. This bid is so descriptive and economical that it would be foolish not to use it.

2. 3♣. What's the problem?

3. 3♠. After the hand you will thank the opponent for allowing you to describe your hand so well.

4. Pass. You have no good bid, so sit and wait.

Now opener has the problem after the bidding goes:

2♣	Pass	2◇	3♣
?			

1. ♠ A K 6 4
   ♡ A K J 7 5 2
   ◇ A Q
   ♣ 9

2. ♠ A K 9
   ♡ A K J 5
   ◇ K J 8 4
   ♣ A 7

3. ♠ K Q 7 4 2
   ♡ A K Q
   ◇ A K Q 9
   ♣ J

1. 3♡. You started with a strong two bid in hearts, so let partner in on that information.

2. Pass. You shouldn't double the opponent on A–x of trumps. Partner will do something intelligent.

3. Pass. What's the hurry? 3♠ would take up a lot of room on a hand where anything might be right. If partner doubles, expecting us to have more clubs, we can then bid our spades. But meanwhile partner can bid a red suit at the three level if he has one.

Defense to 2♣

As we have seen, doubles of 2♣ and 2♣–Pass–2◇ are lead directing. It is fine in theory to interfere with the opponents on their big hands, but be careful. When you play with fire, it is easy to get burned! Obviously vulnerability is the determining factor, although making frisky lead-directing doubles can result in embarrassing redoubled-into-game situations – even when the vulnerability is favorable.

Splinter Bids

Although point count is generally accurate for slam bidding with balanced hands, the key to good slam bidding is evaluating the distributional fit of the partnership hands. A holding of 7-5-3-2 opposite a singleton is ideal, of course, since it means there are no wasted high cards. However, if the singleton faces K-Q-8-4, slam is unlikely unless there is an overabundance of high cards. Cards other than aces lose much of their value when they are present in or opposite short suits.

One player must identify his short suit (singleton or void) so that partner can evaluate the fit. Splinter raises offer the easiest and most efficient way to do this. The phrase "splinter raises" is used because a splinter bid is always a raise of partner's last named suit.

How do you make a splinter bid? You jump one level higher than you would to show a strong hand with a jump shift or reverse. Some partnerships define, a splinter bid as any "impossible" jump bid (except Gerber) where "impossible" means a bid that is not needed to describe a type of hand.

Here are some auctions that illustrate splinter bids. Notice both opener and responder may make these bids. Assume the opponents pass throughout.

By Opener			By Responder		
1)	1 ◇	1 ♡	1)	1 ♡	4 ♣
	4 ♣				

3 ♣ would be a strong jump shift, so 4 ♣ is a splinter bid.

2)	1 ♠	2 ♡	2)	1 ♠	2 ♣
	4 ◇			2 ♡	4 ◇

3 ◇ would show a strong hand with diamonds, so 4 ◇ is a splinter bid.

3)	1 ♡	2 ♣	3)	1 ◇	1 ♡
	3 ♠			2 ♣	3 ♠

2 ♠ would show a strong hand with spades; so 3 ♠ is a splinter bid.

What type of hand qualifies for a splinter bid? Splinters agree partner's last bid suit as the trump suit, so four-card support is necessary. They show a singleton or void in the splinter suit. Since splinters are forcing to game and show potential slam interest, they must contain a good deal of high card strength.

The amount of high card strength depends on the actual auction. Since after 1 ◇ - Pass - 1 ♡ - Pass, opener needs about 20 points to force to game, a bid of 3 ♠ or 4 ♣ should normally show 17+ HCP and a singleton or 15+ HCP and a void. This agrees with the generally recognized method of counting three points for a singleton and four for a void when raising partner's suit with four-card support. Of course, aces and kings and the quality of the trump suit are still the name of the game, so it is quite correct to bid 4 ♣ after 1 ◇ - 1 ♡ with

♠ A 6 3   ♡ A J 10 4   ◇ A K 7 5 2   ♣ 9.

Here are examples of minimum-strength hands with singletons for splinter bids with several auctions. If you are fortunate enough to have a void, the high card requirements can be shaded by about a queen. The rule to remember is: the more strength partner has already promised, the less strength is needed to splinter. Continue to assume that the opponents are too enthralled with your splinter auctions to do anything but pass.

1)   ♠A 7 5 3   ♡K 9 6 3   ◇K J 7 3   ♣5

After a major suit opening bid 4♣. Notice this hand satisfies the three requirements noted above.

2)   ♠A 8 6 2   ♡K Q 6 5   ◇K J 4 2   ♣9

1◇	1♡
1♠	4♣

Remember, 4♣ is a raise of partner's last bid suit. The fact that you have diamonds too is just a coincidence. The minimum for auction 2 is slightly higher because opener usually has only four spades and the 4 - 4 fit requires extra high cards to compensate for the lack of the ninth trump.

3)   ♠A K 8 7 4   ♡Q 8 5 2   ◇5   ♣A 8 2

1♠	2♡
4◇	

Some players would be reluctant to splinter with only 13 HCP points. However, with these controls and holding at least nine trumps, it is surely correct. If partner has

       ♠6 5   ♡A K 7 6 4 3   ◇9 4 3 2   ♣5

you will have a biddable laydown slam with only 20 HCP.

4)   ♠9   ♡A K 7 5 2   ◇A Q 4   ♣Q 7 5 2

1♡	2♣
3♠	

A little additional strength is needed here since you are heading toward an 11-trick game and partner may have only a four-card suit.

5)   ♠K 8 6 2   ♡A K 5 4   ◇8   ♣Q J 8 2

1 NT	2♣
2♡	4◇

Notice that a good hand is needed to splinter here even though partner's 1 NT shows a good hand. There are three reasons for this: the probable lack of a ninth trump, the great likelihood of wasted diamond strength with the notrump opener, and the knowledge that partner's maximum is limited by his opening bid.

How should you respond after partner makes a splinter bid? Since partner has forced to game, the weakest bid is to sign off in the agreed trump suit. This is true even if the splinter bid is doubled. Therefore,

1♠	Pass	4♣	Dbl
Pass			

shows that opener has some slam interest, while

1♠	Pass	4♣	Dbl
4♠			

means opener has no aspirations beyond game. This is logical since passing allows room for cuebidding.

By the way, most people play that redouble by either partner shows first-round control, with redouble by the splinter bidder usually signifying a void. Therefore, with

♠ K Q 8 7 2   ♡ 6 4   ◇ Q 9   ♣ 8 4 3 2

after

1 ◇	Pass	1 ♠	Pass
4 ♣	Dbl		

you should pass and give partner the chance to redouble if he has a club void.

If you are interested in a slam after a splinter bid, you tend to cuebid, although with some hands Blackwood is appropriate. You assume partner has a small singleton in the splinter suit since that holding occurs with far greater frequency than a void or singleton honor. Therefore, remember that your high cards in partner's short suit are not pulling their full weight, especially secondary honors. It is also good to have length in partner's short suit, since the more you have, the more losers you will be able to ruff in his hand.

Try bidding these hands after the auction has proceeded.

1 ♠   Pass   4 ♣   Pass

1)

♠ K J 6 4 2
♡ K 7 4 3
◇ A 5
♣ K 3

Bid 4♠. Your club holding is not good, and you don't have enough strength in the other suits to get interested.

2)

♠ K Q 7 6 3
♡ Q 5
◇ A 5
♠ A 9 3 2

Bid 4◇. You have an excellent holding in clubs with four-card length as well as no wasted high cards. Slam is likely.

3)

♠ A Q 9 5 2
♡ A 5 3
◇ K 4
♣ K J 5

Bid 4♡. Your club holding is not good, but your hand is so strong that you are still interested in slam.

4)

♠ A K J 9 8 7
♡ A
◇ 2
♣ 9 8 6 4 3

Bid 4 NT. This is the kind of hand that becomes monstrous after hearing of the club shortness. Partner must have enough strength in the red suits to dispose of any clubs that you aren't able to ruff.

Now let us consider other auctions in which splinter bids may be used and conclude with some tips to keep in mind when your opponents use splinter bids.

We begin by looking at some auctions that should be played as splinter bids, assuming of course that your partnership has agreed to play them. Remember, a splinter bid is always made one level higher than the natural forcing bid, so normally there should not be any ambiguities between splinters and natural bidding.

1) 1♦ - 2♡
    4♣

Opener would bid 3♣ after the jump shift to show clubs so this auction shows a heart raise with shortness in clubs.

2) 2♣ - 2♦
    2♡ - 3♠

Opener shows a heart suit after the strong artificial opening bid and negative response. Responder can show a spade suit by bidding 2♠, so 3♠ shows something like

    ♠ 8   ♡ Q 7 4 2   ◇ A 8 7 4   ♣ 10 9 5 3.

3) 1♠ - 2♦
    2♠ - 4♡

This sequence differs from the usual splinter auctions, since responder is likely to have only three-card support since he didn't splinter directly over 1♠

4) 1♦ - 1♠
    2♡ - 4♣

After the reverse of 2♡, 4♣ is not needed as a natural bid, so it shows good heart support with short clubs.

Here are some auctions that can also be played as splinter bids by experienced partnerships. However, they are sequences that occur with less frequency, and some pairs may prefer to do without them.

1) 1♣ - 3♡

In Standard this shows a seven-card suit with a very weak hand, but many players now prefer to use this as a forcing club raise with 5+ trumps and at most one heart.

2) 1♡ - 2♡
    3♠

Opener would want to elect this sequence on a hand like

    ♠ —   ♡ A K 8 7 3   ◇ K Q 6 5   ♣ A Q 4 3.

Responder would then know to head for slam with

    ♠ 8 7 4 3   ♡ Q 9 6 2   ◇ A J 7   ♣ 6 5,

but sign off with

$$\spadesuit A Q 6 5 \quad \heartsuit 10\,9\,5\,2 \quad \diamondsuit J\,4\,3 \quad \clubsuit 8\,5$$

3)　1♡ - 3♡
　　5♣

This sequence is similar to 2), except that opener does not need as much strength to make the splinter bid.

4)　1 NT - 2◇
　　2♡ - 4◇

　　If the partnership uses transfer bids, responder would transfer and jump to show something like

$$\spadesuit A\,8\,4 \quad \heartsuit K\,Q\,J\,6\,4\,2 \quad \diamondsuit 3 \quad \clubsuit Q\,J\,3.$$

5)　1♣ - 1♠
　　3♡

Since most players consider the reverse of 2♡ as a one-round force, 3♡ is not needed as a natural bid. Therefore, 3♡ is played as a splinter raise of spades.

6)　1◇ - 1 NT
　　3♣

This would show a hand like

$$\spadesuit 4 \quad \heartsuit A\,Q\,6 \quad \diamondsuit A\,Q\,J\,8\,6\,3 \quad \clubsuit A\,9\,4.$$

If responder has

$$\spadesuit 6\,5\,2 \quad \heartsuit J\,8 \quad \diamondsuit 9\,4 \quad \clubsuit K\,Q\,10\,8\,7\,2$$

he can bid a confident 5♣.

7)　1♣ - 1♡
　　1♠ - 4♣

　　3♣ could be bid to show clubs, so 4♣ is best employed as a spade raise with short clubs.

8)　1♣　- 1♡ or 1♣　- 1♡
　　1 NT - 3♠　　2 NT - 4♣

Both of these auctions show a strong raise of clubs with fewer than two spades.

Another advantage of using splinter bids is that other auctions are clarified because of their absence. Here are some:

1)　1♡　- 1♠
　　2♡　- 3♣
　　3 NT - 4♡

Responder previously used this sequence as his only slam try, both with and without a singleton diamond. Now it clearly denies a singleton diamond because of the lack of a splinter sequence.

2)　1◇ - 1♡
　　3♣ - 4♣
　　4♡

Without the use of splinter bids, there would be no way for responder to know whether opener had three or four hearts. However, with splinter bids, this sequence shows only three hearts, since the assumption is that opener would have bid 3♠ directly with four trumps and short spades.

3) 1♣ - 1♠
    2◇ - 2 NT
    3♠

Again, this shows only three-card support, for the same reasons as in 2) above.

If the opponents interfere, it is not always possible to have sequences available for both splinters and jump shifts. This is especially true when they bid at the two-level. Study the following auctions:

	Opp.		Opp.
1)	1◇ - 2♣ - 3♠	5)	1♡ - 2♣ - 3◇
2)	1◇ - 2♡ - 3♠	6)	1♡ - 2♣ - 3♠
3)	1◇ - 2♡ - 4♣	7)	1♠ - 2♡ - 4♣
4)	1♡ - 2♠ - 4♣	8)	1♠ - 2◇ - 3♡

Some players prefer these to be jump shifts, others believe that they are more useful as splinters. My advice is to treat the jumps to the three-level as natural jump shifts and the four-level bids as splinters. Of course the best advice I can give is that you make sure you discuss these sequences with your regular partners.

Here is another auction that can cause trouble.

    1◇ - 1♠
    2♣ - 3♡.

Although 2♡ is forcing, this auction is needed as a natural forcing bid to distinguish a hand where responder only wished to invite from such a hand as

    ♠A K 8 6 3   ♡A Q 8 6 3   ◇6 4   ♣5.

With

    ♠A J 8 6 3   ♡A J 10 6 3   ◇6 4   ♣5

he would bid

    1◇   - 1♠
    2♣   - 2♡
    Any - 3♡.

Of course, if playing fourth suit game forcing the two auctions would presumably be inverted.

Let's conclude our discussion of splinter bids by considering what to do when the opponents have a splinter auction. Doubling the splinter bid should show more than desire to have the suit led, since you know only one trick can be cashed there. In fact, it is often wise to lead trumps after a splinter auction, since declarer will certainly be planning to ruff out his losers opposite the short suit.

Therefore doubling the splinter bid should show length and strength in the suit, and also a desire to sacrifice if partner has a suitable hand, although you might designate another meaning when the vul. is unattractive.

Splinter bids are now used by almost all good partnerships. They provide an invaluable aid for the partnership to evaluate the fit of their hands. I suggest that experienced players incorporate splinter bids into their partnership, although it is not advisable to try to do too much too soon. Remember, the test of a good partnership is not the number of conventions they play, but rather how well they understand and employ the bids at their disposal.

Questions on Splinter Bids

Question: **Holding**

♠A 10 6 4   ♡A 10 6 3   ◇A 10 5 2   ♣8,

I heard my partner open 1♠. I was all set to splinter when RHO made a takeout double. I bid 4♣ anyway, sure that this was still a splinter bid. My partner passed and obviously this was not our best spot! Who was at fault? My partner's hand was

♠K Q 8 7 5 2   ♡7   ◇K Q J   ♣J 5 4.

Answer: Your partner was to blame. However, perhaps you shouldn't have bid 4♣ if you weren't 100% sure partner would understand. Since bids of 2♣, 3♣ and 5♣ were available to show clubs, there was no reason for your partner not to recognize 4♣ as a splinter bid – but he didn't! This hand should have been a triumph for splinter bids. Over 4♣, opener has the perfect hand to Blackwood into 6♠. This 24 HCP slam could be bid only when opener knows for sure that responder has a singleton club.

Question: **When partner opens a major and I have four trumps, a singleton, and a five-card suit with enough strength to force to game, should I splinter or should I show my five-card suit first?**

Answer: Let's use an example to help us here. Partner opens 1♡ and I hold

♠Q 7 4   ♡K J 6 3   ◇5   ♣A Q 8 7 4.

I would bid 4◇ feeling that the most important thing I could tell partner is about my singleton diamond and my four trumps. In my experience, this has worked out best. It is only fair to mention that many good players would bid 2♣ and support hearts later.

Question: **Playing five-card majors, may I splinter with only three trumps?**

Answer: NO! Since the purpose of splinter bids is to judge whether to bid a slam, we cannot scrimp on the quantity of our trumps. Our short suit is pulling its full weight for slam only if we have enough trumps to ruff all of partner's losers, and four trumps will usually take care of this. However, I have gone down in slams even opposite four trumps on occasion where a fifth trump would have enabled me to take my 12th trick.

Question: **You stated that a double of a splinter bid is lead-directing, showing length and strength in the suit splintered into. Do all experts play it that way?**

Answer: Definitely not. Leading dummy's short suit is far from certain to be the best defense. Also, there is no big advantage in encouraging a sacrifice when the vulnerability is wrong. Therefore some experts use this double to ask for a specific lead in one of the unbid suits. My agreement with Larry Cohen is that a double of a splinter bid suggests a save at favorable vulnerability, otherwise it asks for the lead of the higher ranking unbid suit.

♠ _____ ♠

Fourth Suit Forcing and Artificial

If you and your partner play that a second round jump by responder – raise, preference, rebid or 2 NT – is forcing, how do you handle such hands as the following? You are vulnerable at matchpoints and the bidding goes:

	PARTNER	YOU
	1 ◇	1 ♡
	1 ♠	?

1)	♠ 8 3	♡ K Q 6 4	◇ K Q 8 4 2	♣ 9 3
2)	♠ J 4	♡ A Q 8 6 4 3	◇ 8 5	♣ A 7 4
3)	♠ 10 5 3	♡ K Q 7 2	◇ Q 8	♣ K J 10 5

1) Since a jump to 3 ◇ would be forcing you have the unpleasant choice of overbidding with 3 ◇ or underbidding with 2 ◇. If you bid 2 ◇, you may find partner with

♠ K 6 4 2   ♡ A 5   ◇ A 7 6 5   ♣ K 6 4

and miss a probable game. If you try 3 ◇ partner will bid 3 NT with

♠ A 10 7 4   ♡ A 5   ◇ J 9 6 3   ♣ K 7 4,

but he won't make it.

2) You can force to game by bidding 3♡. However, if partner bids 3 NT with

♠ K 8 7 5   ♡ 5   ◇ K J 7 3 2   ♣ K Q J,

you had better pray that no one doubles. But if you conservatively bid 2♡, you may find partner with

♠ 10 7 6 2   ♡ K 5   ◇ A K 9 4   ♣ K 6 2

and miss another game.

3) You must again choose between the lady and the tiger. If you try 1 NT, partner will automatically pass with something like

♠ J 8 7 2   ♡ A 5   ◇ A K 7 6 4   ♣ Q 3.

and another cold game will go unbid. Yet a forcing bid of 2 NT will propel partner into 3 NT with

♠ K Q 7 2   ♡ 6   ◇ K 7 5 4 3   ♣ A 8 3,

and even Garozzo would be most unlikely to take nine tricks here.

The answer to these three problems is to play that a jump rebid by responder is not forcing to game, simply invitational. Although there is still no guarantee of getting to the best contract, at least you have available a bid that accurately portrays your strength without being forced to choose between an underbid and an overbid.

One thought you may have in mind now is, "OK, this style works well for the hands that have invitational strength, but what do I do with the better hands?" If

1 ◇ – 1 ♡
1 ♠ – 3 ◇

is not forcing, what do we do with

♠ A 7   ♡ K J 8 5 4   ◇ K Q 7 2   ♣ 9 3,

where a forcing 3 ◇ would be perfect? Patience, readers, there is a way to have your cake and eat it too!

First, try two more problems. You hold

4)   ♠ A Q 5   ♡ A Q 8 4 2   ◇ 9 4 2   ♣ Q 3

after   1 ◇ – 1 ♡
                          1 ♠ –

Even if a jump rebid is forcing, no alternative is appetizing. 3 ♠ will certainly get you to 4 ♠ on a probable 4–3 trump fit. 3 ♡ will often be raised on a doubleton, since partner will expect a six-card suit. Jump raising a minor on three small is unattractive: 2 NT is unacceptable with no real club stopper and does not suggest to partner that you are looking for three-card heart support.

What would you do with

5)   ♠ 8 4   ♡ K Q 10 9 3   ◇ A J   ♣ K 8 6 4

after   1 ◇ – 1 ♡
                          2 ♣ – ?

You want to be in game, but the right contract could be 5 ♣, 4 ♡ or 3 NT–and even a slam is possible. 3 ♣ is not forcing; 3 ♡ overemphasizes your so-so heart suit. 4 ♣ is about what the hand is worth, but if partner has

♠ K Q 7   ♡ 8   ◇ K Q 6 5 4   ♣ A 10 5 3

you certainly want to be in 3 NT, particularly at matchpoints.

I think it is now clear that standard methods are somewhat inadequate here. We need a way to allow both invitational and forcing bids to be made, and also need to have an economical bid available for those hands where we are still unsure about the contract and need to exchange information at a low level.

For many years now, new suits by responder have generally been played as forcing, probing bids. Opener must not pass when responder bids a new suit unless opener has severely limited his strength and distribution in an auction such as

$$1 \diamondsuit - 1 \spadesuit$$
$$1 \text{ NT} - 2 \heartsuit.$$

We will use this principle to aid us in our conventional solution to the above problems.

When three suits have been bid by a partnership, it is extremely unlikely that the partnership's best trump suit is the unbid fourth suit. With this in mind, we are now ready to seek the bidding accuracy that was impossible earlier.

The convention is called Fourth-Suit Forcing. We will play that responder's second-round jumps are invitational, and if responder wishes to force to game with a better hand, he first bids the fourth suit and then takes the appropriate action which is now 100% forcing. Also the bid of the fourth suit does not say anything about responder's holding in the suit. It is somewhat analogous to the modern interpretation of the cuebid which shows a good hand and requests information.

Since the fourth-suit bidder does not promise strength in the suit bid, opener must have a stopper himself to bid notrump. It is also very important to remember that a bid in the fourth suit, like a strong cuebid, guarantees a rebid. It would be blowing hot and cold for responder to start the ball rolling, then get tired and quit suddenly.

Let's see how fourth-suit forcing helps us to handle the bidding problem encountered earlier. On

1)   ♠ 8 5   ♡ K Q 6 4   ◇ K Q 8 4 2   ♣ 9 3

after $1 \diamondsuit - 1 \heartsuit$
                                          $1 \spadesuit$

we bid 3 ◇ , after which our partner can pass with a minimum and take appropriate action with a good hand. On

2)   ♠ J 4   ♡ A Q 8 6 4 3   ◇ 8 5   ♣ A 7 4,

we bid 3♡ , again merely invitational. On

3)   ♠ 10 5 3   ♡ K Q 7 2   ◇ Q 8   ♣ K J 10 5

we can jump to 2 NT showing 11–12 points and leaving the decision up to partner. Cᴜ

4)   ♠ A Q 5   ♡ A Q 8 4 2   ◇ 9 4 2   ♣ Q 3,

we are now well placed after

$$1\diamondsuit - 1\heartsuit$$
$$1\spadesuit -$$

by bidding 2♣. Partner can now show some heart support with 2♡. He can also bid notrump with a club stopper, and 3 NT should be a reasonable gamble. Partner can also rebid a five-card spade suit (implying six diamonds) and this likewise will suit us fine. If he rebids 2♢ we will raise that to 3♢ (forcing) and continue the search for the best contract.

On

5)   ♠ 8 4   ♡ K Q 10 9 3   ◊ A J   ♣ K 8 6 4

after $1\diamondsuit - 1\heartsuit$
                                2♣

we try 2♠. Partner can now show belated heart support, which we will carry to game. If he bids 2 NT to show a spade stopper, we will bid 3♣ to identify a hand that is now making a forcing raise of clubs. If partner rebids either of his minors, we will bid 4♣ and play in 5♣ or 6♣, depending on how the cuebidding goes.

Now that we have taken care of responder's problems, let's look at a few hands from opener's point of view. In each case the auction has gone

                       $1\diamondsuit - 1\spadesuit$
                       2♣ - 2♡.

6)   ♠ A 6   ♡ 8   ◊ K Q 5 3 2   ♣ K 8 7 5 2

Bid 3♣ to show 5-5.

7)   ♠ 8   ♡ K 5 4   ◊ A Q 10 7 4   ♣ A J 9 2

Bid 2 NT showing a heart stopper.

8)   ♠ 8 4   ♡ 7 5   ◊ A K J 8 2   ♣ A J 5 4

Bid 3◊. You can't bid notrump without a heart stopper, and a preference on two small would be misleading, so 3◊ is all that's left.

9)   ♠ −   ♡ K J 7 5   ◊ A Q 10 8 3   ♣ K J 9 4

Bid 3♡. This shows your four hearts. You don't want to raise to 4♡ since partner may not have heart length. If partner bids 3 NT, you should abide by his decision and pass since you've already shown your hand.

We said earlier that the fourth-suit bidder guarantees a rebid, but there is confusion as to whether his rebid is forcing.

My suggestion both for simplicity and efficiency is to play "fourth suit forcing to game." It is impractical to come to a screeching halt in the middle of a forcing auction. Also, matters get very complicated when each partner must try to remember which similar sounding auctions are forcing and which are not. A good example of this are the auctions that ensue after opener reverses when responder has a weak hand.

We'll conclude our study of fourth suit forcing by answering some commonly asked questions from the readers.

Questions

Question 1: **I held**

♠ 10 9 7 4 3   ♥ A 7   ♦ A K   ♣ Q 9 4 2

after the bidding had gone

PARTNER	ME
1 ♦	1 ♠
2 ♣	2 ♥
2 ♠	

I bid 4 ♠ expecting opener to have three card support for me. His actual hand was

♠ A 5   ♥ J 2   ♦ 10 8 6 3 2   ♣ A K J 10.

Wasn't he wrong to bid 2 ♠ ?

Answer: If opener needs a heart stopper to bid 2 NT, and at least 5–5 to bid 3 ♣, the only possible alternative to the 2 ♠ bid is 3 ♦. This can't be correct on such a bad five card suit when we've already suggested five diamonds therefore, opener must be allowed to preference on a doubleton honor here. In fact since I would be happy to raise to 2 ♠ immediately with

♠ A 7 3   ♥ 9   ♦ J 8 6 4 3   ♣ A K 7 4,

I tell my partners to assume only two on these type of auctions.

Question 2: **Should "fourth suit forcing to game" be used by passed hands?**

Answer: For myself, I don't even play it as a one-round force! Since I open light, I can't have a hand that wants to force but couldn't open the bidding. Therefore, if I rebid 2 ♣ after

Pass – 1 ♦
1 ♥ – 1 ♠

I'd have something like

♠ 8   ♥ K Q 9 6 4   ♦ 3 2   ♣ K J 8 5 4.

As for others, although I haven't seen the bid used as game forcing when bid by a passed hand, some do use it as an artificial one-round force.

Question 3: **Should opener ever jump after responder bids fourth suit game forcing?**

Answer: Yes, he should if he wants to show his extra values at a convenient level. After

1 ♦ – 1 ♥
1 ♠ – 2 ♣

I would rebid 3 ♦ with

♠ A K J 4   ♡ 6 2   ◇ K Q J 10 7 4   ♣ 8,

3♡ with

♠ A 9 6 3   ♡ K Q 6   ◇ A K 7 4 3   ♣ 9

3 NT with

♠ A K 10 6   ♡ 8   ◇ A 8 7 4 3   ♣ K Q 10.

However, not all good hands should jump. Holding

♠ A K J 6   ♡ A K   ◇ Q 10 7 4 3   ♣ J 5,

I would simply rebid 2♡ and await developments, since all jumps would distort my distribution.

Question 4: **If a bid of the fourth suit is completely game forcing, what do I bid with invitational two suiters?**

Answer: You make an invitational jump in the fourth suit. So after

1◇ – 1♡
1♠,

bid 3♣ with

♠ 3   ♡ K Q 10 8 5   ◇ 6 4   ♣ K Q 10 8 5,

with another king, you would rebid 2♣ then 3♣ to force.

Fourth-suit forcing is now a fixture in the world of tournament bridge. Like so many other conventions, there is considerable disagreement among its followers as to how to use it to best advantage. Hopefully, at this point, the reader will be better equipped to employ this convention skillfully in his bidding arsenal.

♤ _____ ♤

The 2 NT Asking Game Try

At this time, I'd like to concentrate on original conventional ideas involving 2 NT. The world already knows about Lebensohl 2 NT, Unusual 2 NT, Jacoby 2 NT, Transfers over 2 NT, etc. We'll discuss some other interesting possibilities with which most readers are probably not as familiar. The first of these is used after a single major-suit raise. We'll call it the *2 NT Asking Game Try.*

After your side raises a one of a major opening to two, what type of game tries do you use? In the auction 1♠ – 2♠, 3♣, the traditional meaning of the 3♣ bid was merely a *second suit*, perhaps in a hand like

♠ A K Q 6 4   ♡ 5 4   ◇ 6 3   ♣ A Q 8 5.

Then along came the Kaplan-Sheinwold concept of *short-suit* game tries. 3♣ would be bid on

♠ A K J 5 4   ♡ K 5 4   ◇ K J 7 4   ♣ 4.

The modern point of view is for a new suit to suggest where opener has losers and *needs help*. He might bid 3♣ on

♠ A K J 6 4   ♡ A K   ◇ 5 4   ♣ 7 6 5 2.

It seems that this is the method preferred by most players today.

One problem that I noticed with the "need help" game tries was that there were many hands where *I* needed help figuring out in what suit to ask for help! Take a look at the following hands.

1.	♠ A K J 5 4	♡ 8 6	◇ 9 7	♣ A Q J 7
2.	♠ A K J 9 7 2	♡ Q J 4	◇ Q J 3	♣ 9
3.	♠ K Q J 10 6	♡ A Q 7	◇ K 9 6 5	♣ 8
4.	♠ K Q 10 8 7	♡ 8 6	◇ A K 10 5	♣ K 6
5.	♠ A K J 7 4	♡ A K Q	◇ 9 4 2	♣ 6 3
6.	♠ A K J 7 4 2	♡ A J	◇ J 5 3	♣ 9 2

When opener prefers to make a short-suit game try, as in (2) and (3), or a long-suit try, as in (1) and (4), he is in trouble. On (5) and (6), he'd like to make a general game try of 3♠, but that is commonly played as a game try asking for extra help in trumps.

I suppose opener could bid 3◇ on the last two hands and hope for the best. The fact is there are lots of players who might bid 3◇ on all six hands! Pity poor partner, who then must figure out what is the right diamond holding with which to accept the try for game. A small doubleton would be helpful opposite K-9-6-5, A-K-10-5, or 9-4-2, but would be wasted opposite 9-7 or Q-J-3. Even the worth of K-8-6 would be unclear. It is a magnificent holding opposite Q-J-3, but doubtful opposite 9-4-2 or J-5-3.

So not only did I frequently not know in which suit to try, I often didn't know when to acccept as well.

What I'd been missing is the following concept: when a lot more is known about hand A than hand B, hand A should be the one telling, hand B should do the asking. After 1♠-2♠, it's clear that more is known about responder's hand than opener's; so from then on, opener should ask and responder should tell.

(Another important advantage in having opener ask rather than tell involves your opponents. Long-suit, short-suit, and help-suit game tries all give away important information to the defense which can aid them on opening lead and in the subsequent defense. With opener asking, not telling, the defenders know a lot less about his distribution, and anything they learn about dummy's [responder's] distribution won't help them much – they'll see the dummy's entire hand soon enough.)

What should I use as my asking bid? Clearly, 2 NT. Playing five-card majors, it is seldom necessary to stop in 2 NT, as opposed to three of the major, with a known 5-3 fit.

I spent a lot of time thinking about *what to ask for*. I considered having responder cuebid strength, but usually responder's strength is scattered. Finally, I decided to concentrate on responder's *distribution* – specifically, shortness. Since I couldn't afford to wait for singletons (too infrequent), I keyed on doubletons.

So here's what evolved. After 1♠ – 2♠, 2 NT became an artificial game try. Responder would show shortness at the three level if he had some. With 4-3-3-3 distribution, he would bid three of the trump suit with a minimum, 3 NT with a maximum. Opener would now have the following options:

(1) Bid four of the major when appropriate, after being "turned on" by the right doubleton.

(2) Sign off in three of the major when "turned off" – but responder could still bid on with a tip-top maximum.

(3) Bid 3 NT to suggest the possibility of that contract.

(4) Bid a new suit to preserve all options.

In the following examples, I will assume we are using these methods, a la Bergen. . . .

The raise of two of a major is semi-constructive, promising 8 – to 10 points including distribution. The raise promises exactly three-card support, since with four we would have jumped to 3♣ to show a single raise with four trumps. Some readers may not approve of these methods, but obviously the "2 NT ask" can be used with any style raise.

If the following hands seem familiar, it's because I've included some of the problem hands mentioned earlier.

	WEST	EAST
1.	♠ A K J 5 3	♠ 10 8 6
	♡ A K	♡ 9 5 3
	◇ 6 4	◇ K J 7 5
	♣ 8 7 4 3	♣ A 6 2

1♠	2♠
2 NT	3♣
Pass	

When responder showed a flat minimum lacking a doubleton club, game couldn't be a good bet.

2.	♠ K Q J 7 4	♠ A 6 3
	♡ A K 8	♡ 9 7 4
	◇ J 7 3	◇ 8 6 5 4
	♣ K 9	♣ A J 5

1♠	2♠
2 NT	3 NT
Pass	

3 NT rated to be easier than 4♠ as long as responder had at least three diamonds.

150

3.　　　　♠ K Q 10 8 7　　♠ A 6 3
　　　　　♡ 8 6　　　　　　♡ J 7 5 4
　　　　　◇ A K 10 5　　　◇ 9 3
　　　　　♣ K 6　　　　　　♣ Q J 7 5

	1♠	2♠
	2 NT	3◇
	4♠	Pass

With dummy having the right doubleton, game is a good bet.

4.　　　　♠ A K Q 8 7 4　　♠ J 9 3
　　　　　♡ A 6 3　　　　　♡ Q 8 7 4
　　　　　◇ Q 5　　　　　　◇ 10 6
　　　　　♣ 10 4　　　　　♣ A J 7 2

	1♠	2♠
	2 NT	3◇
	3♠	Pass

With the terrible duplication in diamonds, even 3♠ may go down on a bad day, but at least the hopeless game is avoided.

If opener had a better hand, he could bid 3♡ over 3◇ to show that he was still interested. So...

5.　　　　♠ A K 9 8 7 4　　♠ Q 7 2
　　　　　♡ K 6 4　　　　　♡ A Q 9 4
　　　　　◇ 9 5　　　　　　◇ 8 4
　　　　　♣ A 6　　　　　　♣ 10 9 7 2

	1♠	2♠
	2 NT	3◇
	3♡	4♠

Now we'll consider questions we need to resolve to have a complete understanding of the convention. Some of these questions may have already occurred to sharp readers.

1. Is 2 NT still on in competition?

As long as we opened and raised the major to two we ignore competition from either side. Therefore, 2 NT would still be the "doubleton ask" in all of the following auctions:

1♠	Dbl	2♠	Pass
2 NT			

1♡	2♣	2♡	2♠
2 NT			

1♡	Pass	2♡	2♠
2 NT			

1♠	2♣	2♠	Pass
2 NT			

1♡	Dbl	2♡	2♠
2 NT			

2. Can opener ever be interested in slam when he asks with 2 NT?

Yes, but it's rare. Slam is very unlikely when responder can begin with only a single raise, particularly when he can't have four trumps (playing Bergen raises). However, I would bid 2 NT after 1♠ - 2♠ with:

$$♠ A K J 8 6 4 2 \quad ♡ A \quad ◊ 8 \quad ♣ A 7 4 3$$

searching for club shortness.

As we'll see in time, we do have ways for opener to make both long- and short-suit slam tries.

3. Is responder allowed to jump to the four level after opener rebids 2 NT?

Yes, we defined that. A jump to four in a new suit is natural, promising a source of tricks, 5+ cards headed by two of the top three honors. This could get you to 4♡, the right game with:

♠ A 8 6 4 2		♠ 7 5 3
♡ A J 5	opposite	♡ K Q 10 9 6 2
◊ A K J		◊ Q 4
♣ 6 4		♣ J 5

or even to a beautiful minor-suit slam with:

♠ A K Q 6 4		♠ J 5 3
♡ A J 7 4	opposite	♡ Q 6 3
◊ A J 2		◊ K Q 10 7 3
♣ 8		♣ 9 6

Incidentally, if the auction goes:

1♠	2♠
2 NT	4◊

opener should bid 6◊, the safer slam, not 6♠. A ruff can be taken in the hand with short trumps.

4. How do you respond to 2 NT when holding a singleton or void?

The jump to four of the trump suit promises shortness (0 or 1) in the other major. With fewer than two cards in a minor, bid that minor at the three level just as you would with a doubleton. Don't sit for 3 NT if partner bids it — a rebid in your minor suit will indicate that you have fewer than two cards.

5. Which doubleton is shown if you hold two?

The cheaper one, although if your long suit meets the requirements, you always prefer to make the bid that shows a source of tricks.

6. Do those jumps to the four level promise a maximum?

Yes, since you can't afford to go past the three level holding a minimum. Usually, opener's hand is good enough for only a game try.

7. Can the 2 NT asking game try be used in any other type of auction?

The identical structure may be used for Drury. Something similar may also be used when there is a minor-suit opening, responder shows a major and opener raises him.

8. What alternatives does opener have to the 2 NT asking game try?

He can make a short-suit game try. A minimum bid in a new suit shows shortness (0 or 1) and interest in game. After:

152

$$1\heartsuit \qquad 2\heartsuit$$

bid 2♠ with:

♠ 9   ♡ A Q 7 4 3   ◇ K J 10   ♣ A J 4 2

3♣ with:

♠ A 10 4   ♡ K Q J 9 6   ◇ A 10 7 4   ♣ 8

and 3◇ with:

♠ Q 10 4   ♡ A K J 7 2   ◇ 8   ♣ A J 5 4

We'll conclude with some practice hands. Remember that a raise to 2♠ shows three trumps and 8+ to 10 points including distribution. As responder, what is your rebid after:

$$1♠ \qquad 2♠$$
$$2\,NT?$$

1. ♠ Q 6 4   ♡ J 9 8   ◇ K 7 4   ♣ K J 7 4

3 NT, promising a maximum with no doubleton.

2. ♠ A 8 4   ♡ 9   ◇ Q 10 6 5 4   ♣ J 10 7 4

4♠, promising 0-1 hearts.

3. ♠ 8 7 5   ♡ Q J 7 6 4   ◇ K 8 5 4   ♣ J

3♣, promising 0-2 clubs.

4. ♠ 8 4 3   ♡ Q 5 2   ◇ 8 4   ♣ K Q 9 5 4

3◇. You aren't strong enough for 4♣.

5. ♠ A 8 4   ♡ 6 5   ◇ 9 3   ♣ Q J 6 4 3 2

3◇, showing the cheaper doubleton.

6. ♠ K J 10   ♡ K 10 7 3 2   ◇ 9   ♣ 10 9 5 4

3◇, promising 0-2 diamonds. Since you are maximum, you will drive to game.

Responder's 2NT Game Try

Just as I have never liked Standard methods after a single major-suit raise, auctions that develop after:

Opener	Responder
1 suit	1 major
raise to 2 of major	

don't impress me much either.

Additional problems arise here since an eight-card trump fit is not guaranteed! Clearly, opener should raise a 1♠ response to 2♠ with any of the following hands:

♠ K Q 7　　♡ 8　　◇ J 8 7 4　　♣ A Q 9 6 3

♠ A J 9　　♡ K 6 5 4　　◇ A 8 6 4 3　　♣ 9

♠ Q 10 7　　♡ A K 9 4 2　　◇ K 6 3　　♣ 8 5

Also, the principle we mentioned earlier is even more true in this case. "When more is known about hand A than hand B, hand A should be the one responding to hand B's questions." After an opening bid and rebid (which often limits opener's hand), it is clear that responder should ask and opener should tell.

So, once again, I concluded that a 2 NT rebid by responder would be best employed as an artificial force, asking opener for a further description. As we'll see, this usually will be responder's action when he wishes to make a game try or issue a choice of games (3 NT or four of a major).

Before we learn more about this 2 NT game try, we must define what responder means when he rebids in a suit instead. There are only five possibilities, so we can be very complete and precise.

Responder's Non-Jump Rebids Other Than 2 NT

(a) The Other Major

Opener	Responder
1♣/1◇	1♡
2♡	2♠
1♣/1◇	1♠
2♠	3♡

These are natural game tries, promising four cards in the suit and forcing for only one round. Responder is free to pass opener's next bid.

Responder might have only four hearts for the 2♠ rebid, so we'd like to be able to stop in 2 NT with:

♠ 10 8	♠ A J 7 6
♡ A Q 5	♡ K 9 4 3
◇ Q 10 7　opposite	◇ K 5 4
♣ A 8 6 4 2	♣ 10 7

However, responder must have five spades after showing four hearts on the second auction, since he would respond up the line with four cards in each major. A possible hand for him is:

♠ A Q 6 5 4　　♡ K J 6 3　　◇ 9 4　　♣ 8 3.

The need for responder to show his side four-card major is based on the possibility of a 4-4 fit there. Not only would opener raise 1♠ to 2♠ with:

♠ K 7 4　　♡ K Q 9 4　　◇ 8　　♣ A 6 5 4 3,

he would also raise 1♡ to 2♡ holding:

♠ Q 7 4 3　　♡ K Q 6　　◇ 9　　♣ A J 7 4 3.

154

(With such minimum values, it is desirable to limit the hand immediately with a raise.)

When responder holds:

♠ A K 9 5   ♡ A 7 4 3   ◇ 6 4 2   ♣ Q 5,

he might need to bid 2♠ after:

Opener	Responder
1♣	1♡
2♡	

to get to his only eight-card fit.

(b) Opener's Minor

Opener	Responder
1♣/1◇	1♡/1♠
raise	3 of opener's minor

These are also game tries but are *non-forcing* in our style. Responder promises at least four-card support for opener's minor, with only four cards in his major. A reasonable example after:

Opener	Responder
1◇	1♠
2♠	

would be:

♠ A 7 4 3   ♡ 9 6   ◇ A K 8 3   ♣ 8 7 4.

Opener will always bid again if he holds four of responder's major, signing off in three with a minimum and jumping to game with a maximum. With only three-card support, opener can pass, bid 3 NT, three of a new suit, or even reraise the minor with a hand like:

♠ A Q 6   ♡ A 10 6   ◇ J 8 7 4 3 2   ♣ Q.

(c) 3♡ after 1♡ – 1♠, 2♠

This game invitation can also be passed since responder is promising three-card heart support. Of course, opener is also encouraged to bid game in either major, as well as signing off in 3♠ with:

♠ A 8 6 3   ♡ 10 8 7 5 2   ◇ A 6   ♣ K J.

(d) Three of the Trump Suit

It isn't necessary to use this bid as preemptive, since the opponents have already passed up several chances to enter the auction. We use this as a game try, usually promising five weak trumps and asking for extra help in the trump suit. Isn't this the most intelligent way to reach 4♠ with:

♠ A K 9 5		♠ 8 6 4 3 2
♡ 10 8 7	opposite	♡ 6 4
◇ 6 5		◇ A K 9 7 3
♣ A 6 4 3		♣ 8

                                                                     ?

(e) Three of a New Minor

This is our only radical departure from Standard practice. We play this action as a natural but non-forcing game try, promising at least five cards in the suit but only a four-card major. After:

Opener	Responder
1 ◇	1 ♠
2 ♠	

bid 3 ♣ with:

♠ Q 9 7 4   ♡ K 6   ◇ 8   ♣ A 9 7 4 3 2,

or after:

Opener	Responder
1 ♡	1 ♠
2 ♠	

bid 3 ◇ with:

♠ A 9 4 3   ♡ K 6   ◇ Q J 10 9 7   ♣ 8 5.

Opener will return to the major at the appropriate level with four-card support and is free to do what seems best, including pass, with only three cards.

We'll conclude with some well-bid hands using the methods just outlined.

	Opener	Responder
1.	♠ A J 5	♠ K 9 4 3
	♡ A Q 6 3	♡ K 5
	◇ J 10 8 7 4	◇ Q
	♣ K	♣ Q J 10 6 5 4

Opener	Responder
1 ◇	1 ♠
2 ♠	3 ♣
3 NT	

	Opener	Responder
2.	♠ K 5 3	♠ J 8 6 4
	♡ Q 9 6 3	♡ 8 2
	◇ K 9 8 6 4	◇ A Q J 7
	♣ A	♣ K 5 4

Opener	Responder
1 ◇	1 ♠
2 ♠	3 ◇
Pass	

	Opener	Responder
3.	♠ K Q 5	♠ A 9 6 4
	♡ A 8 7 4 3 2	♡ K 10 2
	◇ 6	◇ Q 10 3
	♣ K 10 4	♣ Q 7 3

Opener	Responder
1 ♡	1 ♠
2 ♠	3 ♡
4 ♡	

4.

♠ A 9 7 4	♠ K 8 5 3
♡ A K 8	♡ Q 9 6 4
◊ 9	◊ A K 3
♣ J 7 4 3 2	♣ 6 5

1♣	1♡
2♡	2♠
4♣	

Alternatively, opener could have splintered with 4◊ over 2♠.

5.

♠ A K 5	♠ 6 4 3
♡ K Q 9 5	♡ 10 8 6 4 3
◊ 8 6	◊ K Q J
♣ 9 7 4 3	♣ A 2

1♣	1♡
2♡	3♡
4♡	

6.

♠ K 8 4	♠ Q 10 6 3
♡ A 9 6 4 3	♡ 5
◊ 6 3	◊ Q J 9
♣ A J 2	♣ K Q 10 9 7

1♡	1♠
2♣	3♣
Pass	

7.

♠ K 8 7 4	♠ J 5 3 2
♡ K J	♡ 8 7 2
◊ 9 6 5 3	◊ A K 8 7
♣ A Q J	♣ K 5

1◊	1♠
2♣	3◊
3♠	Pass

Despite his maximum point count, opener knows he should decline the 3◊ game try since his diamond holding is terrible.

Next we will discuss what happens when responder's rebid is *2 NT*. As we stated, we'll use this 2 NT rebid as an artificial force, asking opener for a further description.

You may remember that after an *opening* bid in a major was raised to two, responder answers opener's artificial 2 NT rebid by showing a doubleton if he has one. But after opener has bid two suits, a holding of two cards in an unbid suit would no longer be very newsworthy. Therefore, if opener bids a new suit in response to 2 NT, he promises a singleton (or possibly even a void). Here are the meanings of opener's rebids after:

Opener	Responder
1◊	1♡
2♡	2 NT

(Of course, the concept would be the same regardless of what suit was opened and which major was bid and raised.)

(1) 3♣: This promises club shortness, but with only three hearts. The hand may be minimum or maximum in strength for the single raise. Possible hands for opener:

♠ 10 8 7 5   ♡ A Q J   ◇ A J 7 4 3   ♣ 9 or

♠ A K 5   ♡ A Q 4   ◇ 9 7 6 5 4 2   ♣ J.

(2) 3◇: This bid promises a minimum raise with only three-card heart support and is non-forcing. It also guarantees at least a five-card diamond suit. It usually denies a singleton. Opener would bid this with:

♠ A K 5   ♡ Q 5 2   ◇ Q J 10 9 5   ♣ 9 4 or

♠ A 7   ♡ Q J 10   ◇ K J 9 7 4 3   ♣ J 5.

(3) 3♡: This promises a minimum raise and is non-forcing. Opener will always have a flat hand but he could have either three or four hearts. This would be my choice with:

♠ 9 5   ♡ A K 7   ◇ A J 7 4   ♣ 10 7 4 2 or

♠ 6 3   ♡ A Q 7 4   ◇ A 9 7 4   ♣ Q 5 3.

(4) 3♠: This bid in a new suit promises a singleton, but the hand cannot be of minimum strength, since we are past three of the agreed suit. Opener may have three-card or four-card heart support. Select this bid with:

♠ 10   ♡ A J 9   ◇ K Q 7 5 4   ♣ A 9 6 3 or

♠ J   ♡ A Q 9 8   ◇ A J 9 8 7   ♣ J 10 8.

(5) 3 NT: This shows a maximum raise with only three-card support and flat distribution. Obviously, it is not forcing since we are not yet sure of an eight-card fit. It says nothing about stoppers. This would be my action with:

♠ J 5   ♡ K Q 10   ◇ A 9 7 4 3   ♣ A 10 6 or

♠ 8 7 6 3   ♡ A Q J   ◇ A K 5 3   ♣ 6 3.

(6) 4♣: This is a splinter bid. Opener is showing club shortness with four-card support. Presumably, his hand isn't loaded with high cards, since he raised to only two a round earlier. Two reasonable examples:

♠ A 9 7 4   ♡ A 8 5 3   ◇ Q J 7 4 3   ♣ – or

♠ A 8 4   ♡ K 7 6 3   ◇ K Q 7 5 3   ♣ 9.

(7) 4◇: This bid promises a 4–2–5–2 maximum. Perhaps the diamonds can be used as a source of tricks. These two hands would be acceptable examples:

♠ A 7   ♡ Q J 5 4   ◇ K Q J 5 3   ♣ 9 4 or

♠ A K   ♡ J 7 4 3   ◇ K 10 9 5 4   ♣ K 8.

(8) 4♡ : In addition to promising a maximum with four-card support, opener denies a long or short suit. Therefore, he'll be 4-4-3-2, 3-4-4-2, or 2-4-4-3. (If the opening had been 1♣, a 3-4-3-3 pattern would also be possible.) This hand looks about right:

♠ A 6   ♡ K Q 10 5   ◇ A 10 9 6   ♣ 8 4 3.

Is there any big difference if the opening bid was 1♡ and spades was the suit bid and raised? Not really. After:

Opener	Responder
1♡	1♠
2♠	2 NT

opener's rebid of 3♡ is non-forcing, showing a minimum with only three spades and either six fair hearts or five very good ones. This rebid should be chosen with:

♠ K Q 10   ♡ J 7 6 4 3 2   ◇ A 6   ♣ Q 5 or

♠ A Q 10   ♡ K Q J 10 6   ◇ 6 4   ♣ 8 5 2.

A jump to 4♡ would promise a similar major-suit distribution with a better hand. It is also logical for opener's 4♠ jump rebid to show precisely a decent 4-5-2-2, since he didn't splinter. A good example would be:

♠ A J 7 4   ♡ K J 9 5 4   ◇ A 6   ♣ J 5.

Before we go further, we must consider what kind of hands responder might choose to bid 2 NT with. As far as strength, the possibilities begin with hands suitable for game tries and continue on to some hands with slam interest. (We do have alternate possibilities for the slam-going hands.) Choice-of-game auctions are also possible, usually when responder isn't yet sure whether he wants to play in 3 NT or four of the major. If responder has a hand strong enough to try for only game, it will be one that wasn't appropriate for one of the very descriptive sequences we discussed earlier.

Here are some example hands with which responder would choose to rebid 2 NT after:

	Opener	Responder
	1♣	1♠
	2♠	

1.	♠ A 10 7 3	♡ A 8	◇ A 6 3 2	♣ Q 5 4
2.	♠ A K J 6 4	♡ A 8 5	◇ 9	♣ A 10 6 3
3.	♠ K J 7 5 4	♡ Q 3	◇ A 10 6 3	♣ 8 2
4.	♠ K Q J 5	♡ 9 3	◇ A J 5	♣ 10 9 6 3
5.	♠ A 7 4 3	♡ K J	◇ K J 6	♣ 9 5 4 3
6.	♠ A J 9 7 3	♡ 6 3	◇ K 10 7 4 2	♣ 9
7.	♠ Q 9 6 3	♡ 8	◇ A K 5	♣ A 10 7 4 2
8.	♠ K Q 10 6	♡ 9	◇ A K 7 4	♣ J 6 3 2

Now we'll consider how responder plans to follow up after each of opener's possible rebids. Here is a quick review of the meaning of opener's third bid after:

Opener	Responder
1♣	1♠
2♦	2 NT

3♣ = three spades, minimum hand, five or more clubs
3◇ = three spades, singleton diamond
3♡ = three spades, singleton heart
3♠ = three or four spades, minimum balanced pattern
3 NT = four spades, maximum, balanced pattern (but could be 3-2-2-6)
4♣ = four spades, maximum, 4-2-2-5
4◇ = four spades, maximum, singleton diamond
4♡ = four spades, maximum, singleton heart
4♠ = four spades, maximum, balanced pattern

Keep in mind that our system encourages light opening bids and frequent raises of partner's initial response with three-card support.

After the sequence above, responder holds

1.   ♠ A 10 7 3   ♡ A 8   ◇ A 6 3 2   ♣ Q 5 4

Presumably, our intention was to give partner a choice between 3 NT and 4♠, based on his number of spades. Therefore, if partner's rebid is 3♠, we will bid 3 NT. Of course, if partner can raise 2 NT to 3 NT, we will be happy to pass. If opener rebids 3♣, we'll also try 3 NT. It's possible that 5♣ is a better contract – partner could have:

♠ K 8 4   ♡ 6 5   ◇ K Q   ♣ K J 7 6 3 2,

but 3 NT will usually be best, particularly at matchpoints.

If opener rebids three of a red suit, we will know to avoid 3 NT. We'll rebid 4♣, natural and forcing, suggesting only four spades. If partner can bid 4♠, showing a hand with three very good spades, e.g.,

♠ K Q J   ♡ 8 7 5 4   ◇ 9   ♣ A K 9 7 2,

we will pass and play in the 4-3 fit. If partner's hand is:

♠ Q 8 6   ♡ 9   ◇ K Q 8   ♣ A J 8 7 3 2,

we will settle for 5♣. Hopefully we'll get to 6♣ if opener has a hand like:

♠ K Q 6   ♡ K J 7   ◇ 8   ♣ K J 9 7 3 2.

If opener can jump to the four level, we'll know that we can play in 4♠ since he guarantees four spades. It will be easy to pass 4♠ since opener is known to be balanced. But we'll entertain thoughts of slam over 4♣, 4◇, or 4♡.

2.   ♠ A K J 6 4   ♡ A 8 5   ◊ 9   ♣ A 10 6 3

This would have been a good hand for an original jump shift. Having responded 1 ♠, however, we'll have to make the best of it. Our double fit makes slam very likely, but it can't hurt to learn more about partner's hand with 2 NT. If partner can show a singleton heart by bidding 3 ♡ or 4 ♡, even a grand slam is quite likely. Opener could have:

♠ Q 9 3   ♡ 7   ◊ A 10 6 2   ♣ K Q J 9 4

Rebids of 3 ♣ or 4 ♣ will also be promising, since they show long club suits. We'll be discouraged, though, if partner shows a singleton diamond (admittedly unlikely) since there is bound to be some duplication of values. If partner rebids 3 ♠, we might continue with 4 ♡ in preference to 4 ♣, since the latter would suggest that our spades might be inadequate for a spade game if partner had only three.

(We might bid this way with:

♠ J 7 4 3   ♡ A Q 3   ◊ 8   ♣ K Q J 7 5.)

Note that it might be necessary to play a slam in clubs, particularly if partner were 4-2-2-5. He might have:

♠ Q 9 7 2   ♡ Q 4   ◊ K 10   ♣ K Q J 8 5.

If partner rebid 4 ♣, you would know he had this pattern.

3.   ♠ K J 7 5 4   ♡ Q 3   ◊ A 10 6 3   ♣ 8 2

This time our only possible contracts are 4 ♠ and 3 ♠. If partner can rebid only 3 ♠ after 2 NT, I would pass. (I would bid a game vulnerable at IMPs.) If partner rebids anything else, I would try 4 ♠, but 3 ♠ over 3 ♣ seems sufficient.

4.   ♠ K Q J 5   ♡ 9 3   ◊ A J 5   ♣ 10 9 6 3

It would have been reasonable to bid 3 ♠ a round earlier, but 2 NT is all right since we'd like to hear about a stiff diamond and the spades are good enough to play a 4-3 fit, especially at matchpoints. We'll pass a 3 ♠ rebid and sign off in 4 ♠ after 4 ♣, 4 ◊, or 4 ♡.

It's not obvious what to do over 3 ♣, 3 ◊, 3 ♡, or 3 NT, but regardless of what action you choose, you are in a stronger position than if using Standard methods. Keep in mind that if you bid only 3 ♠, partner can keep going with a maximum.

5.   ♠ A 7 3   ♡ K J   ◊ K J 6   ♣ 9 5 4 3

I would bid only 3 ♠ if partner rebid 3 ◊ or 3 ♡, since no game would seem likely. It's clear to pass 3 NT, but decisions after 3 ♣ or 3 ◊ hinge more on opening bid style than anything else.

6.   ♠ A J 9 7 3   ♡ 6 3   ◊ K 10 7 4 2   ♣ 9

If opener's rebid is 3 ◊, 3 ♠ will be enough. A singleton diamond will not be a good feature if opener has only three trumps. A 3 ♠ rebid will also be discouraging, even though partner might have a diamond honor. I would pass 3 ♠ and bid 4 ♠ over 3 ♡. Of course, if opener's rebid is 3 NT or higher, we'll play 4 ♠.

7.   ♠ Q 9 6 3   ♡ 8   ◇ A K 5   ♣ A 10 7 4 2

Many players would have bid 4♠ over 2♣, but that risks inadequate spade support:

♠ A 7 4   ♡ A 6 5   ◇ 8 3   ♣ K Q 9 6 3

or even missing a cold slam:

♠ K J 5   ♡ A 6 2   ◇ 8 3   ♣ K Q 9 6 3.

If opener rebids at the three level, promising only three spades, I'll bid 4♣ suggesting that we might want to play in that suit.

8.   ♠ K Q 10 6   ♡ 9   ◇ A K 7 4   ♣ J 6 3 2

The spades are adequate for play in a 4–3 fit, although repeated heart leads may be embarrassing. But there is still a chance for 6♣, so the exploratory 2 NT rebid responder chose is correct. It won't help the opponents defend, and 4♠ can still be bid on the next round.

My intentions here would be similar to those on hand (7), although I'm more likely to end in 4♠.

Incidentally, we still play 2 NT as an artificial game try in a competitive auction, or if it is bid by a passed hand. Recently, my partner and I had this auction:

Opener		Responder
♠ A 8 6 4 2		♠ Q 7 5
♡ 8 3		♡ A Q 6 4
◇ K Q 10 6		◇ 8
♣ 9 2		♣ A 10 4 3
	Pass	1♣
	1♠	2♠
	2 NT	3◇
	3♠	Pass

It was nice to have an intelligent way to avoid the bad game.

This concludes our study of responder's 2 NT game try. We've seen that when the partnership's fit is only seven cards long, finding the best contract may be difficult. I feel that this justifies the use of an artificial 2 NT asking game try by responder.

A method which requires a player who has already revealed a lot about his hand to provide even more precise information should always result in a more informative and accurate auction than a "close-your-eyes-and-jump-to-game" approach or a "fuzzy-wuzzy" new-suit game try.

Checkback Stayman

Responding to partner's opening bid of 1 NT is not difficult. Since partner has a well-defined limited hand, if we are balanced we simply add our points to his and bid or pass. Unbalanced hands involve more judgment, but since there are methods to Stayman, sign off, invite and force, responder can usually get the job done.

One would think that after a simple auction like Opener-1◇, Responder-1♡; O-1 NT, R-?, responder would also be well placed. Opener has described a balanced, minimum opening bid with 12 - 14 HCP, lacking primary support for responder's suit. Unfortunately, Standard methods are not advanced and efficient in such a sequence.

Say you have responded 1♡ to partner's opening 1◇ bid, and partner has rebid 1 NT. What do you do with each of the following hands?

1) ♠ 8 4	2) ♠ 9 4 3	3) ♠ K 3 2
♡ Q 7 5 4 2	♡ K 8 6 4 2	♡ K J 7 4 2
◇ A J 7 3	◇ A K 10 2	◇ A Q 7 5
♣ 9 2	♣ J	♣ 5

1) 2◇. No problem. You sign off in 2◇ and partner will pass or correct to 2♡.

2) 3◇, invitational, seems accurate.

3) 3◇, forcing. The right game could be in diamonds, hearts or notrump. This must be the most flexible call.

Do you see the problem? There is no way for 3◇ to be both invitational and forcing. It must be played as one or the other. That means that we must give up either the invitational or the forcing sequence, and that does not leave us well placed.

This is similar to the problem we solved some time ago with fourth suit forcing. We needed a way both to force and to invite after O-1◇, R-1♡; O-1♣, and we could use 3◇ to designate only one of them.

In addition, there are other problems. If O-1♣, R-1♠; O-1 NT, R-3♡ is forcing, and O-1♣, R-1♠; O-1 NT, R-2♡ is a weak signoff, how do we bid an invitational hand with spades and hearts? We are left with an unmistakable conclusion – the methods are unplayable!

Eddie Kantar, who discussed the problem in *The Bridge World* some years ago, recommended that the answer was to use an artificial bid as a Stayman--type checkback. This would also serve to start forcing auctions while eliciting information from opener. Kantar's special bid was 2♣, primarily because it was the cheapest bid, a la Stayman. This did mean that you no longer could sign off in 2♣ after auctions like O-1◇, R-1♡; O-1 NT, R-2♣ or O-1♠, R-1♠; O-1 NT, R-2♣, but that was a small price to pay, just as Stayman precludes a 2♣ signoff after a 1 NT opening bid.

Checkback Stayman has definitely caught on, but some theorists believe that it is better to use the "other minor" as the checkback. This has become known as "new minor forcing."

Both schools of thought have their own followers, and both operate on similar principles, but there are significant variations as to the workings of the conventions.

Since checkback Stayman will involve enough memory work as it is, we will confine our study to the use of 2 ♣ as our Stayman-type checkback.

When Is Checkback Used?

We do not really need to checkback after O-1 ♣, R-1 ♦; O-1 NT, since – - regardless of whether or not opener is stylistically allowed to have any majors after his 1 NT rebid – responder can simply reverse into his major with a suitable good hand. Therefore, responder's rebids will be standard here, with reverses game forcing. The auctions O-1 ♣, R-1 ♦; O-1 NT, R-3 ♣ and O-1 ♣, R-1 ♦; O-1 NT, R-3 ♦ will be defined as invitational.

After all other auctions involving 1 NT rebids, checkback is on. We will assume for the time being that the opponents do not compete; we'll consider the competitive auctions later. Since we have ways to get out cheaply after checkback, we will also employ it with passed hands.

RULE 1

The key to remember with our checkback auctions is that *the only forcing bid is the 2 ♣ checkback bid. We can say that all forcing auctions begin with 2 ♣. However, it is not true that all checkback auctions beginning with 2 ♣ are forcing.* This is crucial enough that it is suggested that the reader reread the previous three sentences.

Here are a couple of examples.

1)   O-1 ♦, R-1 ♠; O-1NT, R-3 ♡

This is not forcing since checkback was not used.

2)   O-1 ♣, R-1 ♠; O-1 NT, R-2 ♣; O-2 ♦, R-2 ♠

This is not forcing even though checkback was used. Why is Auction 2 not forcing? Stick around and you will become enlightened.

What does opener do after his partner bids a checkback 2 ♣? Although it depends on responder's first bid, let's take a sample auction as a starting point. O-1 ♣, R-1 ♡; O-1NT, R-2 ♣. We are assuming that opener could have four spades and/or three hearts. (For those of you who disagree with the four spades possibility, I do not believe it is right to rebid 1 ♠ on something like

♠ J 6 4 3   ♡ 8 7 4   ♦ A Q 5   ♣ A Q 6.)

RULE 2

Here is opener's rebid pattern after the aforementioned O-1♣, R-1♡; O-1 NT, R-2♣.

(Note the priorities, although some would reverse the first two.)

A. Bid 2♡ with three hearts.
B. Bid 2♠ with four spades.
C. Bid 2◊ otherwise.

This is done since responder usually has five of his original major when he checks back looking for three-card support.

RULE 3

If spades had been bid first by responder as with O-1◊, R-1♠; O-1 NT, R-2♣, the responses go like this:

A. Opener bids 2♠ with three spades.
B. Opener bids 2♡ with four hearts.
C. Otherwise Opener bids 2◊.

If you remember the important maxim that supporting partner's major suit is what bridge is all about, you should have no trouble learning and remembering how opener rebids.

RULE 4

What about after O-1♡, R-1♠; O-1 NT, R-2♣ — what happens then?

A. Bid 2♠ with three spades.
B. Bid 2♡ with five good hearts.
C. Bid 2◊ with five poor to fair hearts.

These are clearly easy to remember.
We are now ready to learn about the responder's point of view.

When Responder Doesn't Use Checkback

RULE 5

A jump to 3♣ is a bar bid.

RULE 6

All other jumps, reverses or notrump raises are invitational.

RULE 7

All other bids (rebids of suit; raises of opener's suit, except clubs; and rebids in lower ranking suits, not clubs) are weak and noninvitational.
One auction worth noting:

1 minor - 1♠
1 NT   - 2♡

shows a very weak responding hand, but guarantees 5-5 in the majors. If opener has four hearts and a maximum, he can go on.

This is how we get to game intelligently with

WEST	EAST
♠A 6	♠K 9 7 4 2
♡A Q 10 3	♡K 8 6 5 2
♢A 8 6 4	♢7 5
♣9 7 4	♣6
1 ♢	1 ♠
1 NT	2 ♡
4 ♡	Pass

Before continuing with responder's rules, try some auctions to make sure that you understand how to apply Rules 5, 6 and 7.

1 ♢	1 ♠
1 NT	3 ♣

Responder will have four spades, six clubs and a poor hand. With a hand like

♠Q 7 4 2   ♡8 5   ♢6   ♣K Q 8 7 4 3,

you have to bid 1 ♠ over 1 ♢, and don't you now want to sign off in a club partial? (Remember that 2 ♣ would be forcing and artificial.) The beauty of the 3 ♣ bar bid is that opener can't give a very unwelcome spade preference.

1 ♣	1 ♠
1 NT	3 ♣

This says, "I'm sorry you have to play in 3 ♣ not 2 ♣, but the end justifies the means." You are unlikely to play in 2 ♣ even if you could bid it, since it is so easy for the opponents to balance.

You would usually have five clubs for this signoff at the three-level. With

♠A 10 7 4   ♡J 3   ♢8 6 4   ♣Q 7 3 2,

pass 1 NT and hope for the best.

1 ♢	1 ♡
1 NT	2 ♠

This is only invitational, since no auctions can possibly be forcing without doing the 2 ♣ dance first. Obviously, responder has a hand with four spades, five hearts and 10 - 11 HCP.

1 ♣	1 ♡
1 NT	3 ♢

An invitational two-suiter, 5–5 is practically guaranteed, since we must be prepared to play here when opener holds 4 ♡ and 3 ♢ .

1 ♡	1 ♠
1 NT	3 ♡

166

Invitational, as are all jumps to the three-level with the exception of clubs.

1 ♣	1 ♡
1 NT	2 ◊

Nonforcing and weak. In some partnerships, this would imply five diamonds and only four hearts. Opener's *only* options are a pass or a preference to 2 ♡.

What are the Rules to Remember When Responder DOES Checkback?

RULE 8

If responder's next bid is at the 3-level, it is game forcing.

Exception: When responder has just obtained a major suit response from opener and raises the suit to the 3-level, it is invitational. ("Reraise")

RULE 9

If responder now bids 2 NT, it is invitational.

RULE 10

If responder's third bid of the auction is two of his original major, it is a fairly weak bid and only slightly invitational.

Responder's game interest is limited and distributional, and probably needs a fit plus a maximum.

1 ◊	1 ♡
1 NT	2 ♣
2 ♡	3 ♡

An invitation now that responder knows there is a 5-3 fit in hearts.

1 ♣	1 ♡
1 NT	2 ♣
2 ♡	3 ♣

Responder is making a forcing raise of clubs. He may have only four hearts, but could have more.

1 ◊	1 ♡
1 NT	2 ♣
2 ♡	4 ♣

This is how responder sets hearts as the trump suit on a slam-try hand. 4 ♣ is a cuebid with a hand that is too good to merely say 4 ♡. If responder had jumped to 4 ◊ instead, that would be a heart cuebid showing a diamond control. This auction answers the question, "How do you make a slam try after a delayed major suit raise?"

1 ◊	1 ♡
1 NT	2 ♣
2 ♣	3 ♣

This sequence by responder shows a forcing-to-game hand with hearts and clubs. Responder would virtually always have 5-5 in hearts and clubs since he didn't jump to 3 NT. If opener now bids 3♡, that would presumably show honor doubleton, since the 2♠ bid denied three hearts.

1♢	1♠
1 NT	2♣
2♢	2♡

This is a weak signoff. Responder has at most

♠K 9 7 4 3   ♡A Q 6 5   ♢8 4   ♣6 5

Responder saw a possibility for game if there was a fit, but now that there isn't, opener should pass 2♡ or bid 2♠.

1♣	1♠
1 NT	2♣
2♠	3♡

Responder has a game forcing hand with 5-4 or 5-5 or longer in the majors. He may even be looking for slam.

1♢	1♠
1 NT	2♣
2♢	2♠

Responder had too much to sign off in 2♠ one round ago, but his game interest may be marginal. After all, he didn't jump to 3♠, so the spades are probably nothing special. Responder probably has a distributional hand and was hoping for three-card spade support. Opener may bid again, but shouldn't go out of the way to do so. A sample hand for responder might be:

♠A 8 6 4 3 2   ♡8   ♢Q 5 3   ♣Q 7 4.

1♢	1♠
1 NT	2♣
2♠	3 NT

Why did responder bother with checkback when the knowledge of three-card support did nothing for him? Responder can't be 5-4 in the majors – he would bid 3♡ over 2♠. The only conceivable answer is that the responder has five spades, but is not sure whether to play game in spades or notrump. That would make sense with

♠A K 5 3 2   ♡K 7 4   ♢A 6   ♣8 5 3.

Opener should pass with something like

♠Q 7 4   ♡Q J 3   ♢K 10 5 3   ♣A Q 4

and bid 4♠ with

♠10 9 4   ♡A Q J 5   ♢K Q 10 7   ♣J 6.

More Examples

What would you do with each of the following after the auction by your side has begun

$$1 \diamondsuit \qquad 1 \heartsuit$$
$$1 \text{ NT} \qquad ?$$

♠ 6 4   ♡ K Q 8 7 4   ◊ 8   ♣ Q 10 7 4 3.

Bid 2♡. You may belong in clubs, but there is no practical way to get there.

♠ A 6   ♡ K Q 10 9 6 4   ◊ 7   ♣ Q 10 8 5

Bid 4♡. Game should have some play no matter what partner has.

♠ A Q 7 4   ♡ A Q 6 3   ◊ K 10 5 4   ♠ 8

Bid 2♣. We want to make a forcing diamond raise, while checking on the chance that partner has four spades. Over 2◊ or 2♡ by partner, we will bid 3◊ and await developments. Over 2♠ we will jump to 4♣ or 4◊ to show a control with a spade fit.

♠ 9 4   ♡ A 10 7 4   ◊ 6   ♣ Q J 9 8 4 3.

Bid 3♣. This will end the auction in the correct contract.

♠ A 7 5 4   ♡ Q J 10 6 3   ◊ Q 10 6   ♣ 6.

Bid 2♣. Game is possible if we can find a fit. If partner bids a major, we will invite by bidding three. Over 2◊, we will attempt to sign off in 2♡. This hand is too weak for an invitational 2♠ reverse. The reverse would allow opener to jump to 3 NT on

♠ Q J 2   ♡ A 7   ◊ K 7 4 3   ♣ A 10 7 5,

which we would prefer to avoid.

Interference

Although we can't say that "Checkback" has been carefree and easy so far, at least the opponents haven't gotten into our act and complicated matters. But sometimes they will. How are we going to cope with that?

If the opponents overcall, we simply ignore it and go about our business. All bids retain their previously stated meaning, with the obvious exception that a cuebid of the opponent's suit at the two-level is not natural but a good hand with a small singleton or void in their suit. This can be very helpful in deciding whether or not to play 3 NT.

What if the opponents choose to double 1 NT after an auction like

1 ◊	Pass	1 ♠	Pass
1 NT	Dbl	?	

Most would play this as takeout for the unbid suits, while some purists would treat this as a diamond trap penalty double. The simplest defense is to ignore their double and bid the same way as you would without the double. Redouble would presumably indicate a "good" hand interested in defending, showing that your side has the balance of power.

Should we use Checkback as a passed hand? Sure, why not? Game is still possible. The only difference here is that responder can never produce a forcing auction – all his "strong" 2♣ auctions are invitational. Obviously no passed hand can drive to game opposite a balanced minimum.

Is this Checkback structure feasible for weak notrumpers whose 1 NT rebid shows a stronger hand? No reason why not. They need only adjust their hand strength to the amount of extra strength their partner must have.

Checkback Stayman Quiz

It is now time to discover how much we really know about checkback. I will present you with a series of questions on 2♣ checkback and then provide answers and explanations.

The quiz consists of 25 questions. A score of 17 or better is passing, with 22 or higher considered to be excellent, indicating a superior understanding of checkback 2♣. On questions 1 - 7 you will need to classify checkback-related auctions as forcing, invitational or signoff. Questions 8 - 25 present bidding decisions based on judgment and system. Assume the opponents are out of the picture except on problem 3, where intervention by the opponents is clearly indicated.

Part I

Classify the underscored bid as forcing, invitational, or signoff.

1)
1♣	1♠
1 NT	3♡

2)
1♡	1♠
1 NT	3♣

3)
	Opp		Opp
1◊	Pass	1♠	Pass
1 NT	Dbl	2♣	

4)
1♣	1◊
1 NT	3♣

5)
1♣	1♡
1 NT	2♠

6)
1♣	1◊
1 NT	2♠

7)
1◊	1♡
1 NT	3♡

Part II

On the remaining questions, assume you are playing duplicate with neither side vul. What would you say on each?

8) ♠K Q 7 4 2 ♡8 5 ◇6 ♣K Q 7 5 4

PARTNER	YOU
1◇	1♠
1 NT	?

9) ♠8 ♡Q 10 6 4 3 ◇7 5 ♣A J 7 4 2

PARTNER	YOU
1◇	1♡
1 NT	?

10) ♠7 5 ♡A 10 6 4 ◇A K 7 3 ♣J 5 2

PARTNER	YOU
Pass	1◇
1♠	1 NT
2♣	2♡
3♣	?

11) ♠A Q 9 6 4 ♡A J ◇8 ♣9 7 4 3 2

PARTNER	YOU
1♡	1♠
1 NT	2♣
2♡	?

12) ♠K Q 5 3 ♡8 6 4 ◇9 ♣K J 10 7 2

PARTNER	YOU
1♣	1♠
1 NT	?

13) ♠7 2 ♡Q J 10 6 4 ◇K Q 8 5 ♣9 3

PARTNER	YOU
1♣	1♡
1 NT	?

14) ♠A Q 7 3 ♡A Q 6 2 ◇J 5 4 3 ♣8

PARTNER	YOU
1♣	1♡
1 NT	2♣
2♡	?

15) ♠A J 9 7 2 ♡10 6 4 ◇K J 5 ♣Q J

PARTNER	YOU
1◇	1♠
1 NT	2♣
2♡	?

16) ♠J 5 2 ♡8 6 4 ◇A Q J 6 3 ♣A 5

PARTNER	YOU
–	1◇
1♠	1 NT
2♣	2♠
3 NT	?

17) ♠Q 6 3 ♡Q J 10 7 4 2 ◇J 3 ♣A J

PARTNER	YOU
1◇	1♡
1 NT	?

18) ♠A J 7 3 ♡6 5 ◇9 4 ♣Q 10 7 4 2

PARTNER	YOU
1♣	1♠
1 NT	?

19) ♠A 7 4 3 2 ♡Q J 8 5 4 ◇8 2 ♣9

PARTNER	YOU
1♣	1♠
1 NT	?

20) ♠J 10 7 4 3 2 ♡Q 5 ◇K Q ♣K Q 6

PARTNER	YOU
1◇	1♠
1 NT	2♣
2◇	?

21) ♠A J 5 4 2 ♡Q J 8 7 ◇Q 6 ♣9 3

PARTNER	YOU
1◇	1♠
1 NT	2♣
2♡	?

22) ♠9 7 5 4 3 ♡K Q 6 ◇A Q ♣K Q 5

PARTNER	YOU
1◇	1♠
1 NT	?

23) ♠Q 7 ♡A K J 6 3 ◇A 7 4 ♣10 6 3

PARTNER	YOU
	1♡
1♠	1 NT
2♣	?

24) ♠Q 5 3 ♡A K J 7 4 ◇8 6 3 ♣A 5

PARTNER	YOU
–	1♡
1♠	1 NT
3◇	?

25)   ♠A 8 6 4 3   ♡A 7 4   ◇Q 8   ♣J 10 6

            PARTNER   YOU
            1♡   1♠
            1 NT   ?

Answers to
Checkback Stayman Quiz

Part I

1. Invitational. Shows a reasonable 5-5.
2. Signoff. Jumps to 3♣ are always weak in this system.
3. Forcing checkback. We ignore the double.
4. Invitational. There is no checkback after 1♣- 1◇; 1 NT. Therefore, this is invitational.
5. Invitational. This reverse shows four spades and five hearts with just under opening bid strength.
6. Forcing. Since there is no "checkback" bid after 1♣- 1◇; 1 NT, reverses are forcing.
7. Invitational. With a forcing hand containing long hearts, we can bid 4♡ or checkback via 2♣ first.

Part II

8. 2♣. We would like to bid an invitational 3♣, but that would be a bar auction showing 4 - 6. If partner bids a red suit over 2♣, bid 2♠ and hope that you don't belong in a club partscore.
9. 2♡. 2♣ would start something you can't finish.
10. Pass. This would be forcing if bid by an unpassed hand. Partner's hand probably looks like the one in question 8, and 3♣ seems like the correct contract.
11. 3♡. Partner has five good hearts, with fewer than three spades. Great players can manage with fewer trumps. I would pass opposite a partner who opens light or plays weak.
12. 3♣. This will end the auction in our best spot. Game is most unlikely.
13. 2♡. We are willing to play here even opposite a doubleton. Game is out.
14. 3♠. Partner may have four spades. A bid of 2♠ would not be forcing.
15. 2 NT. Game in notrump is still possible.
16. 4♠. Partner is giving us a choice between 4♠ and 3 NT. He must have five spades, so we reject notrump because of our doubleton and weak hearts.

17. 3♡, invitational. This seems right.
18. 3♣, bar. Hope we make it.
19. 2♡. This shows a weak 5 - 5.
20. 3♠. This asks partner to raise with an honor doubleton. If partner bids 3 NT, we will wish him luck.
21. 3♡, invitational. Partner made the bid that you were hoping to hear.
22. 3 NT. With this strong a hand and such poor spades, notrump should be right even opposite three-card spade support.
23. 2♡. You can't support spades, but can show good hearts.
24. 4♣. Your 1 NT rebid is maximum, although you'd like better diamonds. 3♣ usually would be passed since partner had only an invitational 5 - 5.
25. 3♡, inviting partner to bid game.

Score it up. How did you do? Are you ready to "checkback" left and right, or do you need to *CHECK BACK* on the text material?

♠ _____ ♠

Ace-Asking Bids

Baby, Roman, Key Card, Exclusion, Depo, Dopi, Super, DI, NO – these are neither nicknames for the Seven Dwarfs nor a partial list of the FBI's ten most wanted. They represent some of the conventions relating to those popular ace-asking bids, Blackwood and Gerber.

First we will look at basic Blackwood topics with which every partnership must be acquainted.

Everyone is familiar with Blackwood in its simplest form. After the choice of trump suit has been made and it seems the hands contain enough strength for slam, 4 NT can be bid to insure the presence of at least three aces. The well-known responses are:

5♣	0 or 4 aces
5♢	1 ace
5♡	2 aces
5♠	3 aces

The 4 NT bidder is supposed to be able to tell from his hand whether the 5♣ response shows 0 or 4 aces. If the partnership has all four aces, then 5 NT can be bid to ask for kings and invite a grand slam. The responses to 5 NT are the same as to 4 NT except that responder can jump to a grand slam with a suitable hand.

174

Virtually all partnerships use Blackwood on slam hands in one form or another, but Blackwood is appropriate only for certain kinds of hands. If you will not have a desirable, clear-cut action after partner's Blackwood response, then you probably would be better off cuebidding.

Here are some examples of Blackwood auctions from actual play. Try to distinguish between the good sequences where the use of Blackwood is appropriate and the ones that do not lend themselves to the use of Blackwood.

1.
♠ K Q 9 8 6 4 3 2	♠ A
♡ 8	♡ A 6 4 3
◊ K Q 4	◊ A 7 5 2
♣ 4	♣ A J 8 2
4 ♠	4 NT
5 ♣	5 NT
7 ♠ or 7 NT	Pass

2.
♠ 8	♠ Q 7 4
♡ K Q J 4	♡ 9
◊ 7	◊ A K J 4
♣ A K J 10 7 4 3	♣ Q 9 8 5 2
1 ♣	3 ♣
4 NT	5 ◊
? ? 6 ♣	Pass

3.
♠ A K Q 7 6	♠ J 10 5 3
♡ 9 4	♡ Q J 7 3
◊ A 7 3	◊ K Q 5
♣ K Q J	♣ A 8
1 ♠	3 ♠
4 NT	5 ◊
6 ♠	Pass

4.
♠ A Q 10 6 3	♠ K 7
♡ 9 2	♡ A K 4
◊ A 7 5 2	◊ K J 9 8 6 4 3
♣ Q 8	♣ 7
1 ♠	2 ◊
3 ◊	4 NT
5 ♡	6 ◊
Pass	

On hand (1), responder wanted to be in at least a small slam, so he used Blackwood followed by 5 NT to show possession of all aces. Opener could then bid the grand slam with confidence.

On hand (2), opener would be well placed if responder replied 5 ♡ or 5 ♠, but after 5 ◊ he has nowhere to go, since 5 ♣ was the last makable game. There is a way to discover the number of aces that responder has at a lower level, buy you'll have to wait to discover the method. It is important to remember to think twice about using Blackwood when clubs are trumps.

Another time not to use Blackwood is when you have a void. You would then have no way of knowing whether partner has the "right" ace. Try cuebidding instead, for example:

♠ A K J 8 7 4	♠ Q 10 5 3
♡ –	♡ K J 8 2
◇ 9	◇ A 7 4
♣ A Q 7 6 4 3	♣ K 5
1♠	3♠
4♣	4◇
4♡	5♣
7♠	Pass

Opener did have a nice hand on number (3) after the forcing raise, but Blackwood is never the answer when you have two potential losers in a suit with no ace or king. A better sequence would be:

1♠	3♠
4◇	4♠
5♣	5◇
5♠	Pass

Opener is showing a powerful hand with diamonds and clubs under control. This pinpoints the heart weakness so that the partnership can stop at a safe level, confident there is no slam.

Hand (4) is another example of an effective Blackwood auction. When opener raises diamonds, responder assumes that the trump suit is solid and is concerned only with the number of aces opener has.

One refinement of Blackwood with which most players are familiar is the method of signing off in 5 NT after discovering two aces are missing and you are beyond the five-level of your trump suit. The Blackwooder bids a suit not mentioned earlier in the auction, asking partner to bid 5 NT.

♠ A	♠ K Q 5
♡ Q J 5	♡ K 4 2
◇ A J 9 4	◇ K Q 7 6 3 2
♣ K J 10 7 3	♣ Q
1♣	1◇
3◇	4 NT
5♡	5♠
5 NT	Pass

Although we have reached an agreement about not bidding Blackwood with a void, there is the possibility that the responder to 4 NT may be void somewhere. Here is one of the methods of responding to 4 NT with a void.

Responses to Blackwood with a Void

Number of Aces	Bid
0	5♣.
1	6 of the trump suit or 6 of the void, whichever is cheaper.
2	5♣ (except when clubs are trumps); then identify the void by bidding it at the 5 or 6-level.
3	5◇ (except when diamonds are trumps); then identify the void at the cheapest possible level. The method of showing 2 or 3 aces with a void could be characterized as lying by 2 and then correcting.

Here are a few examples to test your knowledge of the void chart:

1.
1♣	1♠
3♠	4 NT
?	

♠ K J 8 6
♡ A Q 8 3
◇ —
♣ K 8 6 5 4

Bid 6◇. This shows one ace and a diamond void.

2.
1♣	3♣
4 NT	?

♠ A J 6
♡ —
◇ K 5 4 2
♣ K J 8 6 4 3

Bid 6♣. This is the best you can do here since 6♡ would take you past 6♣.

3.
1♡	3♡
4 NT	?

♠ A 10 6 3
♡ A Q 8 7
◇ —
♣ J 8 5 4 3

Bid 5♣. (If playing splinter bids you would have responded 4◇ to 1♡.) Partner will now presumably sign off in 5♡ and you will bid 6◇ showing two aces and a diamond void.

One more thing about responding with a void; if your void is in a suit that partner is known to be long and strong in, it is best not to show it. A void in partner's suit is unlikely to be much of an asset.

There are also conventions to be used on those rare occasions when the opponents interfere with your Blackwood auction. Here are two of the more popular ones.

DOPI (to be used only at the 5-level). After

PARTNER	RHO	YOU	LHO
1 ♠	2 ♣	3 ♠	4 ♣
4 NT	5 ♣	?	

$$
\begin{aligned}
\text{Double} &= 0 \text{ aces} \\
\text{Pass} &= 1 \text{ ace} \\
5 \diamondsuit &= 2 \text{ aces} \\
5 \heartsuit &= 3 \text{ aces} \\
5 \spadesuit &= 4 \text{ aces}
\end{aligned}
$$

DEPO (can be used at any level).

Double = even number of aces (0, 2, 4)
Pass = odd number of aces (1, 3)

The advantage of DEPO for high levels is that the responder is never forced to make a bid at the 6 or 7-level that might place the pair too high.

The assumption made regarding DEPO is that the Blackwood bidder can tell from his hand and from previous bidding how many aces you were dealt.

The Gerber convention is designed so that responder can ask for aces after partner opens the bidding with 1 NT or 2 NT. Since 1 NT – 4 NT and 2 NT – 4 NT are best played as a raise in notrump, inviting a slam, there is no easy way to ask for aces. Therefore, a bid of 4 ♣ is designated to take the place of 4 NT as an ace-asking bid. The responses to 4 ♣ employ the same principles as Blackwood responses:

4 ◇	0 or 4 aces
4 ♡	1 ace
4 ♠	2 aces
4 NT	3 aces

If the partnership has all the aces, then a bid of 5 ♣ can be used to ask for kings. In fact, some players even play that a subsequent 6 ♣ bid asks for the number of queens! As in Blackwood, the 4 ♣ bidder is the one who will place the final contract, which may even be in notrump.

Therefore, all these sequences represent signoffs:

(1)	(2)	(3)
1 NT-4 ♣	1 NT-4 ♣	1 NT-4 ♣
4 ♣-5 ♡	4 ♡-4 ♠	4 ♡-4 NT

Remember that the purpose of Gerber (just like Blackwood) is to tell you if you are missing too many aces for slam, not to enable you to discover if you have the general values for slam. Therefore, the usual hand to bid Gerber with is one containing a long suit. Here are example hands which would bid Gerber over 1 NT and would correspond with the above auctions.

1.   ♠ 8   ♡ K Q J 10 9 7   ◇ K 9   ♣ K Q 5 3

When partner admits to only two aces, you are forced to sign off in 5♡.

2.　　　　♠ K J 10 8 6 5 4 3　　♡ A K 6　　◊ 9　　♣ 5

Again your side has only 2 aces, so game is the limit.

3.　　　　♠ K 6　　♡ K 7 4　　◊ A　　♣ K Q J 10 7 4 2

You can't sign off in 5♣, since that would ask for kings. 4 NT should be very safe.

The only problem with Gerber is that there can be confusion as to whether a 4♣ bid is Gerber or a natural bid showing clubs. Here are a few simple rules which should clarify the Gerber situation so that your partner can always tell when you are bidding Gerber. The overriding principle to remember is that Gerber is always a jump in clubs in an auction where notrump has been bid.

(1) After an opening bid of 1 NT or 2 NT, 4♣ is Gerber.

(2) After 1 NT or 2 NT has been responded or rebid, 4♣ is Gerber, i.e.

<table>
<tr><td>1♡-1♠</td><td>1♣-1♡</td></tr>
<tr><td>2 NT-4♣</td><td>1 NT-4♣</td></tr>
<tr><td></td><td></td></tr>
<tr><td>1♠-2 NT</td><td>1◊-2 NT</td></tr>
<tr><td>4♣</td><td>4♣</td></tr>
</table>

(3) After responder bids Stayman after 1 NT or 2 NT, a jump in clubs is Gerber asking for aces (even if the bid is 5♣), i.e.

<table>
<tr><td>1 NT-2♣</td><td>2 NT-3♣</td></tr>
<tr><td>2♡-4♣</td><td>3◊-5♣</td></tr>
</table>

(4) After 3 NT has been bid, a jump to 5♣ is Gerber, i.e.

<table>
<tr><td>1◊-1♡</td><td>1♡-3◊</td><td>1♠-2◊</td></tr>
<tr><td>3 NT-5♣</td><td>3 NT-5♣</td><td>3 NT-5♣</td></tr>
</table>

On all the 3 NT auctions, 4 NT would be a natural raise, and 4♣ would show clubs. Some players refer to the jumps to 5♣ as Super Gerber.

Another version of Super Gerber can be used to ask for aces when the trump suit is a minor, and Blackwood might take you past five of the trump suit when two aces are missing. Previously we looked at the problems that arose with these hands:

OPENER	RESPONDER
♠ 8	♠ Q 7 4
♡ K Q J 4	♡ 9
◊ 7	◊ A K J 4
♣ A K J 10 7 4 3	♣ Q 9 8 5 2

After 1♣ – 3♣, opener's hand was an ideal one to ask for aces, but after a 5◊ response to 4 NT, the partnership was out of its depth. Instead, opener makes a jump into the cheapest unbid suit (4◊ in this case) to ask for aces, a bid which certainly is not needed in its natural sense. Responder replies to 4◊ or any other Super Gerber bid using the same type of steps as

Blackwood or Gerber.

Step 1	0 or 4 aces
Step 2	1 ace
Step 3	2 aces
Step 4	3 aces

These are the highlights of the Gerber convention, the most important ace-asking vehicle besides Blackwood. Now let us discuss some of the other versions of Blackwood.

Roman Blackwood (4 NT)

As the name suggests, this convention comes our way courtesy of the Italians. It is an attempt to be more precise in showing aces in response to 4 NT. Here are the responses:

5♣	0 or 3 aces
5♦	1 or 4 aces
5♡	2 matching aces
5♠	2 unmatching aces

The matching aces are:
    hearts and diamonds (red suits)
    spades and clubs (black suits)
    spades and hearts (major suits)
    diamonds and clubs (minor suits)

The unmatching aces are:
    spades and diamonds
    hearts and clubs

If the partnership has all the aces, a bid of 5 NT then asks for kings. The responses are then given in the identical manner at the 6 level.

The main advantage of Roman Blackwood occurs when a 5 NT inquiry elicits a 6♡ or 6♠ bid. A grand slam can sometimes then be bid even when a king is missing, provided that the 5 NT bidder can determine that it is not the king of a key suit.

The only other advantage of Roman Blackwood arises when a 4 NT bid receives a two-ace reply and the knowledge of which two aces can enable the 4 NT bidder to bid 6 NT rather than six of a suit with one ace missing. Obviously, this is important only at matchpoints.

Very few American players use Roman Blackwood, and it is not recommended for any but the most practiced expert partnerships.

Baby Blackwood (3 NT)

This is another seldom used convention, because of its low frequency and the fact that it can conflict with a natural bid of 3 NT. After the partnership has agreed on a major suit as trumps, a bid of 3 NT is used to ask for aces and enables the partnership to stay a level lower. Thus with

♠ K Q J 10 8 6 3   ♡ A   ◇ K Q J 4   ♣ 3

after your opening 1♠ bid has been raised to 2♠, you can ask for aces by bidding 3 NT and still play a safe 4♠ if three aces are missing. Without Baby Blackwood, it would not be easy to safely try for slam with this hand. The responses to 3 NT again follow general Blackwood principles:

4♣	0 or 4 aces
4◇	1 ace
4♡	2 aces
4♠	3 aces

Exclusion Blackwood

In contrast to the last two Blackwood offshoots which can be confusing and have limited advantages, *Exclusion Blackwood* is a convention which, when the right hand occurs, can be invaluable. For example, you open 1 ◇ with

♠ K Q 4   ♡ K Q 6 4   ◇ A K Q J 9 4   ♣ –

and your partner makes the very welcome response of 1♡. What usually happens now is that opener makes a few forcing bids which fail to secure the needed information, namely, how many aces does responder have outside of clubs? However, with Exclusion Blackwood:

1 ◇ – 1♡
4♣ – 4♡
4 NT

4♣ is a splinter raise of hearts. The subsequent 4 NT bid shows that opener has a club void and would like to hear about partner's aces excluding the ace of clubs. This will enable opener to get to 6 opposite

♠ 8 7 3   ♡ A J 7 2   ◇ 8 6 3   ♣ Q 5 3

and avoid slam if responder has something like

♠ J 7   ♡ J 10 8 7 5   ◇ 10 3   ♣ A J 9 4

with no need for guesswork.

Also an auction like

1 ◇	1♡	2♡	Pass
2♠	Pass	4NT	

would be based on a responding hand such as

♠ K 7 3   ♡ –   ◇ K Q 10 7 4   ♣ A K J 8 3.

Opener responds to Exclusion Blackwood in the same manner as Blackwood, except that he does not count the ace of the excluded suit.

Exclusion Blackwood can easily be added to the arsenal of any partnership. If a player makes a splinter bid or cuebids the opponents' suit and then bids 4 NT, he identifies a void in that suit and is asking partner how many of the other three aces he holds.

Grand Slam Force After Blackwood

We all know that after 1♡-3♡, 5 NT is the Grand Slam Force, asking partner to bid 7♡ with two of the top three heart honors. What do you do, though, if you need to first find out about partner's aces? The answer is the Delayed Grand Slam Force. After:

$$1♡ \quad -3♡ \text{ (forcing)}$$
$$4\,NT-5♡$$

a bid of 6♣ becomes the Grand Slam Force, again requiring responder to bid the grand with two of the top three.

If clubs are trumps (and you haven't been able to bid Super Gerber), you have to bid five of an unbid suit (forcing partner to sign-off at 5 NT) and then bid 6♣ as the Grand Slam Force.

When It's Their Hand

When your opponents use Blackwood, regardless of the variation, don't just sit there while they do their thing. If your partner will be the opening leader, try to help him out. With

♠ 10 7 3   ♡ K J 8 6   ◇ J 8 2   ♣ 5 4 3,

after:

RHO	YOU	LHO	PARTNER
1♠	Pass	2◇	Pass
3◇	Pass	4 NT	Pass
5♡	?		

you should clearly double. You can't be sure how a heart lead will fare against 6◇, but you strongly prefer it to the lead of any other suit. If you do not double, partner will tend to lead clubs. Therefore, if you have the opportunity to double a Blackwood response and don't, expect to see some other suit led. You shouldn't wait for 100 honors to make a lead-directing double.

"4 NT!!!" – Not "4 NT?"

No discussion of ace-asking bids would be complete without considering those 4 NT bids that are not ace-asking.

The first of these is a convention which has become popular among experts in recent years. This is "D.I." 4 NT (Declarative–Interrogative) which has been used successfully for many years by practitioners of the Blue Team Club. After the partnership makes a few cuebids toward slam, a 4 NT bid announces further slam interest and asks partner to "tell me more." Partner can now continue to cuebid his controls, or sign off if he has nothing further to say. Since controls are always cuebid in ascending order, skipping over a suit denies a control there. D.I. is not recommended for inexperienced players, although placing the emphasis on cuebids rather than the overuse of Blackwood will probably improve bidding skills on slam hands.

Everyone knows about 4 NT as a natural, invitational raise of an opening notrump. The most common examples are 1 NT–4 NT and 2 NT–4 NT. There are also many others, although these often contain some ambiguity when used by inexperienced players. Auctions such as

| 1 NT–2♣ | 1◊ –1♡ | 1 NT–3♠ |
| 2♡   –4 NT | 2 NT–4 NT | 3 NT–4 NT |

should all be considered as raises of notrump. By the way, if partner answers your natural 4 NT bid with a bid at the five-level, he is showing a suit and inviting a slam there if you have support. If you don't you can show your own four-card suit or retreat to notrump.

4 NT is also sometimes used as a natural bid in competitive auctions. For example: 4◊ –4 NT, or

YOU	LHO	PARTNER	RHO
1♣	Pass	1♠	2♡
3 NT	4♡	Pass	Pass
4 NT!			

However, there are other competitive auctions where 4 NT is usually employed as a takeout bid. These are a few examples:

Opp.		Opp.		Opp.	
4♡ - 4 NT		1♣ - 4♠ - 4 NT		1♡ - 4 NT	
	Opp.		Opp.		
2♠	Dbl.	4♠	4 NT		
	Opp.		Opp.		
1♠	Pass	4♠	4 NT		

In each case the 4 NT bid is forcing, and asks partner for his best unbid suit, with the emphasis on the minors. Obviously, partnership discussion is needed to insure that both partners are on the same wavelength.

The most popular of the Blackwood conventions is Key Card. The principle behind it, certainly a sound one, is that for slam purposes, the king of trumps is just as important as an ace. You don't want to be in a grand slam off the king of trumps, and there is likewise no reason to be in a small slam which is at best on a finesse. Therefore, in responding to 4 NT (Key Card), you count the king of trumps as an ace, which means that there are now five "aces" in the deck. For this reason, Key Card Blackwood is sometimes also called Five Ace Blackwood.

The most popular set of key card responses are "Roman Key Card."

    5♣ = 0 or 3 key cards.
    5◊ = 1 or 4 key cards.
    5♡ = 2 key cards without the trump queen.
    5♠ = 2 key cards with the trump queen.

These responses are based on the realization that knowledge about the king *and* queen of trumps is crucial for slam purposes. Roman Key Card enthusiasts feel it is crucial to identify the presence or absence of the trump queen. They also seek to locate the trump queen after the 5♣ or 5◊ response.

In an auction such as:

$$1\spadesuit \quad - \quad 3\spadesuit$$
$$4\,NT \quad - \quad 5\diamondsuit$$

a bid of the cheapest new suit (5$\heartsuit$ here) asks about the queen of trumps.

After the queen-asking bid, responder signs off in five of the trump suit (without the queen) and cuebids a feature (with the queen) on the way to slam in case opener has interest in 6 NT or seven of the agreed suit.

If all five key cards and the queen of trump are accounted for, the RKC asker can bid 5 NT, which

1. Guarantees the above "Big 6."
2. Asks for number of kings.
3. Shows interest in a grand slam.

Responder shows kings in the traditional way. Keep in mind, though, that with Key Card Blackwood, there are only three kings remaining, since the trump king has already been counted.

♠   ♠

Roman Key Card Blackwood

The popularity of Key Card Blackwood has increased dramatically in recent years. Not only do most experts use it, but a significant number of club and tournament players have decided to try it.

The most popular set of Key Card (a key card is an ace or the king of an agreed suit) responses are "Roman Key Card"—i.e.:

5$\clubsuit$ = 0 or 3 key cards.
5$\diamondsuit$ = 1 or 4 key cards.
5$\heartsuit$ = 2 key cards without the trump queen.
5$\spadesuit$ = 2 key cards with the trump queen.

These responses are based on the realization that knowledge about the king *and* queen of trumps is crucial for slam purposes. Roman Key Card enthusiasts feel it is crucial to identify the presence or absence of the trump queen. Holding two key cards, they also seek to locate the trump queen after the 5$\clubsuit$ or 5$\diamondsuit$ response.

In an auction such as

$$1\spadesuit \qquad 3\spadesuit$$
$$4\,NT \qquad 5\diamondsuit$$

a bid of the cheapest new suit (5♡ here) asks about the queen of trumps. If opener instead bids 5 NT, it is assumed that he is not worried about the trump queen. Either he holds the lady himself or he has enough length to expect no trump losers if the queen is missing.

After the queen-asking bid, responder signs off in five of the trump suit (without the queen) and cuebids a feature (with the queen) on the way to slam in case opener has interest in 6 NT or seven of the agreed suit.

Here are a few well-bid Roman Key Card hands to help you understand this important convention.

	WEST	EAST
1.	♠ A 10 8 6 5 2	♠ Q 9 7 4
	♡ 8	♡ A Q 4 2
	◇ K Q J 10	◇ 8 3
	♣ A K	♣ Q 10 3

1♠	3♠ (1)
4♣	4♡
4 NT	5◇
5♠	Pass

(1) Limit raise

Although there are no awards given for getting to a contract of five of a major, any pair would be proud to be able to bid with this accuracy.

2.	♠ K J 8 7 4	♠ Q 9 5 3
	♡ A Q	♡ 8 6
	◇ A K Q J 4	◇ 9 5 3 2
	♣ Q	♣ A K 4

1♠	3♠
4 NT	5◇
5♡	6♣
6 NT	Pass

5♡ asks for the ♠Q and 6♣ promises the ♠Q as well as the ♣K as aces were already shown. How many matchpoints would you expect for 6 NT on this deal?

3.	♠ K Q J 6	♠ A 5
	♡ J 10 6 2	♡ A K 9 7 4 3
	◇ A 8 6	◇ 4 3
	♣ A 5	♣ K 8 5

1 NT	2◇ (1)
3♣ (2)	4 NT
5♡	5 NT
7♡	Pass

(1) Jacoby transfer
(2) Maximum with four trumps and doubleton club

185

East was not thinking about a grand slam when West opened a 14–16 1 NT. But after West's 3♣ bid promised a maximum with four trumps and a doubleton club, the picture brightened. East was more interested in 7♡ after West denied the queen of trumps. With 10 trumps including the A–K, the queen is usually unnecessary, and that increased the probability of West holding more strength outside. Since 5 NT promised no trump losers as well as interest in seven with all aces accounted for, West could bid seven on the basis of his source of tricks in spades without worrying about his weak trumps. It would be the height of greed for East to bid 7 NT even though that contract rates to make. How many pairs do you know who would get to 7♡ on these cards?

Here are a few Roman Key Card auctions without such a happy ending. Although there are solutions to these problems, they are not at all obvious.

4.

♠ K Q J	♠ 8
♡ A Q 9 5	♡ K J 8 6 4 3 2
◇ A 6	◇ K 4 2
♣ Q 9 4 3	♣ K 6

1♣	1♡
3♡	4 NT
5♠	???

4 NT seemed pretty obvious for East over 3♡ – even a grand slam was possible. But West's 5♠ response resulted in an unsolvable nightmare for East.

5.

♠ 6	♠ K Q 5 4
♡ 10 8 6 4	♡ A K 7 3
◇ A K Q 6 3	◇ 8
♣ K Q J	♣ A 7 4 2

1◇	1♡
3♡	4 NT
5◇	6♡

The problem was there was no room for East to ask for the trump queen after the unexpected response of only one key card. We've always known that Blackwood can be a problem with a minor trump suit, but it is clear from these examples that only spades are completely immune from space problems after 4 NT.

6.

♠ A K 8 6 4	♠ 10 7 5 3 2
♡ K 7	♡ A 8 4
◇ A K Q 6 4	◇ J 6
♣ 8	♣ A 10 7

1♠	3♠
4 NT	5♡
6♠	

There was no problem with bidding room here, but a very good grand slam was missed. West knew from the 5♡ bid that the queen of trumps was missing and didn't want to be in a grand slam with the queen-fourth of trump outstanding. East's extra trump changed the odds dramatically and made the grand slam an excellent proposition.

Next we'll solve these problems with an ingenious, yet simple device. We'll also endeavor to attempt to avoid the biggest possible nightmare with Roman Key Card – not being sure what suit is trumps.

Kickback and Redwood

Although Roman Key Card Blackwood is a definite improvement over standard, there are times where it just doesn't cut the mustard.

Remember hands (4) and (5) above? On each of these disasters, the problem was one of space – we just didn't have enough to work with. What's the solution? When a suit other than spades is trump, we must be able to use a bid *below* 4 NT to ask about aces and trump honors, etc.

In his enlightening and revolutionary series in *The Bridge World* entitled "The Useful Space Principle," Jeff Rubens illustrated several areas where bidding room efficiency can be radically improved. The concept which applies to RKC was referred to as "Kickback."

The basic principle of Kickback is that in order to have a truly efficient Blackwood auction; we need to have considerable room to maneuver while doing our asking. When spades are trump, we have three steps *between* 4 NT and the trump suit. That's what we need and want.

In order to achieve this when other suits are trumps, *the ace-asking bid must be the bid directly above the trump suit.* Accordingly, if clubs are trumps, 4 ◊ is RKC; if diamonds are trumps, 4 ♡ is RKC; if hearts are trumps, 4 ♠ is RKC; if spades are trumps, 4 NT is RKC.

Kickback, upon reflection, is not really complicated – it merely is different.

Am I stating that when playing Kickback after any auction where clubs are trump, a bid of 4 ◊ by either player at any time is RKC, and is the only way for the partnership to ask for aces and key cards, etc.? Yes, that's exactly right.

Quite a few experts play that when a minor suit is agreed, a jump to four of the cheapest unbid suit (sometimes one above) is RKC. This is sometimes referred to as Redwood. Here are some sample Redwood auctions:

	WEST	EAST			WEST	EAST
1.	1 ♡	2 ◊		2.	1 ♣	1 ♠
	3 ◊	4 ♠			3 ♣	4 ◊
3.	1 ♣	3 ♣		4.	1 ♠	2 ♣
	4 ◊				3 ♣	3 ◊
					4 ♡	
5.	1 ◊	1 ♠		6.	1 ♣	1 ♡
	2 ♣	3 ◊			2 ◊	3 ◊
	4 ♡				4 ♠	

In (2), the 4 ◊ bid agrees clubs as trumps; in all other cases there was previous agreement. Although examples (1), (4), and (6) are not at full efficiency (because the RKC ask is three steps below, it leaves only *two in-between* steps instead of the three we might need), clearly Redwood is a definite improvement over 4 NT. It is worth noting that Redwood and Kickback both take priority over splinter bids.

1 ♣	3 ♣
4 ♡	

can be played as splinter, but

1 ♣	3 ♣
4 ◊	

is RKC.

Is there any problem with Redwood as opposed to Kickback. Sure, take an auction like

1 ◊	1 ♡
1 ♠	3 ◊

Since Redwood is defined as a jump to four of the cheapest unbid suit, we are up the creek, since the only unbid suit would be even higher than 4 NT. You could therefore play Redwood as a jump to one above the trump suit (even if the suit was bid previously). This feels okay since you never need to jump on these auctions because a bid of three would be forcing.

Here is how the responses to Kickback go. Think in terms of steps rather than specific suits. Just like Gerber, it should be easy with a little practice.

Trump suit Kickback bid		CLUBS 4 ◊	DIAMONDS 4 ♡	HEARTS 4 ♠	SPADES 4 NT
Step 1	0 – 3	4 ♡	4 ♠	4 NT	5 ♣
Step 2	1 – 4	4 ♠	4 NT	5 ♣	5 ◊
Step 3	2 without Q	4 NT	5 ♣	5 ◊	5 ♡
Step 4	2 with Q	5 ♣	5 ◊	5 ♡	5 ♠

We stated earlier that there are two areas of Roman Key Card Blackwood that leave considerable room for improvement. One was that of bidding space, which we have attempted to rectify via *Kickback*. We do need more work with Kickback, especially in the area of grand slam bidding. But first let's turn our attention to the real nightmare of RKC (Roman Key Card Blackwood) – not knowing which suit is trumps.

Sure, life is easy after 1 ♠ – 3 ♠ – 4 NT. You know what suit is trumps and which king should be counted as an ace for key card purposes. But how confident would you be on these auctions?

	WEST	EAST		WEST	EAST
1.	1 ◇	2 ♣	2.	1 ♣	1 ♠
	3 ◇	4 NT		2 ♡	4 NT
3.	1 ♠	2 ♣	4.	1 ♠	2 ◇
	2 ♠	4 NT		3 ◇	3 ♠
				4 NT	

	WEST	NORTH	EAST	SOUTH
5.	1 ♠	4 ♣	4 ♡	Pass
	4 NT			

	WEST	NORTH	EAST
6.	1 ♡	Pass	4 NT

And believe me, these are just the tip of the iceberg. Over the years I have participated in, as well as observed, countless RKC disasters. In fact, for a long while I gave up playing the convention because I couldn't stand the excitement when Blackwood was bid in an auction where the trump suit was ambiguous.

Possible Solutions to RKC Trump Suit Ambiguity

(1) I once had the agreement that 4 NT was Key Card only if a kibitzer who knew very little about bridge was positive what suit was trumps. Otherwise we were in a four-ace situation. This worked fairly well over a period of years.

(2) Another solution is to make the last bid the trump suit for key card purposes. So, after 1 ◇ -1 ♠ -3 ♣ -4 ♣ -4 ♡ , the K acts like the fifth ace. While it can't be denied that, as long as reviews are allowed, the partnership will always get it right, it also must be stated that the ♡ K is probably the least relevant of all the kings on this hand! So, although this method may be better than nothing, choosing some random king and calling it an ace for that deal defeats the entire logical purpose of RKC Blackwood.

(3) Although from a simplistic point of view each of the first two suggestions has some merit, the real solution must be for a partnership to have specific rules. These rules must cover when Blackwood is RKC for an appropriate suit as opposed to regular Blackwood. I certainly do believe that after 1 ♡ -Pass-4 NT, for example there are only four key cards, and a 5 ♠ response promises three aces. If responder wished to make hearts trumps he should first make a forcing raise. For this auction I would probably have something like.

♠ K 6   ♡ 8   ◇ A K Q 10 8 7 4 3   ♣ K 6.

Listed below are the key card rules that govern my partner ship with Larry Cohen. Perhaps your partnership can study these rules and select those which appeal to the partnership.

Bergen-Cohen KC Rules

Roman Key Card is on when:
1. *We open at the four level.* 4♡ – Pass – 4 NT is RKC for hearts.
2. *Opener jump rebids his own suit to the four level.* 4 NT would be RKC for spades after each of the following:

WEST	EAST		WEST	EAST
1♠	1 NT		1♠	2◇
4♠	4 NT		4♠	4 NT

WEST	NORTH	EAST	SOUTH
1♠	2◇	3♣	Pass
4♠	Pass	4 NT	

3. *Responder jump shifts and rebids his own suit.* After

1◇	2♠
2 NT	3♠

spades will be the assumed trump suit for key card auctions, regardless of what the continuations are between 3♠ and 4 NT and no matter which player inquires for key cards.

4. *Jump opposite takeout double.* Although it is rare to try for slam after an opponent opens a one-bid, it can happen. And it is certainly not unusual to look for slam after an enemy preempt. So if anyone bids Blackwood after a takeout double and a jump response, it is RKC in the suit jumped into. Examples:

WEST	NORTH	EAST	SOUTH
1◇	Dbl	Pass	2♠
3◇	4 NT		

WEST	NORTH	EAST	SOUTH
3♡	Dbl	Pass	4♠
Pass	4 NT		

WEST	NORTH	EAST	SOUTH
2♡	Dbl	Pass	4♣
Pass	4♡	Pass	4 NT

5. *We overcall at the four level.*

WEST	NORTH	EAST	SOUTH
3♠	4♣	Pass	4 NT

is RKC for clubs.

6. *We strong jump overcall after their preempt.*

WEST	NORTH	EAST	SOUTH
2◇	3♠	Pass	4 NT

is RKC for spades.

7. *Opener jump rebids to three level* (promising a solid suit) after a two-over-one game forcing response.

190

WEST	NORTH	EAST	SOUTH
1 ◊	Pass	2 ♣	Pass
3 ◊	Pass	4 NT	

is RKC for diamonds, although Kickback players would bid 4 ♡ for RKC.

WEST	NORTH	EAST	SOUTH
1 ♠	Pass	2 ♣	Pass
3 ♠	Pass	4 NT	

is RKC for spades.

8. *If two suits are agreed, the first suit is trumps for RKC purposes.*

WEST	EAST
1 ♠	2 ◊
3 ◊	3 ♠
4 NT	

4 NT is RKC for diamonds even though there is a good chance that spades will become trumps. Obviously, it is possible to have a different rule here, and some experts even play six-card RKC where both kings count as aces when two suits have been bid and raised. This clearly has merit.

9. *Key Card 4♣ (or 4 ◊ with clubs trumps) over preempts.* This convention, which we have already described, is certainly an RKC situation, although different responses are used.

10. *All "Kickback" or "Redwood" auctions are RKC.* Examples:

WEST	EAST		WEST	EAST
1 ♡	3 ♡		1 ♣	1 ♡
4 ♣			3 ♣	4 ◊

WEST	EAST
1 ◊	3 ◊
4 ♡	

11. *After a player makes an unnecessary jump to show a good or solid suit.* Examples:

WEST	EAST		WEST	EAST
1 ♣	1 ♠		1 ♠	2 ♡ (G/F)
2 ♡	3 ♠		2 NT	4 ♡
4 NT			4 NT	

WEST	EAST		WEST	EAST
1 ◊	1 ♠		1 ♡	1 ♠
2 ♣	2 ♡		3 ◊	4 ♣
2 NT	4 ♣		4 NT	
4 NT				

12. *After a notrump opening bid*—1 NT, 2 NT, or 2 ♣ followed by notrump. Any auction where responder asks for aces after showing one suit (such as Texas) calls for RKC with the suit bid identifying the trump suit.

13. *All remaining auctions where the trump suit was agreed by a bid and a raise* (conventional raise or cuebid, as well).

Of course we also have some specific rules when 4 NT is Blackwood but *not* Key Card.

4 NT Blackwood, but not RKC

	WEST	NORTH	EAST
14.	1♡	Pass	4 NT

Could have set hearts, but didn't.

| 15. | | 1♣ | 3♠ | 4 NT |

Regular Blackwood only.

| 16. | | 1◊ | 4♡ | 4 NT |

Regular Blackwood.

Please be aware that other players have differing views on these subjects. Not all would agree that (15) and (16) above are ace-asking bids of any kind.

That's it for now on this subject. However, we are constantly updating and even changing.

What if Blackwood is bid after an auction not covered by the rules above? Then it is regular Blackwood at that time — although we will discuss it afterwards and may add it to our list.

I encourage readers to let me know of other situations where RKC should apply. Although our list is fairly thorough, we know it is not complete.

Do you remember our three Roman Key Card problems?

1.

♠ K Q J	♠ 8
♡ A Q 9 5	♡ K J 8 6 4 3 2
◊ A 6	◊ K 4 2
♣ Q 9 4 3	♣ K 6

1♣	1♡
3♡	4 NT
5♣	?

West's 5♣ response resulted in an unsolvable nightmare for East.

2.

♠ 6	♠ K Q 5 4
♡ 10 8 6 4	♡ A K 7 3
◊ A K Q 6 3	◊ 8
♣ K Q J	♣ A 7 4 2

1◊	1♡
3♡	4 NT
5◊	5♡

The problem: there is no room for East to ask for the trump queen after the unexpected response of only one key card.

3.

♠ A K 8 6 4	♠ 10 7 5 3 2
♡ K 7	♡ A 8 4
◊ A K Q 6 4	◊ J 5
♣ 8	♣ A 10 7

1♠	3♠
4 NT	5♡
6♣	

There was no problem with bidding room, but a very good grand slam was missed.

Here are better bidding sequences.

1.
      1 ♣   1 ♡
      3 ♡   4 ♠
      5 ♡   Pass

4 ♠ is kickback, asking for key cards. 5 ♡ (fourth step) shows two key cards plus the queen of trumps. And there we are.

2.
      1 ◊   1 ♡
      3 ♡   4 ♠
      5 ♣   5 ◊
      5 ♡   Pass

4 ♠ again is the economical key card ask and 5 ♣ (step 2) promises one or four. 5 ◊ is now available to ask for the queen, and 5 ♡ denies possession.

3.
      1 ♠   3 ♠
      4 NT   5 ♠
      7 ♠

If you are wondering about the 5 ♠ response, it is not an error. Whenever the partnership holds 10 or more trumps, they can usually get by without the queen.

> A K 8 6 4 10 7 5 3 2 is fine for 7
> A 9 8 6 4 10 7 5 3 2 is fine for 6
> K J 8 6 4 10 7 5 3 2 reasonable slam
> K J 9 8 6 4 10 7 5 3 2 good slam
> K 9 8 6 4 10 7 5 3 2 slightly inferior slam

Since responder knows that opener has at least a five-card major, treating the fifth trump as the equivalent of the queen will be a problem only if opener has K-x-x-x-x of trumps. This is especially unlikely when responder holds two key cards—there must be something good about opener's hand to warrant the 4 NT bid!

Improved King Ask

"Everyone" plays that if the Key Card Blackwood bidder follows his 4 NT bid with 5 NT he guarantees that all the key cards are present (including relevant trump honors), shows interest in a grand slam and asks about kings.

Most partnerships respond with the number of kings while allowing responder to bid seven with the "right hand." Some expert pairs cuebid kings at the six level, which is certainly an improvement, since knowledge about specific kings is usually more relevant than the bulk number. Many grand slams do not require possession of all four kings. However, a fuzzy agreement about cuebidding is not enough for good grand slam accuracy.

The following discussion assumes that there is sufficient room after the king ask below six of the agreed trump suit. This will be true when spades are trumps. It is also true when we are in a kickback situation, regardless of what suit is trumps.

After we kickback at the four level to ask for aces (key cards), we can ask for kings by bidding five of the kickback suit and invite a grand slam. For example:

$$1\diamondsuit \qquad 3\diamondsuit$$
$$4\heartsuit \qquad 5\clubsuit$$
$$5\heartsuit$$

$4\heartsuit$ = Kickback (key cards in diamonds)
$5\clubsuit$ = Two key cards, no trump queen (step 3)
$5\heartsuit$ = Kickback for kings

The key concepts are: (1) The king ask bid requests responder to cuebid his cheapest king (six of the trump suit therefore denies any kings). (2) After hearing about the cheapest king, the asker keeps asking and the teller keeps telling. Some examples:

1.
♠ K 9 8 6 4 3   ♠ A J 7 5
♡ A Q 5   ♡ K 10 7 4
◊ A 6 4   ◊ 8
♣ 8   ♣ A 10 6 3

$$1\spadesuit \qquad 4\diamondsuit$$
$$4\ NT \qquad 5\heartsuit$$
$$5\ NT \qquad 6\heartsuit$$
$$7\spadesuit$$

After the splinter bid of $4\diamondsuit$, opener loved his hand despite having only 13 HCP. $5\heartsuit$ showed two key cards lacking the trump queen, which caused opener no pain. $6\heartsuit$ promised the $\heartsuit$K while denying the minor suit kings.

2.
♠ A K 9 6 4 2   ♠ J 7 5 3
♡ A Q 7 5 2   ♡ 10 6 4
◊ A   ◊ K 8
♣ 8   ♣ A K 4 3

$$1\spadesuit \qquad 3\spadesuit$$
$$4\ NT \qquad 5\diamondsuit$$
$$5\ NT \qquad 6\clubsuit$$
$$6\heartsuit \qquad 6\spadesuit$$
$$Pass$$

$6\clubsuit$ promised the ♣K, but did not deny other kings. Opener continued to ask with his $6\heartsuit$ bid. Partner would have bid seven with the $\heartsuit$K.

3.
```
♠ A J 10 7        ♠ K Q 8 7 4 3
♡ Q 5            ♡ A K
◊ A K            ◊ 8
♣ A 9 8 5 4      ♣ Q J 6 3

    1♣           1♠
    4♠           4 NT
    5♣           5 NT
    6◊           6 NT
```

Responder was all set for a grand slam after showing three key cards. It seemed very likely that opener held the ♣K. The 6◊ bid firmly denied possession, however. Responder then knew 6 NT was safe but that 7♠ would depend on the club finesse.

Here are a few kickback examples:

4.
```
♠ A              ♠ 9 6 4
♡ A Q 4          ♡ K 9 3
◊ A Q 7 4        ◊ K 8
♣ K Q 10 7 4     ♣ A 9 8 6 3

    1♣           3♣
    4◊           4♠
    5◊           5♡
    5 NT         7♣
```

After the limit raise of 3♣, 4◊ was kickback. 4♠ showed one key card, and 5◊ was the king ask. 5♡ promised the ♡K without denying other kings, since hearts was the cheapest suit over the 5◊ kickback bid. 5 NT asked for the ◊K as a "replacement" bid. (Since there is no way to ask or tell about the king of the kickback suit at a sensible level, notrump has to be the substitute bid for both players.)

5.
```
♠ K              ♠ A Q J 10 6
♡ K 8 6 5 2      ♡ A Q 7 4 3
◊ A K 6 4        ◊ 8 5
♣ A 8 3          ♣ 6

    1♡           2 NT (1)
    3♠ (2)       4♣ (3)
    4◊ (4)       4♠ (5)
    4 NT(6)      5♠ (7)
    5 NT(8)      6♣ (9)
    6◊ (10)      7 NT(11)
```

(1) Jacoby 2 NT showing a forcing heart raise and asking partner for a singleton or a void. If opener does not have a singleton or a void, he can clarify the strength of his opening bid. Incidentally, other responses also would be acceptable on this hand. A jump shift to 2♠ followed by heart support would be fine. A simple response of 1♠ also could work well, and a 4♣ splinter response also is possible.

(2) I have a singleton spade.

(3) A club control. It is far from ideal to cuebid a singleton, but it is mandatory to find out about diamonds. It will be possible to clarify the ace situation later with kickback.

(4) Diamond control.

(5) Kickback, with hearts accepted as trumps.

(6) Either 0 or 3 key cards (step 3).

(7) King ask.

(8) I have the ♠K. (Substituting notrump for spades because spades is the kickback suit.)

(9) Asking for a minor-suit king.

(10) I don't have the ♣K, but I do have the ◊K.

(11) We can take 13 tricks for *all* the matchpoints.

The Grand Slam Force

We conclude our travels through the world of Kickback with a look at a convention that's worth its weight in gold when it occurs. The Grand Slam Force.

As most readers are aware, the GSF is a bid of 5 NT, asking partner to bid seven of the agreed suit with two of the top three trump honors. Failing that, he bids something at the six level without going past six of the agreed suit. Most experts use the principle of "Fast Arrival," six of the agreed suit being responder's weakest action, promising no top honor.

Unfortunately, there are two problems with the above idea. First, we need a more precise schedule of responses so we can reach a grand slam with an adequate trump suit that lacks a high honor (presumably the queen). A combined holding of ten trumps including the ace and king is more than adequate even for a grand slam.

The second problem is, once again, one of space. If we are going to distinguish holdings in the agreed suit at the six level, 5 NT may not allow us enough room to do so, especially when the agreed suit is a minor. We need to find a more economical bid which will enable us to search for ten trumps including the ace-king, or, on rare occasions, even 12 trumps lacking the king!

Once again, the solution comes to us courtesy of Jeff Rubens, who tackled this subject in March, 1981, in *The Bridge World*. Rubens' article was entitled "The Grand Slam Nonforce," since his methods were intended to help avoid grand slams with an inadequate trump holding.

Let's get into the actual responses. For now, we'll assume that spades is the agreed suit and 5 NT has been bid as the GSF. As in Kickback, space is not a problem when spades is the agreed suit. The underlying principle is that, other than the jump to seven with two of the top three honors, *the better your holding, the less you bid*. We will assume that the partnership has at least eight of the agreed suit (since otherwise they would not have selected that suit as trumps).

We must also speak about trump length. For every auction, there is a guaranteed minimum trump length, sometimes based on bridge logic, other times on partnership or conventional understanding. Some examples:

	WEST	NORTH	EAST	SOUTH
1.		1 ♠		2 ♠
2.		1 ♣		3 ♣
3.	1 ♣	Dbl	Pass	1 ♠
	Pass	2 ♠		
4.		2 ♣		2 ◇
		2 ♠		3 ♠
5.		1 ♠		2 NT*
6.		1 ♠		4 ◇
7.		2 ♠		
8.		1 ◇		3 ◇
9.		1 ♠	Dbl	2 NT**

*Jacoby. **Jordan.

In (1), playing five-card majors, opener guarantees at least five spades and responder at least three. In (2), playing 1 NT Forcing, responder shows four. In (3) each partner must have at least four spades. In (4) at least a 5–3 fit can be counted on. In (5) most would expect responder to hold at least four spades. In (6) the splinter bid of 4 ◇ always suggests at least four trumps. In (7) my partnerships allow five-card suits for the weak two-bid, but most others demand six. In (8) the limit raise should be based on four or more trumps. In (9) my partners promise at least four trumps, but some pairs allow responder to have three.

Once we understand the idea of minimum trump length, we can recognize extra length. If you raise 1 ♠ to 2 ♠ with:

♠ 10 6 5 4 2   ♡ K J   ◇ Q 7 2   ♣ Q 7 6,

you have two extra trumps, which we'll refer to as "plus 2." Any efficient GSF structure must take extra length into account, as Rubens' does. The following chart shows his responses. (A few of Rubens' more sophisticated concepts were omitted to avoid overcomplicating matters.)

Responses to 5 NT Grand Slam Force (with spades as the agreed suit)

6 ♣ – ace or king.
6 ◇ – queen, or plus 2 or plus 3.
6 ♡ – no high honor with plus 1.
6 ♠ – no high honor, minimum length.
7 ♣ (or equivalent) – two of the top three.

I included "or equivalent" since some pairs always bid a more flexible 7 ♣ or 6 NT when accepting with two of the top three.

The 6♡ and 6♠ responses are very precise. The 5 NT asker always passes 6♠, and usually converts 6♡ to 6♠ (but can bid seven if the knowledge of responder's extra trump is sufficient). After a 6◇ response, asker will usually know just what to do. The only exception occurs when he wishes to explore for 12 trumps lacking the king, and that's outside the scope of our discussion.

When the response is 6♠, asker has 6◇ available to ask for extra length. The logical responses to this are:

> 6♡ – plus 1.
> 6♠ – plus 0.
> Higher – plus 2 or plus 3.

Are you ready for some clarifying examples? Assume the 5 NT bidder has shown at least five trumps, while responder has promised three or more.

	ASKER	TELLER
1.	A 10 9 7 3	Q J 6
	5 NT	6◇
	6♠	
2.	A K 9 7 4 2	10 6 5 3
	5 NT	6♡
	7♠	

Knowledge of partner's extra trump ensures an excellent grand slam.

3.	A J 9 7 4	K 8 6 3 2
	5 NT	6♠
	6◇	7♠
4.	A Q 10 9 7 4 2	J 8 6 5 3
	5 NT	6◇
	7♠	

When responder promises the queen or two extra trumps, our hero can tell which it is and knows what to do.

If each player has promised at least *four* trumps, then:

5.	A J 9 7	K 8 6 4 2
	5 NT	6♠
	6◇	6♡
	6♠	

"I can do without this grand."

6.	K 10 8 5	A 9 7 6 4 3
	5 NT	6♠
	6◇	7♠

"But this is more like it."

What if a suit other than spades is trumps? Then we use our Kickback principle to save the day by providing the extra bidding space we need.

Since:

	♣ trumps	◊ trumps	♡ trumps
RKC (Kickback)	4 ◊	4 ♡	4 ♠
Then:			
GSF	5 ◊	5 ♡	5 ♠
So:			
Step 1 (ace or king)	5 ♡	5 ♠	5 NT
Step 2 (queen, or plus 2 or plus 3)	5 ♠	5 NT	6 ♣
Step 3 (no honor, plus 1)	5 NT	6 ♣	6 ◊
Step 4 (no honor, plus 0)	6 ♣	6 ◊	6 ♡

So the next time you are fortunate enough to hold:

♠ –   ♡ A K 2   ◊ A J 8 6 4 3   ♣ A K 5 4,

and partner opens 1 ♣ and raises your 2 ◊ response to three, bid a confident 5 ♡, ending in:

7 ◊ opposite K-Q-2, when partner jumps to seven;

6 ◊ opposite Q-9-7-5, after partner replies 5 NT;

6 ◊ opposite 10-9-7, after partner replies 6 ◊;

6 ◊ opposite 10-9-7-2, after partner replies 6 ♣;

6 ◊ opposite K-9-5, after partner replies 5 ♠ and then replies 6 ◊ to your 5 NT inquiry; but:

7 ◊ opposite K-10-7-5, after partner replies 5 ♠ and then replies 6 ♣ to your 5 NT inquiry.

DEVYN PRESS, INC.

3600 Chamberlain Lane, Suite 230, Louisville, KY 40241